Cities of the Hot Zone

Greg Sheridan has been a journalist for more than 20 years and in all that time deeply addicted to travel. In a varied career with *The Australian*, where he is now the foreign editor, he has lived in Beijing, Washington, Canberra and Sydney, and travelled on assignment to Europe, the Middle East and South America. But on an early trip to London he stared out the window of the plane at Singapore Airport and realised he was headed for the wrong place. It was the mysterious cities of Southeast Asia, with their bright lights and dark secrets, that would emerge as his real destination. They would become in time his second home, his ongoing tutorial in life and his abiding preoccupation.

His first trips into Southeast Asia were following the Vietnamese boat people. Later, any excuse to go back would do. Then his life changed forever when he got married and acquired a family, making travel an altogether different experience, an inner journey as well as an outer one, a journey into the secrets of family life, as well as a love affair with the sparkling, strange and inexhaustible cities of Southeast Asia.

He has written two previous books on Asia: *Tigers: Leaders of the New Asia-Pacific* (1997) and *Asian Values, Western Dreams* (1999).

Cities of the Hot Zone

A Southeast Asian adventure

Greg Sheridan

ALLEN&UNWIN

First published in 2003

Allen & Unwin
83 Alexander Street
Crows Nest NSW 2065
Australia
Phone: (61 2) 8425 0100
Fax: (61 2) 9906 2218
Email: info@allenandunwin.com
Web: www.allenandunwin.com

National Library of Australia
Cataloguing-in-Publication entry:

Sheridan, Greg, 1956- .
   Cities of the hot zone : a Southeast Asian adventure.

   ISBN 1 74114 224 5.

   1. Sheridan, Greg, 1956- . 2. Journeys - Asia, Southeastern.
   3. Cities and towns - Asia, Southeastern. 4. Asia,
   Southeastern - Description and travel. I. Title.

915.9

Set in 11/15 pt Galliard by Bookhouse, Sydney
Printed by Griffin Press, South Australia

10 9 8 7 6 5 4 3 2 1

For my wife, Jessie, who inspired these travels,
and for our sons Ajay, Lakhvinder and Jagdave,
boon companions on these journeys
and many others.

Contents

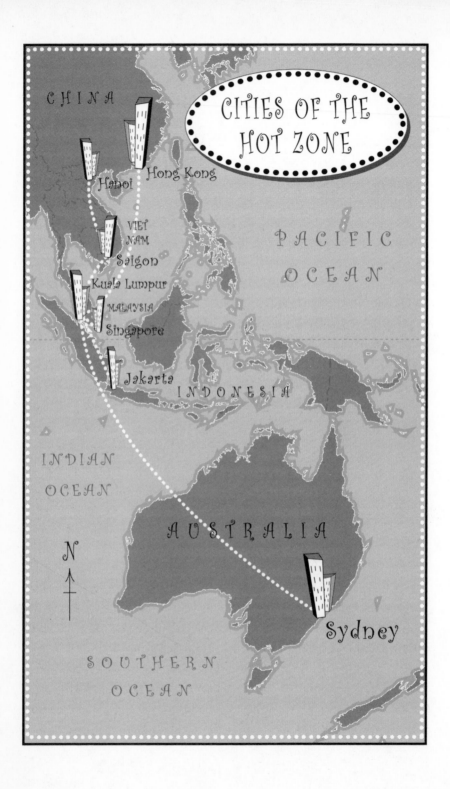

Prologue

Ever since I was a kid I wanted to move, to be on the move, to travel. When we moved house when I was about twelve, I was jumping out of my skin with excitement. We lived in Sydney Airport's flight path and I never heard a plane roar overhead that I didn't want to be on. Trains were full of romance. Even the bus seemed interesting.

In my childhood, airports were impossibly glamorous. My two uncles (Michael and Tony) loved airports so much they sometimes took us out to Sydney Airport just for a milkshake, just to look at the planes. In those days there was no question of us actually flying anywhere—that was way too expensive. Just being at the airport, the sound of the planes and all the hustle and bustle, was fantastic. At ten years old in an airport I felt like James Bond.

Early on I knew that one of the best bits of travel was coming home. As a kid of about eight or nine I remember being at school, almost weeping with loneliness for my mother. I loved her extravagantly and couldn't bear to be parted from her for the day. But no sooner would I get home than I wanted to be off again on new adventures, down to the shops, sometimes back to school with mates to play ball. As a teenager I talked my parents into sending me to boarding school for a year (they couldn't really afford it but it was a cheap boarding school) mainly because it was somewhere new. I always regretted the places I'd left, just as I always missed my mother at school, and returned to them often—but the prospect of somwhere new was irresistable.

And so my adult life has become a series of trips—not the constant travel of the permanent correspondent, but endless trips taken from home base. You see, I also love routine. I know that routine is the friend of health and achievement and satisfaction. But I construct elaborate routines only so that I can shatter them with travel, new trips to new places and new trips to old places. I particularly love travel to cities, especially cities where I've been before. Coming back to a city gives you two of the main pleasures of travel at once—the pleasure of departure and the pleasure of return, the mingling of something new with something familiar.

Anticipation and nostalgia are not the opposites they're sometimes thought to be, but lightly disguised twins.

Although I still have everything to learn, I know a few things now and one of them is this—bachelor life is overrated. Travel taught me this. I discovered it when my wife, Jessie, and our three sons and I took a combined work–holiday trip to Kuala Lumpur, the capital of Malaysia. Jessie grew up in Kuala Lumpur and has family there and the city became our base for up to a couple of months every Christmas for four or five years. We never went there for more than a couple of months, never less than four weeks. It became our second home, and 'living' there was a different experience from visiting.

From KL we would journey through other Asian cities, mainly in Southeast Asia, sometimes a little further afield. These journeys took place from the late 1990s to the early years of the new century. These cities are now a big part of my life. It's the story of these journeys that I'm going to tell in this book.

The terrorist attacks of September 11, 2001, the infiltration of al-Qaeda terrorists into the region, the Bali bombings of October 2002, the exposure of the terrorist group, Jemaah Islamiah, even the SARS epidemic, didn't change my attitude to these Southeast

Asian cities. I love them, plain and simple. And when I'm away from them I long to be back in them. They offer the sweet taste of unpredictable possiblity every time I visit. Islamic extremists are part of the regional scene, but actual terrorists are an infinitesimal minority. Statistically, you're in more danger every time you drive your car in a big city than you are from terrorists in Southeast Asian cities. That's not to say I don't take terrorists seriously, but they shouldn't stop you travelling. Mostly I've had fun in these cities, though undoubtedly there is a more sombre note there now than when I first began travelling in them.

I've always lived in big cities, generally close to the centre. Many writers love the tranquillity of the countryside. There they can invite their souls. Maybe I have a deformed soul but mine is stirred by the clash and clang of cities. Big cities, it seems to me, are the natural habitat of mankind, where we all rub up against each other and see what we're really made of.

I know all about bachelor life. I studied it for my first thiry-six years and became a modest expert on it. Then unaccountably I got married and acquired three kids and forgot all about bachelorhood. Now we were taking big overseas holidays together. In the past I'd mostly travelled alone. As a reporter I didn't even like travelling with photographers and I was positively phobic about sharing a hotel room. I'd lived as a bachelor in wildly different cities, in Washington, Bejing, Sydney and Canberra, and for shorter periods in New York and London, and so long as there was a cafe, some music and a book, I didn't mind my own company a bit.

But a few years of marriage change your point of view. Jessie and the boys left before me and I hated being in our house on my own. I couldn't wait to join them.

Travel with a family is different from travel on your own. But for now it's the excitement of the move that overwhelms us as we begin on a journey to discover not only the cities of the hot zone, but to discover ourselves more deeply as well.

Kuala Lumpur

The Enigma of Arrival, or Someone Lost My Horse

Frankly, the journey didn't start all that auspiciously. Through some vagary of airline scheduling or seat availability Jessie and the boys were leaving a day before me. I drove them to Sydney Airport and went through the usual bedlam of checking in. I was with them as they were putting their hand luggage through the X-ray machine.

The security man, an older guy, grey-haired and gravelly of voice, called me over.

'Excuse me, sir. Is there anything in your family's hand luggage you'd like to tell us about?'

'No, everything's clear. Why, one of the kids hasn't brought a bomb with him has he? Hee Hee.'

'Would you just step around here and have a look at this, sir?'

You can't complain about politeness like that—all this un-Australian business of calling me 'sir' and so on—but the guy's voice was definitely starting to acquire an edge. I stepped around and saw what his problem was. There was a hand gun in the luggage.

'Are you familiar with that, sir?'

He reversed the X-ray's treadmill, opened the bag and there was a metal, snub-nosed .38 revolver. It was a toy of course but it looked absolutely authentic. What's more I'd never seen it before.

'Boys!'

Jagdave, our youngest, sheepishly came up and claimed ownership. I gotta tell you, Jagdave is a cute kid, everybody likes him. But if there's a kid who can cause mayhem, it's him. I often think he must have read St Francis's prayer backwards: *Where there is tranquillity, let me sow chaos; where there is peace, let me bring confusion.* You get the drift.

After a relatively short period where I felt like an al-Qaeda terrorist who wouldn't confess, the security guy accepted it was all a mistake made in good faith, but warned us it was not a good idea to take guns on airplanes, which seemed perfectly reasonable. The choice was they could confiscate the gun, package it up securely, put it on the plane and the family could apply for it in Kuala Lumpur or I could take it home.

I took it home.

I was leaving the next day but still I missed my family more than I expected after they'd gone. Before it had always been me, as the travelling journalist often away on assignment, who left *them*. Even when I was on the road I always had them to ring up, write postcards to, worry about in a dad sort of way. This was a new experience, them leaving *me*. Anyway, I thought, at least after these several years of marriage I'll enjoy the secret pleasures of bachelorhood for one night. That is to say, I'll put my feet up on the lounge, I'll choose whatever I like on the TV, or if I don't want to watch TV I'll read a book without feeling anti-social, I'll eat what I like and I'll spread some mess around. Boy I sure know how to have a good time.

But that's not the way it worked out. As I opened the door, it felt creepy to be on my own in the big old place. The house 'ate up my head', as Jessie would say. For a start, I didn't know what I was supposed to do—read the papers, watch TV, do some work, ring someone up. I became a slug, mysteriously attached to the lounge, unable to move for long periods, simultaneously reading and watching the TV and not doing either properly.

I ate the curry Jessie had prepared for me then left my dinner plate on the coffee table in front of the TV. At first this seemed like a liberation from the confining domestic routines. But after an hour or two I thought, 'God what a mess this lounge room looks with dirty old plates lying around.' So I did the washing up anyway. Then I found I didn't go to bed, but I wasn't staying up for any reason. Late night televisision is the pits. I couldn't wait to get going.

After years of travel for profit and for pleasure, for newspapers and for fun, for conferences and reporting assignments and interviews and weddings, I've developed a fairly straightforward attitude to airplanes. As far as I'm concerned there are basically just two types of air travel. One is an idyll of luxury. You envelop yourself into a kind of snug-fitting sofa-cum-bed, which oozes its way around your body and caresses you gently through the skies. A whole bevy of friendly and frequently attractive staff attend to your every need. The food is good. Champagne and caviar are there if your taste runs in that direction. You're not expected to do anything. The phone never rings. You can take a gentle stroll now and then, read your book, watch your choice of first-run movies, or nod off whenever all this puts you in the mood.

That's business class.

Then there's economy class, which as most people know is a form of state-sponsored terrorism, a cruel and unusual punishment which should be outlawed by some Geneva Convention. In economy class you're always wedged in next to some big fat guy whose hips and stomach and massive upper arms and elbows spread across into your tiny space. And the big fat guy, despite consuming vast quantities of the airline's cardboard food and sundry drinks, has a limitless bladder capacity so he never gets up, which means you too can never leave your seat as the prospect of trying to climb over him is geometrically implausible. The seat in front is inches from your nose at best, and its occupant wants to spend the whole journey with his seat leaning back so that you're pinioned into your seat. In the row behind you, two blokes are drinking and belching at a furious pace, determined to rinse every drop of free alcohol out of the flight. And the more they drink the louder they talk. Never more than a couple of rows away, an infant squalls. Sometimes there are extra tricks, like the air-conditioning leaking above your head so that a slow, steady drip of water keeps you both awake and wet for the duration of the flight. Sometimes your leg-rest is broken and hangs down on your feet so that your tiny space is diminished even further. Often the reading light doesn't work. And so on.

Flying to Kuala Lumpur that day I am travelling with Air Lauda and they're not too bad. But there is an institutional dishonesty about airports these days which is weird.

Half an hour before the plane is due to take off I'm at the departure gate and the staff are saying the plane is on time and everything is going according to schedule. But as all the passengers can readily see, the plane hasn't even landed yet.

We take off a couple of hours late.

The plane leaves in the late afternoon and lands about midnight KL time, or three in the morning Sydney time. The Air Lauda crew are got up in fairly wacky outfits. They're all young and wearing, male and female alike, black jeans, black formal blazers, ties and, it being Christmas season, red Santa Claus caps.

KL's old airport, at Subang, was crowded and dusty and a little bit grotty. And sometimes things didn't work too well. Its only advantage was that it was close to the city. The city's new airport, KLIA (Kuala Lumpur International Airport—Southeast Asians love acronyms, which somehow sound modern and techno-logical)—is an incredible, huge, glass barn. And it's a long way from town.

KLIA is the biggest airport in Southeast Asia, which is the sort of thing Malaysians like to brag about. It's much bigger than the city or the nation need. But they'll grow into it in time. A pilot pal of mine told me about flying a freighter into KLIA and the ground crew directing him with all kinds of Bravo Foxtrot Delta signals and codes to turn here and turn there on the runway's apron. He looked up and saw that the place was completely empty except for him and answered back 'Just tell me which gate you want me to go to.'

Anyway there's no point being a smart aleck about KLIA because Malaysia's extravagance is the traveller's friend. KLIA, by the standards of almost any of the places I've been, with only the partial exception of Singapore, is the most sublime airport experience you'll have.

It is, admittedly, vast, so if you're old and feeble it's best to order a wheelchair or a buggy. Otherwise the long walk is just what you want when you step off a plane. The chrome and glass and tiles and whiteness not only suit the tropics, they are a splendidly old fashioned, attractive vision of the future. They're like something out of Arthur C. Clarke or Isaac Asimov. Your vision of the future is a good guide to your view of the present and there's nothing post-modern or cutely self-referential in KLIA. It's not embarrassed about being big, it doesn't mind pretty. On the way to a speeding bullet train, which takes you from the outer ring of the airport to its core, you pass fabulously up-market jewellery and toiletry stores, seemingly endless Delifrance coffee shops and a pretty good book shop.

This is no trivial matter. Airport bookshops are cultural transmission belts in Southeast Asia. Some Southeast Asian countries are democracies and some aren't. Folks from the non-democracies who get to travel pick up all kind of banned or just locally unavailable stuff in the big bookshops at the hub airports. Singapore Airport's lavish bookshops are still the market leaders but both KL and Hong Kong, when they got new airports, also got new and bigger bookshops.

KLIA has other charms. It has somehow incorporated several small tropical gardens into its design. I don't know how they do this while maintaining the air-con everywhere else. (Oops: 'air-con'. As well as acronyms, Southeast Asians love word abbreviations, so 'air-conditioning' is universally 'air-con'. A high commission is a high com. The Ministry of Defence is MinDef. You'll catch on.)

The bullet train from outer KLIA to inner KLIA is spectacular. I get into the front carriage, the nose of which is glass and affords a great view as we speed between the two terminals. The modernist, old-fashioned–futuristic, science fiction atmosphere of KLIA is reinforced as we zap into central, all brightly lit, glass panels twinkling at us, radars rotating, a few aricraft doing their thing at the gates.

Customs and immigration are quick. It's 12.30 a.m. KL time and there aren't too many people around. A young Malay woman is on the immigration counter. She wears an airport uniform and a *tudong*, the modest headdress many Muslim women wear in Malaysia. Perhaps she's a young mother. She looks absolutely dead-beat, as if she could drop off at any second. But she stamps the passport quickly enough, which is the main thing.

As I walk out of the airport to the road-side taxi-stand I am hit by a sudden, furnace-blast of hot, sticky air. It is the taste and feel of Southeast Asia. Whenever I come back it is always a jolt, an instant pulse of heat and presence and possibility. Straight away my glasses fog, in seconds the sweat starts to form, the body starts to tingle.

It's good to be back.

Taxis are well organised at KLIA which is a great contrast to the touts and hucksters and general chaos you encounter at a lot of other regional airports, like Manila or New Delhi. KLIA's system is a little bit bureaucratic but it means you don't get ripped off and you stand almost no chance of being mugged by the cab driver, something which happens disconcertingly frequently in other parts of Asia. I walk to the official counter and tell them my destination. I buy a ticket which I later give to the cab driver and there is no charge beyond the ticket, certainly no one ever expects a tip and there is no dispute about the fare. That is not to say that KLIA doesn't offer some eclectic sights and sounds. It is one institution that the nation's three main races—Malay, Chinese and Indian—share fully. Malaysians who are not on business trips tend to get met by large family delegations. Many different types of Malaysian are to be seen at the airport. That night the oddest is a stocky Malay girl in her late teens or early twenties, her hair dyed a flaming orange, and wearing a blue T-shirt which bears the words, 'Excuse me he lost my horse'. Utterly baffling.

Quickly I seek the order of an airport limousine taxi (don't be fooled, all the airport taxis are limousine). For a trip into town the cost is about 80 Malaysian ringgit, which is about A$30 or US$20.

The system has only one drawback. The cabs that travel between the airport and the city are dedicated to that task. That means the cab drivers, routinely working long shifts, have one of the most boring jobs in the world, endlessly repeating the journey back and forth, back and forth. To relieve the boredom of their job, and to make a little more money, they drive at death-defying speeds along what is admittedly a high-quality freeway. The journey should take 90 minutes to two hours, but my driver that night cuts it down to an hour. It doesn't matter. I'm too tired to worry, and doze fitfully in the cab.

It's 2 a.m. by the time I finally check in at MiCasa Hotel Apartments, in Ampang, just near the US embassy and ten minutes from the centre of town. I've stayed there a lot, so I'm a familiar sight to the staff, mostly Malay and Indian, and they welcome me back warmly. Adnan, the Indian assistant manager, always seems to be there when I come in and always seems happy to see me. He remembers what I do for a living, remembers my relatives, shrewdly though discreetly discusses politics, and offers advice on the city. Tall, broad-shouldered, slim and magnificently moustachioed along Errol Flynn lines, he is the embodiment of the MiCasa.

I have to be honest with you about hotels. I am beyond the backpacker stage. I no longer stay in $10-a-night hotels and have moved past the period in my life when I'm happy to squat on friends' lounge-room floors. This is even less appealing if you're travelling with a wife and three kids. But while I like luxury as much as the next man I'm not routinely a five-star-hotel person. They're just too expensive. They can also be a bit impersonal, though I'm not against them in principle. Jessie and I are middle-range budget travellers. At the MiCasa you can negotiate long term rates and this time, because we're staying for a couple of months, the cost is around A$500 a week. That's good value, especially considering it includes a vast buffet breakfast each morning.

I've certainly stayed in more luxurious places than the MiCasa but it has become my second home. It is the place in the world I like to stay best after my own house in Sydney. It's not an especially lavish building. It consists of two main accommodation wings, seven storeys high, and a large foyer area open to the weather at either end, which can be tricky if you get a tropical downpour coinciding with strong winds.

But the MiCasa is an institution of great charm. It is halfway between a hotel and an apartment block. This means service is friendly rather than fawning. Staff are happy to do things for you, and the place is small enough that they know who you are, but they're not dripping all over you trying to get you to use services you don't need. It doesn't pretend to do all the things a hotel does. There's no well-stocked mini-bars, room service is limited, I've never quite worked out how the laundry runs.

The design of the place is a surprisingly effective Somerset Maugham colonial style. The common floors on the ground level are all in a quiet, dark green marble. Without using much space the place has cultivated dense tropical gardens, or at least, through the shrewd use of palm tree clusters and flower beds, the suggestion of dense tropical gardens. Everywhere there's an effort to make use of the sunshine and the warmth. A long connecting corridor has one side entirely composed of retractable, louvred doors. The rooms themselves follow this style, with floor to ceiling brown louvre shutters which pull out on hinges. Although the rooms are air-conditioned, they also have fans set in the high ceilings. Ceiling fans are ubiquitous in Southeast Asia. Any middle-class home that doesn't have air-con has ceiling fans. In the MiCasa they must be mainly for show. They have about them that indefinable sense of luxury and the slowness of a quieter time. The furniture is rattan or dark wood. The paintings are serene and sometimes voluptuous Malay jungle and *kampung* (village) scenes. Lots of foreigners use the MiCasa, but its greatest tribute is that lots of Malaysians stay there, too—from sharp-dressing Chinese wheelers and dealers down from Penang on business, to middle-class Malay families visiting KL for a wedding or a holiday.

This trip, Jessie and I are at the MiCasa while the three boys stay with their grandmother, Balwinder Kaur, in her apartment at Pandan Indah, a suburb five or six kilometres away. Jessie is joining me at the MiCasa later in the day, having stayed the first night with her mum. Jessie was born in Singapore and grew up in Malaysia, first in Melaka, then in KL. She is of north Indian, specifically Punjabi, extraction. Our three boys, Ajay, Lakhvinder and Jagdave, were all born in KL when Jessie was in her first marriage, before I knew her. But they have been my sons now for a long time. They're great guys. You'll just have to take my word on that. I'd say my sons are the best men I know, which is not to say they can't drive you mad sometimes.

After a few hours sleep, I catch a cab round to Balwinder's apartment. It's up one flight of stairs in a big concrete block on a main road opposite a huge shopping centre called Fajar. Balwinder's apartment is typical of the decent, middle-class housing so many Malaysians now enjoy. Her block contains all the main races, Malay, Chinese and Indian. Her apartment is smallish by Western standards, but attractive. It's three bedrooms over two storeys. Kitchen, combined living–dining and balcony downstairs, three bedrooms and two bathrooms upstairs. Balwinder lives there with Jessie's two sisters, Amy and Dipi (shortened versions of their full Punjabi names—Amarjeet and Hardip).

Amy and Dipi, like Jessie, are beautiful young women. High cheek bones, large almond eyes, long dark hair, tall and statuesque in the Sikh manner, they are delighted to see us. Amy works for a German multinational, Dipi is a stewardess with Malaysian Airlines. Once the two sisters came to visit us in Sydney and spent a day helping at the canteen at the boys' school. Our phone ran hot that night as teachers called to find out, not to put too fine a point on it, if Jessie's sisters were married.

Balwinder's flat may be small, but it is spotlessly, gleamingly clean. In the tropics you either clean relentlessly or the fecund bugs and ruthless mould get the better of you. It is noisy from the traffic outside and brightly lit by fluorescent lights inside.

The walls reflect Balwinder' diverse life. Pride of place goes to a photo of Balwinder as a young bride, seated beside her husband, who died when Jessie was a child. In the photo he looks just what he was—tall, sleek, an imposing Sikh paratrooper in the Malaysian Army.

A much larger print is of an avuncular-looking man in a long, grey beard and full turban, surrounded by an orange glow. This is a representation of the great Sikh leader, Guru Nanak, who decreed the wearing of beards and turbans for men, and transformed his people into mighty warriors.

Further down the room, just near the doorway, a kangaroo skin is attached to the wall, a souvenir of a daughter's visit to Australia.

The apartment's location is good. There's a light rail transit (LRT of course) stop nearby at Cempaka and the huge Fajar shopping centre is air-conditioned. Outside Fajar every night are countless satay stick and other food stalls and Malaysians of every race and plenty of foreigners routinely take the air there, browsing and grazing at their leisure. The boys don't repine at Balwinder's. They enjoy being fussed over by their grandmother and two glamourous aunties. Most days they come and swim at the hotel pool. Every day we eat together, either at the hotel or a food stall or Balwinder's.

Eating is a big deal in KL. It's a food city. Balwinder, to whom I am devoted, loves me and dotes on me and one of the ways she does this is by cooking me endless feasts. That day for lunch we have what is literally my favourite dish in the world, Punjabi chicken curry. The family has to tone down the chilli quotient a bit for my lame Western taste. At restaurants Jessie routinely asks for a bowl of fresh-cut chillies in soy sauce to add to whatever she's eating. Over the years of our marriage my taste has grown more robust but I still can't match her penchant for consuming pure rocket fuel. Balwinder has got the spices just right in this meal.

I have a deal with the boys that they do some reading and study every day in the school holidays. After lunch they go upstairs to fulfil their end of the bargain. Jessie, her mother and sisters have a long, animated chat in Punjabi about everything they haven't caught up on over the last several months. I go over to the sofa and pick up the day's *New Straits Times*. I have determined on this trip to find out something of Islamic fundamentalism and extremism and what various Malaysians think of it. In the next few days my search will begin. But today, tired after my late night, I find the sound of the women's voices, from which I can pick up the meaning of only a few words, a gentle lullaby, the laughter interspersed with more serious passages, sometimes all of them talking at once in a kind of strange unconscious harmony, sometimes a solo aria being performed. I drift into sleep and shamelessly snooze the entire afternoon away.

In Search of KL

The Days of Walking Dangerously

Jessie and I welcome two old friends to the MiCasa. The Australian novelist Chrisopher Koch, author of *The Year of Living Dangerously*, that classic of journalists and Sukarno in the madness of Jakarta in 1965, and of several other acclaimed novels, is coming with his wife, Robin, for a first holiday in Malaysia.

I feel a little apprehensive. Chris is one of my closest and oldest friends. I love him like a brother. I'd trust him with my life. But he's never been to KL before, and Robin only once many years ago. They are coming now wholly on my recommendation. Maybe I've oversold KL. Can any city possibly live up to the recommendations I've given to this place?

Breakfast is a very affectionate reunion for the four of us. It is also an absurd feast. Anyone who is used to the parsimonious, pitiful offerings that pass for a continental breakfast in Europe, still less in England or even the US, will be bowled over by the splendour, the artistry, the oomph and passion of the Malaysian hotel breakfast. Every hotel I've stayed at in Malaysia serves a buffet breakfast and from three stars to five, they're all lavish.

At the MiCasa you take breakfast at the Tapas Bar and Bistro. Of course there's a choice of cereals and toast and all that sort of stuff. There are also chilled fruit juices, orange, pineapple, watermelon, plus a vigorous medley of tropical fruits—papayas, different types of melon and the rest. Then there is a whole wall of hot dishes—beef bacon (they don't serve pork in Muslim Malaysia), eggs, hash browns, chicken sausages, baked beans. There is congee, the Chinese porridge which many Malaysians like. There's fried noodles, chicken curry, hot beef rendang. There's a chef standing by a grill who will mix you any kind of exotic omelette, or fry your eggs just so. Then, just to demonstrate the energetic eclecticism of Malaysian eating there is tray after tray of cup cakes, Danish pastries, and bread rolls of every description.

Is it excessive? Of course. Malaysians like their buffet breakfast, and their high teas in the afternoon. Why it is that more Malaysians are not rotund is a mystery, though they are slowly getting more rotund. But if you are going to eat to excess, the best time to do so is at breakfast. KL is a popular holiday destination for Arabs, having the right combination of Muslim flavour and Western diversions. Arabs escaping their summer are the only people who can think that KL's pitiless tropical heat is quite mild. Now I don't wish to engage in any offensive ethnic stereotyping here but it seems to me that it's a brave man who stands in the way of an Arab family and its breakfast buffet.

I advise Chris and Robin that the best way to deal with the MiCasa breakfast is to take your time and indulge yourself to your heart's content but follow it up by a vigorous day's walking, drinking lots of water and skipping, or at least going very light, on lunch.

Chris decides he likes the MiCasa. The staff are well spoken and courteous, his room is gracious. 'My boy,' he says, 'you have led me into paradise.'

Jessie and Robin agree they're going to need lots of energy that day and get into some kind of weird espresso coffee fetish. They drink about six doubles each and are pretty much bouncing off the ceiling by the time we leave for a day's walking tour of the city.

Mid-morning the four of us set off. We walk down the thundering Jalan Tun Razak (a huge thoroughfare named after Malaysia's first

Prime Minister). The dense humid air is infused with traffic fumes. We turn left towards Kuala Lumpur City Centre and the Petronas Twin Towers, the tallest buildings in the world (couldn't you guess).

Within minutes Chris and I are sweating in the way of Western men in the tropics. Do women sweat less than men or what? Jessie and Robin somehow look poised and relaxed long after Chris and I have come to resemble ambulatory oil puddles.

The twin towers are worth a look. In the marvellous Sean Connery movie, *Entrapment*, one of few international films set in Kuala Lumpur, not the least of the beautiful characters on screen are the locations—New York, London, Scotland and KL's twins. In one memorable scene the twins are shown rising from a rancid riverside slum, as Connery and his luscious co-star, Catherine Zeta-Jones, take a cruise on the muddy river.

'Isn't it beautiful here?' the dishy Welshwoman asks, irony dripping, the implication being that it's foolish of the Malaysians to waste money on big prestige projects like the twin towers when people lack basic housing. There's only one problem. The river scene was filmed in Melaka, 120 kilometres away, and the image of the twins super imposed on it.

There are no slums, and incidentally no river, at the base of the twins, which are in the middle of a business not residential district. At the base is actually one of Southeast Asia's loveliest public spaces, the gardens of the Kuala Lumpur City Centre. KLCC is a huge, multi-storeyed shopping complex surrounded by a park with a large, clear, artificial lake and connected wading pool. It's probably kitsch to confess this but I like these Southeast Asian shopping complexes enormously. They may lack the so-called authenticity of the village market beloved of tourists, but what they signal is the arrival in Southeast Asia of stable, enjoyable, middle-class life. The only people who mock middle class life are bohemians who take its comforts for granted, aristocrats who feel they are above its quotidian mix of small pleasures and routine obligations, some extreme Greens, who believe bourgeois consumption is unsustainable and therefore shouldn't spread, and left-over Marxists who rightly see the embourgeoisement of society as the enemy of the revolution. Oh, and sometimes religious fanatics, be they Christian or Muslim, who idealise a narrow, agrarian poverty as a better environment for maintaining morals.

I'm sorry, I guess I'm a rootless cosmopolite as far as all that goes. Show me a few big city shopping malls and I'll show you some societies getting their acts together.

KL has certainly become more middle-class in the years I've been visiting it. Nowhere is more bourgoeis than KLCC. In the huge city park at its base, every day there are families in abundance, dad pushing a stroller, kids frolicking. The buildings are edged on two sides by alfresco restaurants. At night they're raffish and fashionable, a haunt for KL's beautiful people. Chinese and *mat sallehs* (white folks) drink beer and wine while Malays enjoy endless varieties of coffee.

It wouldn't be quite right though to leave the twins defined solely by the greenness at their base. Up close and personal the twins themselves are an astonishing abundance of chrome and steel and glass. There is a Gotham touch there somewhere, like a giant *Batman* movie set. At night, always brightly lit, they can resemble two giant Daleks from *Dr Who*. On other nights, viewed from other tall buildings, they look like giant toffee apples poking through the fairy floss of low clouds.

Walking down to Little India we never lose sight of the twins. They dominate from every corner. John Naisbitt in his celebration of Asian economic success, *Megatrends Asia*, hailed the twins as exemplars of Asia's modernisation. Michael Backman in *Asian Eclipse*, written after the 1997 economic downturn, wrote of them thus: 'Largely vacant and mostly composed of elevator shafts on account of their height, they are symbols of excess and inefficiency.' It is of course an inherently silly business building the world's tallest building. But we Australians certainly went through that phase. For a long time everything we built was the biggest, best, brightest or whatever in the Southern Hemisphere, which simply reflected the fact that there are few rich, developed countries in the Southern Hemisphere.

Jessie and I lead Chris and Robin down the hill away from KLCC. We avoid for the moment the night-life entertainment district known as KL's Golden Triangle and head instead for Little India. These old parts of KL—Little India and Chinatown—are densely alive. Their architecture and visual style have avoided the sanitising effects of replanning or government design. Generally I'm pretty much in favour of development and modernisation but I hope KL never, ever redevelops these areas. Even in purely commercial terms a couple of enclaves of the living ancient are an important attraction in most big international cities.

Of course, KL, truth be known, has very little of the living ancient about it. Of all Southeast Asia's big cities it is perhaps the greenest and most naturally lovely, but it's not very old. Nor, traditionally, did it possess any great romance. It hardly figures in Somerset Maugham's short stories about the old Malaya. Penang, Melaka and of course Singapore, and endless isolated rubber plantations, yes, but in Maugham's stories Kuala Lumpur is just a dusty administrative centre, almost always off-stage.

My particular devotion to KL is, I'll admit, a little eccentric. *Kuala Lumpur* means muddy estuary and it was originally a tin mine. You can't get much less romantic than that. It was only really founded in the mid-nineteenth century, when tin deposits were discovered in abundance and it became a Chinese mining town.

The Government has filled it with grand monuments and built many national icons and some of this is an attempt to capture some of the prestige of antiquity which exists all around it, from the densely fecund jungles to the older cities of the peninsula. Similarly its countless biggest, best, fastest, longest, largest, looniest hotels, government centres, amusement parks, towers, airports, bridges and all the rest are an attempt to capture the spirit of modernisation. It wants to be both modern and venerably antique, not dusty and indeterminately middle-aged.

It's not hard for KL to feel like a giant Disney theme park. The outsider can react to this in one of two ways. He can sneer in smug self-satisfaction at its foolish pretensions (that's pretty much the standard response of Western smarties) or he can delight in the almost child-like quality of enjoyment that so many of these buildings, bridges, towers, et cetera give to the city's inhabitants.

Chris is a trim guy, lean and fit for a man in his later sixties, but he comes originally from Tasmania, where it is never really hot and he is finding the heat of KL hard going. Maugham once wrote of 'the various tones of the heat' in Malaya: 'It was like an Eastern meoldy in the minor key, which exacerbates the nerves by its ambiguous monotony; and the ear awaits impatiently a resolution, but waits in vain.' It doesn't get as hot in KL as it gets in India or parts of Africa, but it never gets cool. It seems always to hover around 30 to 33 degrees Celsius, with occasional spikes upwards. KL weather is the Don Bradman, or Babe Ruth, of its class: its performance never falls far below a high number. If you're from a temperate climate it certainly takes a bit of getting used to. Karim Raslan, one of KL's best young writers, has contrasted the New Zealand sun, which can be soft even when it's warm, to the KL sun, which, he said, beats upon your head like a hammer striking an anvil.

So before we embark on an exploration of Little India, we seek the shady side of a street running between Little India and Chinatown. Chris thinks my suggestion that we find an air-conditioned coffee shop a good idea. We pass a narrow but modestly affluent-looking place called the Kowloon Hotel. The four of us venture into its lobby which is indeed blessedly cool. At the end of the lobby is the hotel's main restaurant. It bears an admirably explicit sign: Coffee House.

Not much ambiguity about a place called a coffee house, you might think, that's where you come for coffee.

There are no other customers at this pre-lunch time so we take a seat and soon enough along comes a small, toothy, Indian waiter, formally attired in correct evening dress, to take our order.

Chris asks for a black coffee.

'Oh, no sir, I am sorry, unfortunately at the moment we are not having any coffee.'

This produces a rather perplexed silence. How many coffee houses don't serve coffee?

The waiter has a suggestion, which causes him great joy as he sees it solving the problem altogether: 'Sir I could offer you some Milo. That would be very nice, isn't it?'

We decline this kind offer but remain friendly with the waiter who is disappointed he can't satisfy our wants.

'What I love about Indians,' says Chris, 'is their attachment to British empire comfort foods like Milo, the sort of thing matron would bring to a sick boy in the boarders' dormitory.'

We wander a little further down the street and come upon the Coliseum Cafe, one of KL's most venerable establishments. The Coliseum is a low, two-storey Chinese shop-house building. The ground floor of the main building is set a few paces back from the road. The footpath outside is covered by the building's second storey and further protection from the sun is afforded by twin arches on to the road. It stands next to what was once a Coliseum Cinema and must once have been a chic, up-to-the-minute nightspot. The cafe is two rooms wide, one a bar and the other a restaurant.

It must date from colonial times. It's the sort of place that could have come into being only in a British colony. It is not air-conditioned but has numerous if fairly lazy ceiling fans loping rather than whirring around. The rooms, although giving an unmistakable air of decay (though perhaps a decay that has neither progressed nor reversed in decades) are nonetheless high and airy. The walls are decorated mainly with old black-and-white newspaper cartoons. The staff is mostly Chinese, the furniture lower middle-class imitation Edwardian English drawing room, weirdly anonymous brown vinyl easy chairs, low couches, high-backed wooden seats for the tables which are covered in white tablecloths with Worcester sauce bottles their only other adornment. I first went there for lunch way back in 1992 with Australia's then high commissioner to Malaysia, John Dauth. He ordered bangers and mash, I ordered steak and chips. This English stodge is surprisingly popular in corners of Malaysia. The waiters then were Chinese and of such antiquity as to be unbelievable. The waiter who served Dauth and me that day looked as though he had escaped the Boxer Rebellion. Scrawny, stooped, tufts of grey hair protruding at odd points from his wizened face, his hand trembling from who knows what— Parkinson's disease, old age, a hangover from late-night mahjong —a good deal of the coffee was in the saucer by the time it made its perilous voyage in his hands to the table. But you had to admire the old geezer for still being on the job. You just can't beat the Chinese work ethic.

Now, Chris, Robin and Jessie have a coffee while I drink a lukewarm Pepsi (I don't trust the ice). The waiters now are still Chinese, still in uniforms of white shirts and black trousers, but of a completely different generation, perhaps the old guy's great-great-grandchildren. But they maintain his fine tradition of sturdy gruffness towards all customers. It's one of the few places in tourist-conscious KL that has a lot of foreign visitors and no pretence at modern service standards.

I love the Coliseum Cafe.

Fortified by our caffeine injections we head down to Jalan Masjit India (*Jalan* means 'street', so the name is literally 'Street of the Indian Mosque'), the heart of Little India itself. The scene on Jalan Masjit India is indescribably colourful. This area used to be overwhelmingly ethnically Indian, when I first came here you could think yourself in old Madras. Now there are many more Malays and plenty of Chinese too, but the area retains its Indian flavour, especially through the shops. This is typically KL, shopping areas with particular ethnic associations are not enclaves of exclusion but an offering which all Malaysians can enjoy. Many of the Indians are *mamaks*, or Indian Muslim migrants, and their descendants. On both sides of the broad street are maybe a thousand stalls, with brightly coloured tarpaulin shade cloths, selling more-or-less everything. Behind the stalls are more established shops. These too have an Indian flavour—bookshops, flower shops, a sports store selling seedy looking Indian cricket bats and high-quality Australian cricket balls, lots of gold shops, drapery stores and of course endless, endless clothes shops. Although this is a good market and a cheap one it is not predominantly for foreigners. The overwhelming bulk of the people are locals.

Most of the crowd are women, laden with shopping bags containing groceries and meats and countless other household items. Many of the Indian women are in Punjabi suits—harem pants and long, flowing blouses over them. Punjabi suits are worn by Indian women of all religious and ethnic backgrounds because they are more practical than saris. Nonetheless a distinct minority of women are in saris.

The colour here comes from the people.

And their clothes.

Both the Punjabi suits and the saris are extravagantly coloured, green and red and gold, even purple. There are scarves laced in gold, and much gold on wrists and necks.

There are no mini-skirts here. In KL it's mostly the Chinese who wear mini-skirts and they don't wear them in traditional markets. But not all the Indian women are in traditional dress. Many younger Indian women are in spray-on jeans and designer tops. As always in KL the modern and the traditional jostle and blend.

'There's an awful lot of women wearing Muslim headdress,' Chris comments.

It's true. In the nearly 20 years I've been visiting Malaysia the proportion of women wearing the *tudong* has risen steadily. Religious observance is clearly on the rise.

The view in Jalan Masjit India is dominated by a tall, mustard-coloured apartment building bearing the curious title, Selangor Mansions. This is a decayed but lively place. Every apartment has a balcony, and from every balcony hangs washing. It is occupied mainly by *mamaks*, many of them seamstresses. The building is not air-conditioned, but from every open window—and every window appears to be open—you can see fans whirring away. What vivid, unrecorded life goes on there! It reminds me of the Bombay apartment building, inhabited mostly by Parsis (a tiny religious minority in India), in Rohinton Mistry's classic dissection of a self-contained community, *Tales from Firozsha Baag*.

The Malay women also contribute greatly to the colour quotient in Jalan Masjit India. They may cover up but no one wears black and no one wears a full face covering, more just the *tudong* which can be as little as a headscarf or as much as a traditional Western nun's headgear. But Malay women want to be fashion plates even if they're being modest. Their headdress and their robes are often white but there are also vibrant pinks, greens, even purples. Jalan Masjit India this day is incredibly crowded. The mixture of KL's three races, plus guest workers from Indonesia, Bangladesh and Africa, and even a few tourists, is exactly what a city should be. It is precisely the opposite of Osama bin Laden's puritanical view that only Muslims should walk on Muslim streets. Here we all walk together.

Beyond exhausting Chris and Robin, and walking off our breakfast, there is a purpose to all this tramping around. I want to enquire into Islam and the life of the city. But I have a rooted belief in the importance of just walking around a place and letting its smells and impressions seep in through the pores of the skin, taste a place, see it, smell it. The impression you get of a city as you walk around is totally different from the way it feels if you are just riding around in taxis all day.

I am obsessively drawn to bookshops. What are the local folks reading? Jessie wants to bargain for perfume for herself and cologne for the boys. She wants me to go away while she does this because the shopkeepers won't bargain properly if they see a Western man in the picture. Instead I stroll into a long, narrow bookshop. The most prominent book is a five-volume encyclopedia of *jihad*, with what seems to be a picture of a violent Palestinian protest on the cover. There is a book on Javi, which is Malay written in Arabic script. Malay is normally written in Roman script, so the study of Javi is an esoteric pastime. Its popularity has declined across the Malay world, except to some extent in neighbouring Brunei and among some religious folk who believe it helps them learn to read the Koran in the original Arabic.

Another book is called *Relaxation: Enhancing Your Better Self*. It's hard to know who this is aimed at. The Chinese in Malaysia are not known for relaxation whereas the Malays already seem among the most relaxed people on Earth. Another book seems more directly aimed at Indians—*The Medicinal Powers of Gold*. It is a small paperback printed on ancient, grey paper. I open it at random and read the following passage: 'I returned with the most irritating and intolerable itching on the third quadrant of my inner groin. I was naturally anxious to see whether the preparation of our first tincturation had any beneficial effect.' Is it genetically possible for anyone other than an Indian to write a sentence like that?

Jessie then goes on a food buying spree. Jessie is slim and beautiful and no matter what she eats she remains that way. (I, on the other hand, only need to nod at a coffee and cake and resemble immediately, as she so kindly puts it, a 'double Dunlop'). When Jessie returns to KL she cannot resist eating all the food from all of KL's ethnic groups. We walk round the corner to Masjit Jemaak and enter a long, low, cavernous and sinisterly dark shop which specialises in Indian sweets, which Malays and Chinese also buy in large numbers. After picking up a couple of kilos of supplies to keep the family properly sugarated, Jessie then, at a street stall, buys a supply of tapioca savouries and a thing called dodol. I haven't come across *dodol* before. It is a traditional Malay sweet allegedly made of raw sugar and coconut milk. It is dense and viscous. I am frankly reluctant to try it as it looks like a congealed oil slick. The only food I've ever come across that it remotely resembles is the black pudding my Irish relatives made me eat long ago in Galway, and that is made from pig's blood.

As we walk from the *dodol* stand we pass a stallholder shouting '*Ayam Percik! Ayam Percik!*' which means broadly speaking freshly grilled chicken available here. I am proud of my small Malay vocabulary and can recognise *ayam* as 'chicken'. But when he sees me this lean, wiry Malay stallholder changes his call to 'Chicken, Chicken'. This seems appropriate as Jessie is always telling me I have 'chicken skin' because I am so white, for which I can thank or blame the aforementioned Irish connection.

Chris and Robin have put up with our walkathon a long time. I'm not especially a sporting type but walking, provided it's at an amble, is one form of exercise I am happy to undertake for hours at a time. Chris walks more purposefully but finds too long in the pitiless KL sun vexatious. Coordinating your walking rhythms is one of the greatest challenges to joint holidaying. Around the corner from the *dodol* stand, in Leboh Ampang, the other spine of Little India, we pass a row of traditional Indian tea-houses. There are stores selling Hindu religious artefacts; images of Ganesh, the elephant-headed god with the body of a baby, are popular. Most of the stores play Tamil film music, a high-pitched, high-energy affair. The heavy traffic crawls past, buses and trucks belching and grinding through their gears, motorbikes farting viciously, car horns tooting. It's noisy and cacophonous. We pass by a row of moneylenders—dark, mysterious establishments with narrow doors and po-faced men sitting behind low tables. At last we take refuge from the noise and the car fumes in one of the tea shops that has half its area air-con and half under fans. Here we eat *tosai* which is like a pancake made of lentils, freshly fried in front of you and then you dip it in dahl or chicken gravy. You're meant to eat *tosais*, like so much other Malaysian food, with your bare hands. The restaurant has a sink in its main area to wash your hands after the meal. Out the back the bathroom latch doesn't work and the kitchen, dark, dank and forbidding, is not very reassuring. But the *tosais* are beautiful to taste and I've never known anyone get a tummy bug from this *tosai* shop.

After lunch we walk five minutes out of little India and across to Chinatown. There is a big, multi-storeyed shopping mall with a food court on the top floor, but Chinatown is dominated by row upon row of tiny, terraced, two-storey shop-houses—residence above, shop below, with stock pouring out in profusion across the narrow footpaths. There are Chinatowns like this all over Southeast Asia. The persistence, strength and spread of this form of commerce, this culture, is a tribute to the unbelievable energy of the Chinese small trader.

The main market in Chinatown is in Petaling Street. Some weeks later I call on an old friend, Jawhar, the deputy head of the Institute of Strategic and International Studies. Jawhar is fiddling with his watch: 'I'm sorry, my watch seems to have stopped, this is a Petaling Street Rolex and I'm very proud of it. It's supposed to last for one year.'

I know just how Jawhar feels. I've bought a lot of watches at Southeast Asian Chinatowns, never for more than A$7. If they last for a year I feel I've done very well indeed. If they last for less than a day I go back and make a fuss and the stallholder always kindly replaces the defective item with another one (does he then re-sell the defective model?). Between a day and a year I'll take my chances.

This day in Chinatown Chris talks me into buying a straw hat in the shape of a homburg, what I would think of as an elderly gentleman's topee but Chris insists is both smart and practical. Chris buys one too and says it keeps the sun off his face and his head cool. I find mine itchy and annoying, and the sense of it always pressing on my outsize head irksome. I can't get over the idea that it makes me look even more an out-of-place Western prat. I later contrive to leave it at Balwinder's apartment where it rests to this day as far as I know.

Chris and I bargain manfully at Chinatown but we are rank amateurs compared with Jessie. One great thing about bargaining with Chinese merchants though is that they really want to do business with you. The initial price the merchant asks naturally is only meant to be taken as an opening bid, a notional point at which to start the conversation.

Walking along Petaling Street the four of us are subject to constant entreaty.

'You come in my shop, *lah*!' one portly Chinese woman in ill-fitting shorts and a large, dirty, white T-shirt shouts. Malaysians of all races add 'lah' to the end of many sentences. It is the monosodium glutamate of Manglish. It adds flavour without any other discernible function and has unknown side effects.

'I give very good price for you, *lah*. Good barg'in, special new brand, can do special deal for you, *lah*.'

Jessie looks at a coat hanging on a clothes stall and begins the bargaining process.

'How much is this?' Jessie asks.

'Eighty ringgit only, very good price, special one, *lah*.'

'Eighty ringgit? My goodness that's ridiculous.'

'Gentleman can buy for you.'

The situation is hopeless. The bargaining process has been fatally polluted by my presence.

'Some of these *mat sallehs* will pay whatever the Chinese ask,' Jessie comments with scorn. She banishes me again before she starts the intricate, delicate, wary game with another trader further down the street.

Chinatown isn't solely about commerce, though you might get that impression. There are clan houses, celebrating members of one broad family, united generally by a family name, revering rather than worshipping their ancestors, although certainly seeking their helpful intervention in the affairs of this world. These clan houses are much festooned with dragons; joss sticks burn, decorative, valuable-looking vases sit in splendour, sculptures of ancient ancestors stand guard, furtive triad associations are suggested—they cry out to be rendered in Western film as the haunt of the mysterious East.

Chinatown also contains the jumble and the muddle of old KL. Amidst all this Chineseness is the Sri Mariaman Hindu temple, with its grand marble entrance, dark oak doors, riotous, soaring towers of voluptuous statuary and, on this day, a young, male devotee, naked from the waist up, draping strings of flowers around side altar statues of Hindu deities.

Finally we take mercy on the Koches and head back to the MiCasa for rest and recreation. I make a few phone calls to Islamic politicians and clerics. The pattern of our days thus establishes itself. A lavish breakfast, a hearty walk, a little gentle business in the afternoon. The boys come to the hotel and swim most days, and we dine with the Koches or repair to Balwinder's flat.

A few days later Jessie, her sister Amy, our son Ajay and I tramp around the more formal, newer, civic parts of KL, some of it left over from the British but most of it designed by Malays to represent Malaysian nationalism. We start at Merdeka (independence) Square. Merdeka Square is a pretty, green *padang* (field) in a city with a lot of pretty greenery. Incongruously (or perhaps congruously) for the square celebrating independence, it has a cricket pitch in the middle of it. And, almost inevitably, as the sign informs us, the world's third-tallest flagpole. (*Aieeeeyaaaaahhh!* as my Chinese friends would say.)

Opposite Merdeka Square is the Supreme Court building— a stylish Moorish number. The profusion of Arab and Moorish architectural styles in KL dates from an attempt to find a distinctive non-British cultural expression for the majority Muslim population. There is an element of cultural cringe here. Traditional Malay architectural styles have not been much used, as if to bear out V.S. Naipaul's thesis, which he advances in *Beyond Belief: Islamic Excursions Among the Converted Peoples*, that Islam in non-Arab countries promotes a local cultural inferiority complex because it regards all non-Arab history as second-rate at best.

Traditional Malay architecture was built in wood. To some extent therefore it didn't obviously furnish models for grand public buildings. But its motifs could have been incorporated into more official Malaysian architecture, a process which is still only really beginning. Generally I like Malaysia's public buildings, their space, their bold colours and their frank enjoyment of themselves, but too often there's a feeling that you're getting a secondhand version of the Middle East, rather than something that emerges naturally out of Malaysia itself.

A short walk from the Supreme Court takes us to the National Mosque, would you believe it—the biggest in Southeast Asia. It is a huge, elegant, white building with a striking blue roof. Under its shadow seems quiet and calm, cool and welcoming, though as we approach its doors we find it is closed to visitors that day. Despite many attempts, I've never actually been to a mosque in Malaysia which is open to visitors when I'm there, which suggests that really they'd be just as happy if non-Muslims didn't visit.

We cross the road from the mosque and enter the Islamic Art Exhibition Museum. After the torrid heat we give thanks for the air-con. Islamic art, eschewing representation of the human form, doesn't have much of a profile in the West. This museum is mostly empty of visitors but we find it strikingly handsome, white and distinctly Middle Eastern in ambience. It is full of quiet courtyards and gardens, and contains endless intricate models of great mosques around the world, as well as a fine general collection of Islamic art. There is an exhibition showing how Islamic design principles blended with Malay styles in the building of mosques in Malaysia, typically emphasising the vertical pillars of the main prayer hall and the Malay-style roof. But this seems to have more to do with the past than with today.

All these fairly splendid public buildings do give KL the feeling of an endless theme park for grown-ups. Nowhere is this truer than in the five-star hotels. These modern palaces of luxury are derided by politically correct, touchy-feely international travellers as soulless and uninteresting. Nothing could be further from the truth. That attitude also misses the social role they play in the society locally. They are not purely, or even necessarily mainly, for international visitors. Wealthy Malaysian businessmen and powerful Malaysian politicians just love to take you to lunch, or indeed to be taken to lunch, at a five-star hotel. KL, as I say, is a city that takes food pretty seriously, and the restaurants in the five-star hotels are more chic than all but a tiny handful of restaurants not in hotels.

For all KL's races the wedding is the high point of human activity. A surprisingly large number of Malaysian families can afford to hold a wedding reception (often after prodigious saving or even the liquidation of precious family assets) in a five-star hotel, or if not then a four-star or a three-star. These hotels are markers of social significance.

Their restaurants and foyers and shopping arcades afford a lot of pleasure even to people who cannot afford to buy anything there, or only very rarely. Many, many KL families, deep into the modest end of the middle class, once in a while treat themselves to a hotel high tea. The KL high tea is an institution, blending British and Malay and Indian influences. In Western stories of the old planters' lives lunch was often followed by a sleep during the worst heat of the day which was then followed by tea. But today's KL high tea really has very little to do with afternoon tea as this is understood in the West. Instead it is a huge banquet served as a buffet around the middle of the afternoon. The traditional Malaysian way of consuming this meal is to have little or no lunch beforehand and then consume the buffet over several hours, thus incorporating dinner as well. The high point of the buffet is tea *tarik*, a sinewy, sweet milk tea which in its preparation is pulled from container to container.

From time to time, at conferences and the like, I've stayed at some of KL's five-star hotels. Quite the most remarkable is the modestly named Palace of the Golden Horses.

The Palace of the Golden Horses is the over-the-top, super-duper, mega-deluxe, gorgeous, wedding cake king daddy of five-star hotels. It is a huge property on the highway to the airport and is much favoured for official conferences. It is built on an old tin mine. The mine has been flooded to form an artificial lake. There is the obligatory golf course and luxury swimming pool complex. The building is huge and truly looks like a Moorish palace built by an especially opulent and indulgent sultan. It could've leapt straight out of a Disney cartoon version of *A Thousand and One Arabian Nights*. I strain to hear Scheherazade spinning her tales. There are countless minarets and arched balconies around its many layered floors. There are wings and alcoves protruding in all directions. The vast foyer is done out in the most sumptuous marble. Exquisite chandeliers disappear into the impossibly high cathedral ceiling. Everything is on a grand scale. The walkways arched in stone are expansive. There are many actual statues of golden horses and much of the trim—handles on bathroom doors and the like—also involve miniature horse statues. There seem to be endless staff, and so many meeting rooms and corridors and shopping arcades and function centres and business centres, as well as a bewildering array of restaurants and coffee shops, that it is quite easy to get lost in its labyrinthine expanses.

I stayed there once for two days attending a regional security conference. Who can deny that this unaccustomed luxury was fun for a couple of days? During that conference I was riding up in the lift when Henry Kissinger got in. Although accompanied by a flunky or two, he was clearly a bit lost, having trouble, as I was, finding the function room for the conference session he was meant to be attending.

'I think the builder of this hotel maybe didn't pass design school,' he rumbled in that deep, double bass Germanic accent of his. With all due respect to the great former statesman I think he approached the Palace of the Golden Horses in the wrong spirit. The Palace, like so much of modern KL, is the absolute opposite of the post-modern, minimalist aesthetic which dominates Western taste these days. Everything in the West has to be ironic and self-referential. We wouldn't be caught dead expressing enthusiasm or indulging unironic delight.

At the Palace of the Golden Horses the thing is not to look for chic but to let yourself go, to think of it as the ultimate playground of your lost childhood. One night Jessie and I went to the Italian restaurant at the Palace. By KL standards it was certainly expensive, but not prohibitive. And there was a live jazz and blues band, imported from Los Angeles. There's nothing all that remarkable about that, except that most hotel bands in Southeast Asia are local or Filipino. The LA band was just another part of what KL offers.

Officially KL has a population of only 1.5 million. Of course it is much larger, counting all the illegal, legal and semi-legal guest workers, from Indonesians and Bengalis on construction sites to Filipina and Indonesian maids and *amahs*. But the small population is also just a question of definition. The city of Petaling Jaya is contiguous with KL and really just a suburb of KL. So too is Subang

Jaya near the old airport. So in effect is the new administrative centre of PutraJaya and CyberJaya, the centre of the Government's Multi-Media Super Corridor. There are other population centres nearby and part of the Klang River valley. The point of which is that KL is the centre of an urban conurbation of several million. It presents itself as a small city and, traffic jams notwithstanding, it's accessible and manageable, but it is also really a big city with all the diversity and excitement a big city offers.

My impression is that most KL'ers are proud of their city and enjoy all the amenities which have come their way in recent years. None of this is to deny the underside of KL, like the underside of any big city. There are red-light districts, Chow Kit and Bukit Bintang at night. The dignified Islamic Cemetry is sometimes littered with syringes as it's a favoured shooting-up spot for drug addicts.

I'm not alone in delighting in KL. Many of the smartest young Malaysians have chosen KL over London, New York and other possibilities. Take Karim Raslan. Karim has been a friend of mine for years. He is Eurasian, with a Malay father and an English mother. He comes from a distinguished Malay family and identifies himself fully as Malay. He was educated at Cambridge, for a time wrote leaders for the *Times of London*, and was called to the Bar in Inner Temple.

He is something of a KL phenomenon. He seems to be in and about everything. He is originally a lawyer but has been desultory at best about the practice of law. He is good-looking in a rather Cambridge way, sort of a Malay Hugh Grant look, and stylish, and speaks with a cultivated contemporary English accent. While desultory about the law he is fantastically active about everything else. It's one of the odd features, a strength in some ways, of a developing country that its leading people can be active in a number of fields. Karim is also a syndicated columnist and short story writer who one day will take the world by storm with a great novel.

But he is also on the committee of various economic think-tanks and is to be found at economic conferences and seminars. Rather strangely he is involved as well in regional security think-tanks and conferences. He is deeply engrossed in the KL art scene, attending gallery openings, helping young artists. He is regarded as an expert on the political face of Islam and is certainly much quoted on this. Karim exercises a prodigy of ubiquity. Is he a gifted polymath, a well-rounded generalist, or is there just a touch of the blarney about him as well? I always feel that whatever possible event I could conceive of attending in KL, from a seminar on the role of dance in opera to a technical economic discussion on capital controls or a symposium on the implications of missile defence for the proliferation of nuclear weapons on the Korean peninsula, Karim would be there. As far as I can tell he is generally kind to everyone but certainly makes an effort to help outsiders seeking a way into KL.

Perfectly formed in every way, Karim could have been all kinds of success in England but he chose to come back to live in KL. I ask him why: 'There was just a thinness to life in England, compared with Malaysia. Of course what you love most about Malaysia you sometimes hate most, its drama and unpredictability. In terms of what's happening artistically it's just waiting to be discovered. It's as rich as the Caribbean but on a much bigger scale—as rich as V.S. Naipaul's Port of Spain.'

As Karim readily admits, food played a part in his decision to live in KL. He once wrote of his time in England that he was astonished to be 'in a country so frigid and mean that when people invite you for tea they really do mean tea and nothing else'.

KL for him, as for me, could sometimes appear to be nothing more than 'a succession of meals, so many meals that there were times when I realised I'd eaten breakfast, a mid-morning snack, lunch, tea, dinner and supper . . . '

Karim also enjoys the intensely gossipy nature of Malay society, as he once wrote: 'KL is also a succession of gossip, of stories that floated in the air, linking everyone, high and low. From the songstress who slept with the politician who slept with the pretty TV journalist who slept with the princess who slept with the stable boy (but don't tell anybody!) who slept with the bored *mak datin* housewife [datin is a Malay fedual title, like an English life peerage, given out to vast numbers of worthy citizens] who never slept with her bored *datuk* [male version of datin] husband who slept with his secretary (we men are so boring) who slept with her boyfriend who slept with his best friend who slept with the checkout girl at the supermarket at Cheras who slept with the gangster who slept with the callgirl who slept with the record producer who slept with the songstress—and so it went on.'

Karim's love of KL's art, politics and gossip is admirable, inspirational. But art, politics and gossip are to be found in all big cities. I have come to KL this time seeking something else. I have two purposes, to have a family holiday, and to learn something more of Islam and its political arm and how it plays out in Malaysian politics and society. In short, I want to find some *mullahs*. All this tramping around KL isn't going to do the trick. Tomorrow I will set out in earnest, in search of political Islam.

Desperately Seeking Islamic Fundamentalists

Finding political Islam in KL is not really difficult. Understanding it is another matter altogether. Islam is a tricky business in Malaysia. Malaysia consists of the Malay peninsula and eastern Malaysia, which comprise two states, Sabah and Sarawak, on the western side of Borneo. Something under 60 per cent of Malaysia's population is Muslim. Somewhat more than this are classified as bumiputeras, literally sons of the soil. Bumis get all kinds of advantages, from preference in education to lower interest rates for housing loans to special consideration in government share issues and lots and lots of other goodies as well.

The indigenous people of Sabah and Sarawak are classified as *bumis*, though not all of them are Muslim. So are the indigenous people, the *orang asli*, of the peninsula, and of course the majority Malays. Malays means ethnic Malays. Malaysians means citizens of Malaysia. About a quarter of Malaysians are ethnic Chinese and a little under 10 per cent Indian.

Ethnicity, religion and class have been an explosive cocktail in Malaysia's history. When Malaya was given independence in 1957 the British handed over rule to the Malay aristocracy. Nine Malay states have royal families. The sultans of the various states take it in turn to be king. At the time of independence the vast majority of Malays were poor, rural, *kampung* dwellers. Dr Mahathir Mohamad, who ruled the country for more than twenty years from 1981, was the first commoner ever to be Prime Minister.

The British were happy to hand over power to the Malay aristocracy in part because they seemed such good chaps. Many of them had spent time in England and imbibed English social attitudes. Whereas rather a disturbingly large number of Chinese, not only in Malaya but all through Asia, were communists. There was a time when British authorities in Asia, Australians even more so, had a tendency to view Chinese as almost genetically predisposed towards communism.

The different races, and even the different social classes among the races, had distinctly different spaces in the old Malaya. The towns were dominated by the Chinese, who were traders and tin miners and industrialists. Until very recently even Kuala Lumpur itself was a majority Chinese town. Then there were the Indians. They were mainly Tamils who worked as rubber tappers on the vast rubber plantations. There was also a small Indian professional class, often Sikhs or some other Indian minority who didn't have much in common with the Tamils.

These groups didn't mix much. They had their own separate customs. Middle-aged Malaysian Indians have told me they were told as kids not to wander into the Malay *kampungs* or they might be beaten up. I'm sure such beatings were not very common but I have no trouble believing that some parents told their kids not to venture into the other race's space.

In the early days the Malay aristocracy had the political power and the Chinese had the commercial power. When the Chinese looked as though they were making a real bid for political power as well there was a fierce and bloody outbreak of communal violence and in 1969 hundreds of Chinese were killed in race riots. Part of the anger came from Malays at the bottom of the heap who felt the Malay aristocracy weren't doing enough for them.

So since the early 1970s Malaysia has had the New Economic Policy. This is the policy which gives the *bumis* favoured treatment. Its critics think it's not only unfair to the other races, especially the Indians who don't have the economic clout of the Chinese, but that it's actually played to the Malays' weaknesses, making them dependent on government and in some ways even less competitive with the Chinese. Its supporters argue that giving the Malays a stake in the economy has brought social and political stability to Malaysia. No one certainly can argue with the fact that Malaysia has had spectacular economic growth over the last twenty years and that with a bigger pie, everyone's slice is larger.

How does Islam fit into all this? Malays are proverbially an easy-going people, polite, relaxed, hating confrontation and going to great lengths to avoid it. On the other hand 'amok' is a Malay word and implies that Malays can lose their tempers too and it's best not to be around when they do.

The negative racial stereotypes in Malaysia are that Malays are lazy, Chinese are economic animals who would sell their grandmothers if the price was right and Indians drink too much. The positive racial stereotypes are that Malays are nature's aristocrats, cultivating gentle arts of conversation and hospitality, Chinese are industrious and Indians are great entertainers, as in Hindi movies, popular with all Malaysia's races.

Their critics would say Malays in some measure can have a triple chip on their shoulders. Number one, even after 30 years of *bumi* favouritism they're still not as succesful as the Chinese. Number two, like all Muslims they believe that Islam is the highest cultural and spiritual achievement of the human race, yet Islam does not rule the world and even in Malaysia, with its multi-racial population and guarantees of religious freedom, the position of Islam is equivocal. And number three, as Naipaul would argue, being Malay rather than Arab, they're prone to insecurity about their Islamness, or at least some uncertainty about what constitutes authentic Islam.

A clever journalist, Rehman Rashid, in his scinitillating memoir, *A Malaysian Journey*, points out that the overthrow of the Shah of Iran in 1979 had an electrifying effect on young Malays, especially university students. But then the promise of the Iranian revolution seeped away in the face of the brutal misrule of the ayatollahs and Malays clung more strongly to their traditions of moderation and tolerance.

Now we have the emergence of al-Qaeda and the forceful response of the United States. While the overwhelming majority of Malaysians obviously abhor terrorism of any kind, and I have always found KL an uncommonly peaceful and safe city, there is also a lot of popular anti-Ameircanism in Malaysia.

The contest for the political loyalty of the Malays is partly a contest about whose version of Islam is the best, the truest. At the level of electoral politics, it's fought out between the party that leads the ruling coalition, the United Malays National Organisation, and the Islamic Party, PAS, which wants, formally at least, to implement an Islamic state including shariah law. UMNO favours the existing Malaysian compromise—all people are free to practise their religion, Muslim laws about family matters and fasting during Ramadan apply only to Muslims while the country has a British-style non-religious common law for everything else.

I am advised by a young lawyer, a devout Muslim activist I know from contacts with some of the Opposition parties, to go and see Professor Jaafar bin Mohamad at the Islamic University. I ring the good professor to make an appointment. He works in the law faculty. I pick up a cab outside the MiCasa and a long drive across town takes me to the university. I'm surprised at what a scruffy-looking campus it is. The day I am there is a public holiday and there are only a few people hanging around. The guards tell me the law faculty is in the central spine building, down across the courtyard, turn right and it's the last building you see. OK, off I go and ten minutes' walk puts me at the central spine building. Jaafar has told me his office is on the third floor, but the third floor turns out to be the science department.

Perplexing.

All the female students I see are wearing *tudongs*, most of the males the *haji* cap which indicates they have made the pilgrimage to Mecca.

All the students I approach are polite, none is helpful. There is a quality of smiling Malay indifference, to be found at times, it must be said, in government offices, which is serenely sweet, perenially polite and maddeningly unhelpful, an almost inhuman geniality resistant to any blandishment or inducement to get involved in your bureaucratic difficulties. None of the students has ever heard of a Professor Jaafar, nor indeed a law faculty. After approaching too many students I feel I'm beginning to look like a creep, some weirdo Western guy trying to pick up students at the Islamic University of all places. I'm just about to give up when finally one student tells me the Islamic University has two campuses—this one, at Petaling Jaya, and another at Gambok. Exercising a prodigy of decisive intervention on my behalf, he tells me there is a student welfare centre that is open that day.

I trudge over to the student welfare centre and approach the counter. I'm looking for Professor Jaafar, I say, could they tell me whether he is at this campus or at Gambok. This enquiry puts the woman behind the desk into a panic.

'Just wait, uh?' She hurries down to the back of the room for a series of whispered consultations with her colleagues. Finally a man emerges from the huddle to tell me, without consultation of any staff directory or any such, that they have never heard of any Professor Jaafar but he is certainly at the Gambok campus. I'm quite happy to go to Gambok, which is way over the other side of town, but would like to confirm that Professor Jaafar is actually there before I set out.

I eye the phone on the desk. Could I ring the professor to confirm he's there?

This request completely flummoxes the people behind the desk as it appears they will actually have to get involved in some way in my dilemma. Another series of consultations ensues up the back of the room. We are involved in a tense little Malay drama here, the determination of the low-level bureaucrat to do nothing that is not in the script. The drama elicits a stroke of genius from the head man behind the counter.

'This is only an internal phone. It cannot be connected to an outside line.'

We both eye the phone. Can any phone really be so set up? But he has achieved his objective of complete non-involvement in my concerns. There is a creativity in this determined bureaucratic passivity which is admirable in its way.

I find a public phone and ring Professor Jaafar. Where are you? he says, I am waiting for you. Didn't you know the Islamic University has two campuses? He doesn't apologise for not telling me this but says merely that most cab drivers should know by now that the main campus is at Gambok. It's too late for me to get to Gambok before he leaves for the day. The good professor kindly suggests that I go back to my hotel and rest. We arrange to meet a few days later.

The day of our rearranged appointment I have some business that has taken me into the city and decide to take a cab from the rank at the Shangri-La Hotel. Taxis can be difficult to obtain at certain times of the day and hotel ranks are sometimes the best bet. The first taxi takes me round the corner and down the street and then the engine cuts out. The driver smiles at me and says his taxi has been playing up that day. I should pay the fare so far and he could radio for another taxi to take me to Gambok.

Asking the taxi company to dispatch a cab is notoriously the least effective way of getting one in KL so I give him a couple of ringgit and walk back to the hotel rank. Only a short time in the queue and I get another cab: 'Can I go to the Islamic University, Gambok campus, please?' I ask as we drive off.

'No, Islamic University Petaling Jaya,' replies the Malay cabbie.

'No, you're wrong. I know there's an Islamic University campus at Petaling Jaya but I want the one at Gambok. Bugger me I'm having a bad day with cabs today. The last driver I had, I'd just told him where I wanted to go and the damn cab broke down and I had to walk back to the hotel. Can you believe it?'

By then we are just about where the first cab broke down. The driver pulls over to the side and in what seems a great rage, though he is speaking very quietly, says: 'No, get down, I don't want to take you.'

'What? I wasn't criticising *you* I was just telling you about the previous cab driver whose car broke down. Normally the cabs in KL are fine, it was just this particular car that was the difficulty, surely there's no problem with me telling you that?'

'We are a simple people, good people. Just pay me two ringgit and get out.'

And so, hang-dog, I walk back again to the hotel taxi rank. Somehow I had offended Malay national pride by my remarks and he wasn't going to take such arrogant Western neo-imperialism anymore.

On my third attempt I am suitably chastened. This time my request to the driver is meek and servile. KL's taxis are pretty cheap and most of the drivers are more or less cooperative but all that anti-Western rhetoric in the newspapers must have some effect. When I first visited KL in the mid-1980s taxi drivers didn't routinely try to rip you off for small amounts on the fare. Now, sad to report, they sometimes do. They are also, like many cab drivers around the world, incredibly nosy, frequently asking about your marital status, profession, income, reasons for being in the country. But today is the first day I have transgressed nationalist sentiment in quite this way, provoking what I think is a most un-Malay confrontation.

The third cab does take me to the Gambok campus of the Islamic University. There are uniformed guards on the campus gate. They want to know my purpose and whether my entry has been cleared in advance. But these people at least do know of Professor Jaafar and finally they do let me in, even pointing me to the correct building, and giving me a pass saying I am an authorised visitor. Which is just as well because as I wander over to the building I am questioned by another guard. Learning is obviously a precious business in KL, it's so well guarded.

The Gambok campus is green and lovely, perhaps a touch austere, the buildings plain concrete but with blue tile roofs and high arches, the spacious green fields mostly empty. But there is a denseness to tropical greenery, even just a green field, which an eye from a temperate climate can never fail to marvel at.

Walking to Jaafar's office I pass a classroom, all the boys on one side of the aisle, all the girls on the other side. On a wall in the corridor is a large poster reminding students of the university's rules:

- Girls must wear head cover which does not show neck, hair or chest.
- No dating or coupling or close proximity.
- No smoking, smoking is a bad and unhealthy habit.
- No tight pants.
- No jeans.
- No long hair for boys or very short hair.
- No getting back after 11.00 pm.
- No eating or drinking during Ramadan (the Muslim fasting month).
- Students must display matriculation badges at all times.

The last rule was the only one I saw breached on campus that day.

I climb the three flights of stairs and find Jaafar's office but alas it's empty and locked. This is all getting a little annoying but it gives me a chance to read a sign plastered over the small window on his office door. The sign contains five declarations, which obviously guide the professor's work. They are:

I   Knowledge shall be propagated in the correct spirit, leading towards the recognition of Allah as the absolute Creator and Master of Mankind.
II   The recognition of Allah as the Creator and Master of Mankind represents the absolute apex in the hierarchy of knowledge.
III Knowledge is a trust from Allah and its development shall be in conformity with the purposes behind Allah's creation of the universe.

IV Knowledge should be utilised by man, as the servant of Allah and viceregent (khalifah) on Earth, in accordance with the will of Allah.

V The quest for knowledge is regarded as an act of worship.

I write a note for Professor Jaafar but give up my quest to speak to him. In a way the sign on his office tells me the most important things about his outlook anyway. He is operating within a closed intellectual system. The mere operation of human reason, the mere presentation of Earthly evidence, can in no significant matter ever trump the authority of his scriptures or, presumably, the authority of his teachers. What in the West is sometimes called the scientific method, and what the Chinese sweetly call 'finding truth through facts', is no match in Professor Jaafar's mental universe for the awesome power of religious authority.

Islamic scholars are often quite kind to infidels. They don't mind taking the trouble to enlighten them. But for the Islamic scholar the encounter can have no real intellectual value. What possible contribution can an infidel, operating without the benefit of scripture or tradition, contribute to the scholar's knowledge?

It's easy, and pointless, to ridicule Islam over this kind of thing. Many European Catholic universities, not so long ago, would have had rules, and an outlook, not so different from those at the Islamic University. The conflict between liberal enquiry on the one hand and tradition and authority on the other is hardly unknown in Western history.

Nor are my sympathies absolutely with contemporary Western liberalism on all these issues. The student code at Gambok strikes me as needlessly restrictive. I personally find jeans only an aesthetic, not a moral, offence (just kidding). But I'm not convinced the absolutely anything goes ethos of so many Western universities, with their rampant promiscuity, drug taking and the rest, is such a good thing either. At least on the level of social behaviour quite a lot of Western parents might prefer their kids were safe at a place like Gambok.

Next day Jaafar rings me at my hotel to confirm, he says, our appointment for later that afternoon at Gambok. There is an unmistakably sheepish quality to his voice, which suggests to me it is at least barely possible that he is being a tad economical with the truth. I tell him about my excursion to his office. Ah, he says, he hasn't been back to the office and so hasn't got my note yet. He doesn't apologise for the mix-up or make any offer to reschedule the appointment and I think it best to let the idea slide. Has Professor Jaafar practised his own form of unbeatable, passive Malay resistance? Did he think it useless to talk to an Australian? Or were the stars just against our meeting? Christmas is a couple of days away and soon the Koches must return to Australia. My quest for Islamic fundamentalists can wait.

White Christmas in a Hot Climate

There's something I should be quite upfront about. I'm a Catholic, a rock chopper, a mick, a harp, a tyke, a bog trotter, whatever you want to call us. And I have to tell you I believe in it all. That's one reason I'm not completely unsympathetic to institutions like the Islamic University. I don't think the religious outlook is altogether unreasonable. I'm not a very good Catholic. No one should judge Catholicism by me. I don't practise all that much or very well but even after all the Church sex scandals and all the general disarray and rampant tomfoolery of the Catholic Church in most Western countries, I still believe in it all. Like most people in the West I think my religion is pretty much a private matter. I don't consider myself a foot soldier in the Church's battles nor do I hold myself bound to follow the official Church line on contentious issues.

But the bottom line is, whether wanting to or not, I believe in it all. I believe the Church is true. When my time comes I'll want a priest if there's one around and I say a few prayers every day. So shoot me.

All that is a lead-in to telling you that Jessie and I wanted to go to Christmas mass in KL that year. Whatever the role of Islam in

Malaysia's politics, the Malaysian Government, and KL as a city, make sure they respect and celebrate the main festivals of the main religions: Hari Raya at the end of Ramadan for the Muslims, Chinese new year for the Chinese, Deepavali for Hindus, Vesakhi Day for the Sikhs and so on.

In KL establishments that deal with foreigners, like hotels, Christmas is a real big deal. There are choirs, some with Malay members, singing Christmas carols at many of the big hotels. All the shops have Christmas decorations and many are playing Christmas music. When people see a white person they assume you're vaguely Christian and wish you happy Christmas.

I actually think a good bit of this ecumenism comes from the natural Malaysian liking for a party, an enthusiasm greatly amplified by all the partying KL goes in for. KL'ers like anybody's party on an any excuse. And with all the main festivals the members of the religion concerned practise the delightful custom of an open house. This was originally a Malay Muslim custom but has been appropriated by the other races. I have been to lots of Muslim open houses at the end of Ramadan. At the open house the accent is on food, hospitality and celebration. The Prime Minister holds a public open house for thousands of people who come by and shake his hand and have something to eat and drink.

The Prime Minister and other senior politicians also hold a private open house for smaller numbers of people. One year Jessie and I went to the private open house of Anwar Ibrahim, who was then Deputy Prime Minister. He later fell out spectacularly with Mahathir and ended up in jail on corruption and obstruction of justice charges. But that day at Anwar's official residence all had been sweetness and light except that Jessie nearly caused a diplomatic incident by moving to shake hands with the Saudi ambassador. He withdrew his hand in a panicky flourish and explained that as a representative of the Saudi Government and a good Muslim he could not touch a woman's hand. The other thing I remember about that open house is that whenever I next met anyone whom I had seen there and reminded them (that is, after

Anwar's jailing) of our last encounter they said no, you must be mistaken, I wasn't there.

We telephone around the Catholic churches to find our Christmas mass and take a taxi to the bottom of the small hill on the edge of Little India, at the top of which stands St John Nenas Catholic Cathedral. There are thousands of people gathered for Christmas mass. In a straggling line all the way up the hill are beggars—not a great number, just enough to make a distended chain. Many have physical deformities. Almost all of them outside the church that day are Indian. You don't see many beggars in KL. Occasionally on the pedestrian overpass at Ampang shops near our hotel there will be a middle-aged woman sitting with a cup in her outstretched hand, and yesterday, unusally, there was a young man occupying that spot. It seems fair enough for beggars to hope they might find some charity on Christmas Day.

St John Nenas, a plain white structure, is not very distinguished architecturally and looks a bit run down. Today it is bursting at the seams. Jessie and I don't get seats but we are lucky to find a place to stand inside the church. Such a big crowd in such sweltering heat is not easy to manage but the church copes well. All the doors and windows are thrown wide open and many fans whirr in the ceiling. It's not too bad.

Naturally there are no Malays because all Malays are Muslim. Other than the absence of Malays the mass is multi-racial. There are hundreds of Indian Catholics there, and a lot of Chinese, but probably the biggest single group is the Filipinas, who mostly work as domestic servants in KL. The occasion has a typically Filipino festive air. All the collectors of the two donation plates are Filipinas in red Santa hats, which is something, I have to tell you, I've never seen in a Catholic cathedral anywhere else. Some of the hymns are in Tagalog, some in English, hymn sheets are distributed and everyone sings lustily.

The Indian priest preaches a lovely sermon mainly in English, but, oddly enough with a bit of Malay thrown in, about the difference between a faith of plastic decorations that you only get out once a year and faith which is deeply rooted. I seem to be the only white person in attendance, a situation in which I often find myself in in Asia, but the good natured, culturally mixed-up, modestly raucous and entirely cheerful service appeals to me as quintessentially KL.

Cecil Trelawney and the Deadly Durian

Venerable Melaka is one of those enchanting Malaysian cities—
Penang to the north is another—where European empires washed
ashore hundreds of years ago, never penetrating far into the interior
jungles, and eventually washed away again, to be replaced in their
turn by successor empires, European and Asian, and eventually by
independence. Melaka is also the site of the oldest Malay sultanate,
whose soldiers fought fiercely against the original European invaders.
These rising and receding tides have left their traces, seemingly
delicate but somehow indelible, across all the centuries. In Melaka
there are surviving Gothic churches, grand colonial mansions, cannon
on hilltop, the odd prison cell and a small Eurasian population.

It's an easy drive down the highway. Just out of KL, our driver,
a Tamil named Sami, leaves the highway to take us through some
Malay *kampungs*. So close to KL, yet these kampungs look as
though they haven't changed much in decades. The traditional
Malay house is a ramshackle little affair of brown wood, built on
stilts two or three metres above the ground, to allow some
movement of air, some natural cooling. It may have its living space
divided into only one or two areas. Ablutions occur outside the
house. Within the *kampungs* vividly coloured bantam hens wander
around. I can never work out how villagers keep track of the

ownership of particular hens, and how the hens avoid the cars. Only the presence of the odd car, and the sealed road on which we are driving, marks the *kampung* out from a scene travellers might have witnessed a hundred years ago.

We leave KL mid-morning and arrive well-timed for an early lunch. We follow directions to a Peranakan house which has been transformed into a restaurant. The food is Malaysian Chinese and very good. Peranakan is the characteristic architecture of the Baba community, a mix of Chinese and Malay. The Peranakan style house is distinctive and well adapted for the climate. It has a central well with an enormous ceiling while separate stairways lead to rooms at the front and rooms at the back which have no connection apart from the ground floor. The middle space is kept clear from the ground floor to the building's uppermost level. The furniture is dark lacquered wood with a tiled floor. Chinese-influenced housing, adapted for cities and towns, generally creates many more small spaces than the Malay house which is more communal.

In Southeast Asia, the saying goes, the sea unites and the land divides. The jungle was so dense and so inpenetrable that it was easier to move around by boat than overland. The easiest internal travel was by river. Melaka was a great trading town, and as well as waves of European colonisers it attracted Chinese traders. Now many of the central blocks are dominated still by countless small Chinese shop-houses, these days selling artworks, antiques, knick-knacks, furnishings, souvenirs and just about any small item you can think of.

It's a port town and everything tends towards the sea. After lunch the four of us tramp around the main historic sites—Dutch, Portuguese, English. The old gothic ruin has a commanding view out over the Straits of Melaka, one of the busiest trade waterways in the world. The hilltop also contains a former tomb of St Francis of Assisi, for a while his body was kept here and then later taken away.

Melaka has had a housing boom and there are new condos and resorts. We walk across a big field, in which a huge Brahmin bull with fierce horns is grazing rather menacingly, to the new, modern, multi-storey shopping complex and look in on the bookstore to see if it stocks any of Chris's novels. Alas it doesn't although I've seen his books in many other bookstores in Southeast Asia.

Walking back to our car we pass a line of Chinese shops and restaurants opening on to a wide footpath. Chris is struck by the perfect onomatopoeic quality of so many Chinese names when rendered in English. This thought is provoked by the sign Madam Fat So's Restaurant. Another says Mee Meat Balls (*mee* being noodles).

A stall here is selling durians.

The durian is a dangerous fruit.

Durians are about the size of a large pineapple and are hard and prickly on the outside. Jessie remembers durians from her childhood and delights in the idea of tasting the fruit again. We pay seven ringgit for a large durian. The durian seller uses a broad-bladed knife, like a small machete, to cut the top open for us and we carry it in a plastic bag back to the place we are to meet Sami and the car. Sami is a tolerant and easy-going Tamil but his smile collapses, his face crumpling into a grimace when he sees we are carrying a durian.

'Sir, it will make a most unpleasant smell in the car.'

'Don't worry, Sami, we've thought of that. We'll put it in the boot. It certainly won't be any trouble there.'

Jessie's plan is that the four of us will share the durian as a treat when we get back to KL. Sami is unconvinced but not willing to insist that our actions will inflict economic and physical pain on him, as he knows they will.

How to describe the smell of the durian? Some wiseacre once said that eating a durian is like consuming a strawberry ice cream in a particularly filthy bog. The durian doesn't smell at all until it is cut but then it takes the most fearful revenge. It emits the most aggressive smell to be found in the natural world. Its power is unbelievable. Sami is driving a big car and the durian is securely locked in the boot. It is only a few minutes after we drive away, however, that the first sense of something wrong comes to us.

At first we think there might be something amiss with the car's air-con. Then we wonder if we are passing an especially pungent drain. The ethereal tendrils of the durian's smell power have reached quickly out from the boot and into the car's cabin.

'Perhaps we should throw the durian away after all darling,' I suggest to Jessie. But Jessie is frugal with money and frugal with food and she won't hear of such wanton waste.

As each stage of durian smell saturation is reached we believe it can't get any more powerful. We are wrong. Time after time a whole new burst of energy infuses the smell. It is like some magical creature from the forest in Tolkein's *Lord of the Rings* and we are incompetent hobbits unable to deal with its powers.

The durian has a powerful psychotropic effect on Chris's novelist's imagination.

'Cecil Trelawney was a tough old planter, but that evening he was feeling liverish. There was something strange about the durian his wife had placed before him at breakfast on the verandah of their isolated jungle home,' Chris intoned.

There in front of us he was composing a short story in which a planter's wife poisons the planter, confident that the smell of the durian will smother any tell tale aroma of the poison itself.

Sami, playing our Gandalf, suggests: 'Perhaps you could eat the durian now, on the way back to KL.'

We all agree and at the next convenient spot we pull over to the side of the road. But how can we eat anything that smells like that? We tumble out of the car and although the durian is soon exerting all its powers, they are less affecting in the open air. We take the durian from the boot and tear off the outer skin. Then, in one of those incredible tricks that nature is always playing on us human beings, the taste of the durian is sweet and lovely, like a smooth, sweet custard. There is a lot of durian to go round and Sami joins in. As this is a trucker's roadstop there is a waste bin in which to deposit the durian's mortal remains.

But the durian lives on. For all the journey back to KL the best efforts of the air-con cannot shake the smell. Sami tells us he will have to disinfect the car with burning charcoal before people will ride in it again. When we get back to the hotel we notice for the first time a sign saying NO DURIANS ALLOWED. This sign transcends language by having a durian in a circle with a line drawn across it, like the ghostbuster sign. Although I have never noticed them before over the next few weeks I see durian-buster signs all over KL, all over Malaysia.

The bad news when we get home is that our middle son, Lakhvinder, is ill with fever. He has been battling this fever all week and has had two trips already to a nearby clinic. But tonight he is much worse, constantly vomiting, weak as a kitten and nearly delusional. At one point he is lying on the lounge at Balwinder's house when he looks up and sees a small picture, which Balwinder keeps on her television, of Jessie and me standing by the Sydney Opera House with Sydney Harbour in the background.

'Vedi Masi [elder aunt],' he says to Jessie's sister, 'you better put that photo away, Mummy and Daddy might fall into the water.'

There are few things in the gamut of parental experience worse than having a child seriously sick. All of a sudden you realise the limitations of the protection you can really provide for your kids. Lakhvinder's derangement has really got us scared. A dreamy and intelligent kid, he has always had the habit of talking in his sleep. Once when he was very young I went to check on him in the middle of the night. He looked up from his bed.

'Dad, Dad,' he cried urgently, 'there's something I've got to tell you.'

'What's that, Lakhvin?'

'Um, um, drive carefully.'

But talking in your sleep is different from waking delusions and we are worried to bits about him. After dinner, Jessie and I take him once more to the medical clinic.

The clinic is busy and there is a wait, the three of us sitting on a bench outside the doctor's office, Lakhvinder's expressive face, normally so ready to smile, now so glum and miserable and inert. We see a young Malay doctor, smooth-skinned with pious moustache and goatee, assisted by a nurse. He seems wise and thorough and reassuring. He examines Lakhvinder thoroughly and concludes that he is suffering from viral fever. The medicine he had given before had not worked because of Lakhvinder's constant vomiting. So he gives Lakhvinder an injection to stop the vomiting and prescribes the medication in syrup form which will be easier for him to take and keep down.

Lakhvinder is sick once more that night but then a couple of days later, in the afternoon, just like someone turning on a light, he wakes from a sleep and the fever has lifted. He's better. He's still weak and subdued for a few days but each day gets stronger.

Our relief is overwhelming. It's the most sick he's ever been.

When he's fully recovered we decide to have a few days in a resort in Penang, off the northwest coast of Malaysia. Resorts are like five-star hotels, if you're a chic, sensitive, culturally atuned, touchy-feely, Western traveller you should be beyond resorts, no longer interested in their simple hedonism. But I gotta tell you resorts are great for families. The other thing about resorts in Malaysia is if you're using Australian or American dollars they're pretty cheap. Of course there's a locals' price and a foreigners' price. Often there are different prices for different foreigners, with Brits and Americans charged more than Australians. In any event they are far cheaper than similar accommodation in Australia or Europe or North America.

The Koches come with us, their last excursion before returning to Australia. Penang is like Melaka only more so. It is a bigger city and has some things Melaka doesn't have, like a huge electronics industry and some first-rate universities. It is a beautiful little island. The main city, Georgetown, contains a huge, lively Chinatown and even its own Little India. There is the grand Eastern and Oriental Hotel, built by the same people as built the legendary Raffles in Singapore and to some extent in a similar style.

In the main street of Georgetown, leading up to the E & O Hotel, are a string of wonderfully inappropriately named hotels, yearning strangely after Western associations. There is the Waldorf Hotel, on which every bit of lettering other than the name is in

Chinese characters, and the White House Hotel, which certainly doesn't look much like the White House. And the Soho Pub, which does look dark and enclosed like a pub in London's Soho but why would you build such a pub in Malaysia?

We stay at a resort on the tourist strip on the beach at Batu Ferringhi. The kids love it, glorying in the water sports, the gym, the volleyball, the archery and table tennis and mini golf and cable movies and endless great food and the long, bargain-rich night markets. The cool traveller often affects not to like to be in a place 'spoiled by tourists'. Tourists, like anything else, can be irksome in excess. But I enjoy places that have plenty of tourists. It's best if, like Penang, they have some industries independent of tourism and if the tourists themselves are a mixture of nationalities and age and income groups. But the presence of tourists means the restaurants will be pretty good, things will work and there will be plenty of locals in well-paid jobs.

Every night at our resort Jessie and I go late to the hotel lounge to listen to some music and have a nightcap. This is our first holiday at a big resort and we discover that, rather like cruise ships, they are a field of fantasy.

A resort is a bit less intense than a cruise ship but you still have the sensation of being on a journey with a semi-randomly selected group of international travellers around whom a misty film of intrigue and romance inevitably settles, at least in the imagination.

We find we are observing, and perhaps being observed by, a certain regular crew of fellow guests. We label them one by one. There is the Chinese drug dealer with the American wife. There is the beefy Australian who likes Japanese girls (we deduce this from his habit of staring fixedly and intently at two Japanese single women who also nightcap each evening in the lounge). There is the middle-aged Italian couple with the beautiful-people son with the Oedipal complex. He later morphs into 'the only son' or, more briefly, 'junior'.

Although we never speak to any of these people they become disturbingly prominent in our conversation and our imaginative lives. The people we do talk to or become friendly with of course are instantly disqualified from fantasy status.

At the resort each night I read from James Hilton's novel, *Lost Horizon*, about the original Shangri-La. I feel very much like the novel's hero, losing the will to leave, gradually captured by the hypnotic rhthyms of the day and the fantasy guests we've invented.

Soon, too soon, it comes time to leave and we take a taxi to the airport. The driver is ebulliently Chinese.

'You see that sign, "AWAS"? You know what it mean?'

'It means "Beware",' I reply, proud of my elementary Malay.

'No, no, mean beware because All Woman Always Shopping. Ha Ha Ha Ha Ha.'

His stream of self-directed and frankly chauvinist Chinese humour is unstoppable and he continues his patter all the way to the airport.

'Know why Chinee woman always gamble in casino? So husband no money for second wife. Ha Ha Ha Ha Ha.'

We farewell the Koches, who I think have enjoyed Malaysia. At KL they transfer to the airport hotel and fly back to Australia next morning. The frivolities of Christmas and New Year are over. I will now renew my search for Islamic fundamentalists and an explanation for their politics.

Fellow Travelling with the Fundamentalists

A few years back, in 2000, I had gone bush on the trail of the fundamentalists in Malaysia. I flew to Alor Setar, tiny provincial capital of the state of Kedah, deep in the north of the Malaysian peninsula. Its airport looks like the airport of any small town in rural Queensland, a tiny terminal, a small garden lovingly tended. Our plane from KL that day is rerouted for no accountable reason through Penang, so I'm an hour late. This turns out to be a stroke of good fortune. I'm in Alor Setar to interview Fadzil Noor, the federal leader of the Islamic Party, PAS.

No one should underestimate PAS. It has several hundred thousand grass-roots members, it controls two of Malaysia's state governments and, with a couple of dozen federal MPs, is the main Opposition party and the alternative government. The PAS activist who is meeting me at the airport is a friendly, round, young Malay named Jusuf.

He is a school teacher and school teachers have traditionally formed the backbone of Malaysian politics. Jusuf is a pleasant and obliging young man. The day I spend in his company is agreeable. He couldn't be more helpful. We set out for PAS headquarters but on the way there he sees Fadzil Noor in a car travelling in the opposite direction, passing us going away from PAS HQ as we are going towards it. This turns out to be my good fortune because Jusuf turns the car around and follows Fadzil to his home.

It is of course much more interesting to meet the PAS leader at home than at the party premises. During our drive I am a little disconcerted at some of Jusuf's views.

'You know the new Russian leader, Putin? You know who he works for?'

'No,' I reply. 'Who does he work for?'

'The CIA.'

Naturally.

'You know who really runs the world?' Jusuf asks much later after we have established some rapport.

'Who?'

'The G7 and the Zionist lobby.'

Of course.

Jusuf was once a strong supporter of Dr Mahathir and his United Malays National Organisation but then a friend sent him a tape of the famous and fiery Islamic preacher, Hadi Abdul Awang, now the chief minister of Trengganu state. After listening to a series of these tapes Jusuf came to realise, he says, that Mahathir didn't really understand Islam.

Jusuf's story is a tiny part of the huge battle that's under way across Southeast Asia, across the world, for the political allegiance of Islamic communities. Alor Setar is a typical battlefield in this war of competing world views. It is Mahathir's home town, the sort of place he must win if he is to halt the advance of PAS in the Malay heartland. It is also a microcosm of the Malaysian social structure. In the centre of the city is the small central business district, predominantly Chinese, politically owing allegiance to the Malaysian Chinese Association which, with UMNO, is a key part of the governing coalition. There is one big hotel, one big shopping mall, a big office block and many smaller shops run by Chinese traders.

On the road from the airport to town are some lavish mansions and numerous sizeable bungalows. These are owned by UMNO supporters. There is some dignified civic architecture—the state parliament, the chief minister's residence, the sultan's palace. There are many, many mosques and every Malay woman I see wears the *tudong*. Further from town the houses become more modest, there are some concrete townhouse-type dwellings and then you are among the traditional *kampung* houses of their brown wooden construction.

It's necessary to go to Alor Setar to appreciate KL, to understand KL as part of the Malaysian nation. The average income in Alor Setar is a fraction of the average income in KL. The level of amenity is far lower. There is much less to do. KL is to Malaysians in Alor Setar what New York is to the pious mid-West, an infinitely distant den of wealth, vice, glamour, wickedness and power.

Jusuf takes me to Fadzil's home and explains that my plane was delayed. Fadzil is gracious about this and welcomes me into the downstairs sitting room. He orders up some tea and biscuits. He is a hospitable and gracious man and would like to chat to me but doesn't have very good English. Our interview is delayed as we wait for an interpreter to arrive.

The most interesting thing I learn that day is the nature of Fadzil's home. It is the most modest of any political leader's that I've ever seen. It is little more than a traditional *kampung* house, the wood painted a strange mustard colour and rendered only slightly more commodious by having the ground floor walled in to make a spacious living area.

Fadzil, educated in Cairo, was a lecturer in Islamic law before becoming a politician. His living-room walls are decorated with scrolls of quotes from the Koran. This modest home may well be the key to much of PAS's appeal. Whatever one thinks of accusations of corruption in Malaysia there is no doubt that most of its leaders live well, while many Malaysians outside KL, and some within, are poor. In some the hierarchical Malay psychology accepts this and even sees it as a sign of the competence and consequence of the leading men. But in others it causes resentment. The contrast with the material modesty of PAS leaders like Fadzil is obvious.

Fadzil, an older man with Islamic moustache and goatee, soft spoken, slightly built, dressed that day in an informal sarong, does his best to dispel my fears about fundamentalism and intolerance: 'People voted for PAS because they lost trust in UMNO which takes care of themselves first and divides the nation's wealth among cronies. People believe in PAS's integrity. They will see how we perform in both Kelantan and Trengganu. We can have Chinese and others in our coalition because our common goal is justice.'

Fadzil's words are soothing but when you read the PAS newspaper, *Harrukah*, you find disturbingly anti-Chinese senti-ments. Some time after our interview the predominantly Chinese Democratic Action Party split up the opposition coalition because it could not stomach PAS's plans to impose Islamic *shariah* law and make Malaysia an Islamic state. Kelantan under PAS has languished economically and the PAS Government in Trengganu has mightily upset the small Chinese minority with what they regard as discriminatory measures. Despite all the PAS claims that women are treated equally with men in Islam it is PAS's formal policy that women shouldn't stand as parliamentary candidates.

I ask Fadzil about PAS's commitment to impose Islamic law and he appears to dissemble: 'Even if we won power we would look at priorities, the issue of justice would be the first priority and freedom of expression. Islamic fundamentalism is a Western concept. In Islam, fundamentalism merely means we go on principle, we want justice, we are tolerant and moderate. PAS accepts the principle of democ-racy. We can join with any group which is not doing harm to Islam. Chinese and Indians have rights which we would respect—the right to their religion, the right to property, the right to vote. The West should change its image of Islam and see Islam as a friend not an enemy.'

Sadly, some months after our interview Fadzil died as a result of heart disease. He had long been recognised as a moderate within PAS which has many far more extreme voices. His words to me that day were reassuring but perhaps not wholly convincing.

After the al-Qaeda terrorist attacks in the US in 2001, PAS seemed to place the blame on America. When the US took military action against the Afghanistan Taliban regime which had sponsored Osama bin Laden and al-Qaeda, PAS organised rowdy demonstrations outside the US embassy in KL. Some of its leaders called for *jihad* against the US.

I was surprised to find—as was the whole world after the Bali terrorist attack in October 2002, which killed eighty-eight Australians and more than two hundred altogether, and after the discovery of a plot in Singapore to blow up the US, British and Australian embassies, among other targets—that in Jemaah Islamiah there was a well-organised Islamic terrorist network in Southeast Asia with close connections to al-Qaeda. What was even more startling was to find that some of these JI figures had spent a lot of time in KL, as had some other al-Qaeda operatives, and that a small number had links with PAS, although there is no suggestion PAS's leadership knowingly encouraged any terrorist links or activities.

I have always been treated courteously and kindly by PAS people. That day in Alor Setar I was completely in their hands, as so many Western journalists following up stories have placed themselves in the hands of Islamic fundamentalists, and in the country at that time were numerous JI and al-Qaeda operatives.

On this latest trip to KL I go to see Dr Mohamad Hatta Mohamad Ramli, a central committee member of PAS. As seems to happen with all my Islamic fundamentalist interviews the fates conspire against the logisitics. The PAS office at the back of the Tacawal Hospital, not far from central KL, which I have visited before, has shifted across the road. As I am standing on the footpath figuring out its new location I am comprehensively crapped on by a pigeon, which is never a good way to begin a meeting. When I finally locate the PAS office it seems deserted. It is an office spread over several floors of a narrow building. I ring the buzzer on each floor but each door is tightly locked and no one answers the buzzers. Miraculously, on the top floor, after ten minutes ringing the buzzer a man does come out, his hair wet as though he's just had a bath.

He rings Dr Hatta for me and finds he's been delayed at home by a repairman come to fix his roof. He lets me wait in the second-floor PAS office, where one of Dr Hatta's colleagues had been present all the time but obviously under instruction not to answer the buzzer.

When Dr Hatta arrives I'm keen to get the PAS take on the war on terror and the new international issues arising from it. Dr Hatta is a sophisticated man, often brought out to present the PAS view internationally. But what I find when talking to him is a bewildering and nearly farcical wilderness of conspiracy mirrors. These conspiracy theories are incredibly widespread among Southeast Asia's Muslims and they indicate more than anything a disconnection from reality, a willingness to believe what is convenient, no matter how far-fetched, rather than what is obvious. It is another triumph of the closed intellectual system over the mere claims of evidence and reason.

The Bali bombings, Dr Hatta comments, were 'very well planned and well organised, very professional'.

He continues: 'It looks like it was planned by a highly specialised group. And we have heard the American Navy stopped by in Bali. The nature of the bomb was C4 explosives. It's not a common thing so people try to link it with the presence of the US ships.'

But can he, or anyone, really genuinely believe that the hideous bombings in Bali are the work of the US Navy?

'I'm not saying anything,' Dr Hatta replies, not very enigmatically.

He also seems not to believe even in the existence of Jemaah Islamiah despite endless testimony about its networks, and the well-established evidence that its spiritual leader, Abu Bakar Bashir, spent years in Malaysia in effective exile from Indonesia under former-president Suharto. Despite being at the heart of Islamic fundamentalism in Malaysia for years Dr Hatta says he is not aware that Abu Bakar Bashir ever spent any time in Malaysia.

'I would like to ask whether these groups are really structured. Jemaah Islamiah is a new thing. I never heard of it before. Before this [recent publicity] I never heard of Jemaah Islamiah. Abu Bakar

Bashir started off as its leader, now he's portrayed as its spiritual adviser. I wonder whether this is a promotion or a demotion.'

I ask Dr Hatta straight out whether he believes Osama bin Laden and al-Qaeda were responsible for the terrorist attacks in New York. His response is evasive but seems to favour the weirdest conspiratorial interpretations. 'Whether I believe or not is immaterial. Maybe they [al-Qaeda] are around in some corner of the world, it's difficult to say. If they were planning everything [the September 11 attacks] in Afghanistan, they were very smart people. And all their satellite phone communications and planning were not picked up by the Americans. We are surely giving too much credit to simple people in Afghanistan.'

At the time we are speaking, bin Laden's voice has recently been authenticated in a taped message to the world, proving he is alive. Dr Hatta doesn't accept this evidence at all, suggesting instead that he is really dead, and that the Americans are pretending he's alive, deceiving the world.

'I'm quite sceptical whether he is around or not. I knew during the Afghan war he would not die. If he's alive, the so-called war against terror must go on. If not, you've got to create another villain. So he needs to be alive.'

I ask Dr Hatta how he assesses the former Taliban Government in Afghanistan: 'The Taliban took over at a very difficult time. The Taliban were basically fundamentalist Muslims who tried to rule Afghanistan in the best way possible. Of course, it's nothing compared to our democracy.'

And the way the Taliban treated women?

'A lot of things happened to the women in pre-Taliban days— rapes and so on. The Taliban came in and tried to protect the women, maybe in an extreme way by keeping them at home.'

In fairness to Dr Hatta, all human beings have a deep capacity to believe as true what they think is in their own interests. One of the few compliments George Orwell ever paid himself was to say that his greatest virtue was his willingness to face up to hard and unpleasant truths. Orwell was certainly right. He could do it and it is a rare quality. We all tend to believe that our side has been wronged. I can bore people to sobs over the historic injustices suffered by the Irish.

The overwhelming majority of Muslims, it goes without saying, have nothing to do with terrorism or violence. Most have not that much interest in politics. But it is telling that among people like Dr Hatta, who define their politics by Islam, there is a strong tendency to find an excuse even for al-Qaeda, or to believe a construction of events, no matter how preposterous, which finally has the United States as the villain, the author of all suffering.

But it would be wrong to leave Dr Hatta as merely an amalgam of conspiracy theories. He is a personally gentle man, always well dressed without being dapper, and, like many Islamic activists, a man of deep principle and obvious sincerity and commitment.

He comes originally from Perak. His father was a '*kampung* man', that is, just a fellow who did odd jobs around the place and had no fixed profession. It was a large family, seven brothers and sisters. Dr Hatta's parents encouraged study, of both the Koran and worldly subjects, and he won a scholarship to the MCKK, the Malay College of Kuala Kangsar. MCKK is a revered institution in Malay life. It is sometimes called, at least by Malays, or at least by its own old boys, the Eton of the East. It was the preferred school for sons of the Malay royalty and educated no end of Prime Ministers and cabinet ministers. For a time it had a perverse practice of not charging fees for the sons of royalty, who obviously could afford them, but charging fees for the sons of commoners. But there was a system of scholarships and, like Anwar Ibrahim, Dr Hatta went there as a scholarship boy, which was an enormous source of pride for his family. His son carried on the family tradition and also attended MCKK.

The family had high hopes and conventional aspirations for their son and he studied medicine, so that the Dr before his name does not come from some shonky honourary doctorate, or a PhD in politics or some such nonsense, but from real medicine. His wife too is a doctor and they have seven children of their own, ranging in age from infants to young adults. It is a large and busy and happy household. His mother lives with them, and a maid.

Dr Hatta's father had been a PAS activist at the *kampung* level, even though PAS was weak in Perak. Dr Hatta himself joined PAS in 1983. Men like Dr Hatta are gold for a political party. The teacher and the doctor are greatly revered in Malay society. They are expected to be wise, sober and learned. In 1998, after many long years of activism, Dr Hatta took a big pay cut, hung up his stethoscope and went to work for PAS full-time.

'We decided to form a think-tank within PAS and I needed to be involved. On my part it was an important decision to stop working for the Government medical service and take a big loss in income. In UMNO you can earn a living from the party, in PAS it's not a tradition for leaders to live off the party. I can't say whether I'll ever go back to medicine, there's so much to do.'

As a kid he not only went to government school during the day but Islamic school after the normal school day was over. At university he was active in the student union and the student Islamic group. There are many ways in this life to self-respect and self-improvement. In Dr Hatta's family, it has been the Islamic way.

Like most Islamist political activists Dr Hatta makes no distinction between religious and political activity, or at least not the distinction that is second nature to Western thinking: 'Politics is part of the reason [for becoming so active] but PAS is an Islamic movement. It's not government we were looking for but to continue the struggle for Islam. PAS is just the natural expression of this. We want to have political Islam in power, so that we can manage ourselves under an Islamic system, which will be good government with good ethics.'

The word struggle is for Muslim fundamentalists what the word revolution once was for Marxists. It is everywhere in their speech and thinking.

Dr Hatta continues: 'We foresee that we will struggle along democratic lines. It won't be imposed by force. We want to establish a system under which Islam is enshrined as a way of life, including *shariah* law applying to Muslims. At the moment, *shariah* law applies mainly to family matters. Under us it would apply to all facets of life, commercial law, criminal law, all aspects of life.'

He is unapologetic about standing against many trends that are regarded as part of modernity, such as greater liberalisation in what can be broadcast, a so-called 'open skies' policy.

'If you talk against an open skies policy you're seen as restrictive but people must be informed, films categorised, people not forced to watch what they don't like. There should be more Islamic TV channels. TV programs here and in the West are the same, there is a lot of violence and mistakes. I am not ashamed to say to my children, this is not Islamic. We can't stop them watching [pay] TV and all that. But we say to them "Kissing in films is unIslamic." We tell them and when they see it they turn their faces away and are embarrassed.'

You cannot under estimate or denigrate Dr Hatta's commitment, sincerity or idealism. It seems tragic that the ideological interpretation of his religion takes him so far away from people who should be his friends in the West and leads him into embracing mad conspiracy theories about international politics.

The fault is partly the West's, in its failure to reach out with a sophisticated and sympathetic message to moderate Muslims. It is the West's fault in another way too. Much anti-Americanism in the Muslim world, and elsewhere, apes the exaggerated criticism of America, and especially the mocking cynicism as to motives, to be found in the liberal American press itself, especially *The New York Times*. In KL during this visit I see in several Islamist offices the books of Noam Chomsky, whose mad conspiracy theories about the infinite wickedness of Washington resonate deeply in the Muslim world. The fact that Western democracies are self-critical is one of their great strengths but sometimes the critique is unbalanced and reflexively cynical as to Western motives. It's not surprising that Muslim activists prone to be hypersensitive about the West take many of their cues from such material. But the fault too lies partly with PAS and its ideological leanings.

While I'm in KL I ask PAS for a briefing on its economic policy and go to see a Dr Dzulkifli. Dr Dzulkifli is a pleasant fellow but the guy just won't, or can't, engage about modern economics. Our conversation is hopeless. When I suggest that the strict application of *shariah* law to Muslims will also affect non-Muslims, because it will affect the interaction of Muslims and non-Muslims, he flies into something like a rage and loudly declaims on a famous case from the Koran when the caliph had his armour stolen by a Jew but because the evidence was insufficient the *shariah* court declined to convict and so 'the Jew got to keep the armour'.

Another question about economic policy produces an answer beginning: 'Remember when the Muslims were fleeing Syria . . . '

Of course, the Muslims fleeing Syria—the natural starting point for any discussion of contemporary economic policy.

All great religions, and Islam is certainly a great religion, provide principles and inspiration for good policy. But no ancient sacred text provides a handbook on how to run a modern economy.

For many Malays, in many parts of Malaysia, Islam and Islamic institutions do provide something like a total environment. I take a taxi out to see Dr Siddiq Fadzil, a university academic specialising in Islamic thought and the Malay world, at his home in Kajang. He is a former president of ABIM, the Muslim youth movement which came to UMNO when Anwar Ibrahim did but returned to PAS when Anwar was jailed.

Kajang is a suburb of KL, but it's a long way out and the area is semi-rural, with poorly sealed roads, farm fields, clumps of jungle and groves of palm trees. The cab driver has a lot of trouble finding the address and I pay him to stay and wait for me until the interview is over, thinking it would be just about impossible to find a taxi to take me back. Dr Siddiq's house is in Jalan ABIM and there is a big ABIM school nearby. This is obviously a real community, a cluster of Islamic institutions.

Dr Siddiq's house is a big, imposing, two-storey white bungalow with a blue-tiled roof. It is set far back from the street on a big block of land behind an ornate fence. A Mercedes sits in the drive. The house, as I knock on the door, seems utterly quiet. A small man, barefoot, shabbily dressed in a sarong, and so slight and unassuming that I take him to be the house servant, comes out to meet me. It is Dr Siddiq.

We enter the front room and he offers me a drink.

Dr Siddiq's house, like many in Malaysia and Indonesia, looks Western but has one distinct design feature that is not Western. Despite its size you enter not into a hallway or an entrace area as such but into a front parlour. It's definitely not the family lounge room but is designed to receive guests who are not intimate friends of the family. How far you penetrate into the house depends on how close you are to the family. Many people who are kind enough to invite you to their house nonetheless make sure you stay in the front room, to preserve the private, sacred nature of the family home.

Dr Siddiq's interest in Islamic matters began at secondary school. He joined ABIM in 1971 but became really active when he graduated in 1974.

'We witnessed a wonderful re-flowering of Islam. ABIM was meant to champion the Islamic resurgence. We appreciated the cause of the Iranian revolution [in 1979, which brought the Ayatollah Khomeini to power] but we don't think such a revolution is appropriate here.

'The difference between Malaysia and Iran is that Malaysians are Sunni [Iranians are Shia]. In Malaysia we cannot produce an Ayatollah Khomeini. In the Shia tradition an Islamic *mullah* is infallible. In the Sunni tradition they are not.

'Malaysia is a multi-racial country and needs a special approach of Islam. We have to convince them [the non-Malay races] that we do not want to oppress them. We have to present a smiling face of Islam and learn from our past history. Islamisation in this part of the world took place in a subtle and gradual way and we believe in the relevance of that too.'

That line about the 'smiling face of Islam' somehow makes me shiver, though it's meant to be reassuring. Dr Siddiq says the main Islamist forces in the nation have lost faith in the Government, and the religious figures who still support it are merely 'accommodationists' without vision or authority.

He is keen to emphasise the predominantly national nature of Malaysian politics, but nonetheless says: 'There is an Islamic resurgence around the world and we respond to that. With modernisation and urbanisation and industrialisation there seems to be a process of Westernisation. But this brings new moral and social problems and that drives Malays to resort more to their religion.

'Parents who are too much Westernised may have no control over their children, or don't have skill in educating their children. Of course everyone is facing the same problems. Westernisation and globalisation have produced the most isolated homes. In the past only urban areas had the foreign influence, now it's everywhere, in the *kampungs* too. In the past we considered the *kampungs* a fortress—I myself am a *kampung* boy, my father was a farmer.'

There's no doubt the fundamentalists in Malaysia are less severe than the fundamentalists in the Middle East. Increasingly, though, through the internet, travel for study, and perhaps above all money from the Arab world subsidising fundamentalist schools, charities and other organisations, the Middle East is exerting a greater influence on Malaysian Islam.

The Arab television station, Al Jazeera, is broadcast for several hours a day on pay TV. Perhaps for the first time large numbers of Malays are becoming deeply socialised in the Israeli–Palestinian dispute. Islam is being globalised as much as any brand name and many of the old, tolerant, syncretic traditions of Malay Islam are under threat from the new globalising forces of Islam emanating from the Middle East. But the fundamentalists remain a minority in Malaysia, and a minority even among Malays. Not the least of the forces that reject them and challenge their claim to represent the authoritative interpretation of Islam are KL's feisty, formidable feminists and I set out now to track them down.

I Am Woman, Hear Me Roar

The Sisters Don't Agree

Karim Raslan has been out of town. In London or New York or somewhere. His existence is peripatetic and frequently internationalist. It is a blessing to find him in KL. He is so endlessly courteous and helpful that when I ring and say I'd like to see him and talk about Islam and where to find some feminist groups he sends a car and driver to pick me up. The driver takes me to Karim's home, which consists of two apartments—one for his books and office, and one for his home. Instead of just chatting, however, he has an evening's entertainment set up for me. First we drive out to the exquisite home of an Australian couple who have set themselves up as patrons of the visual arts.

The husband is a panjandrum of the business world and they use their own money to provide a residential scholarship for a year for a promising young Malaysian artist. The scholar gets his or her own quarters on their compound, the use of whatever materials he or she needs, a modest stipend and at the end a full exhibition in the family gallery downstairs, which is in a kind of cellar so that it can remain easily air-conditioned in order to protect the works of art.

Karim wants to visit briefly because he is borrowing their house in a week's time for a function he is hosting. The house is one of the most serene and beautiful I have seen. Two major pavilions are connected by a long covered walkway. The whole house is set in terraced gardens with quiet water features. In the main house, which sprawls across several levels, the maximum effort has been made to invite in the light and air, with relief from the heat mostly being provided by fans, though no doubt there are air-conditioned areas.

It is altogether a lovely ambience. Here you could invite your soul. But as we get out of Karim's car a less lovely sight confronts us. Several large dogs bound up. While not exactly blood-curdling, the canines are seriously less than friendly. Dogs are common in larger KL homes, as in many big cities, for security.

'Hullo,' Karim says to the mutts slowly and melodiously. Within seconds he is tickling the dogs under their chins, rotating their muzzles, patting them on their heads. I am impressed at Karim's many talents. Does he attend seminars not only on the role of dance in opera, missile defence and currency stabilisation but also on the art of calming savage dogs?

We have a drink at this lovely home and then head into one of KL's central shopping centres. Karim has invited me to dinner with Marina Mahathir, the daughter of the Prime Minister and one of her country's best-known feminists. We meet at a Chinese seafood restaurant in the shopping complex. Marina is with her husband and two children, their *amah* who helps look after the baby, and two friends visiting from England, whom she knew at university. It is an indication of Marina's liberal politics that the two friends from London spend part of the night complaining about how Tony Blair is too socially conservative.

Marina is a fascinating Malaysian and in her own way offers considerable resistance to the interpretations of Islam promulgated by PAS and its fellow travellers. She has been the chairperson of her country's AIDS council and frequently appears on TV, in advertisements and chat shows, to argue the case for AIDS sufferers. She also writes a regular newspaper column and is one of the most liberal mainstream voices in Malaysia.

Despite being much more liberal than her father on social issues she remains a loving daughter on good terms with her dad. She credits her father, through his medical background, with quickly coming to understand the AIDS problem. She points out that on religious issues he has always been regarded as a liberal and intervened deisively to have domestic violence legislation passed.

That night at the Chinese restaurant I don't burden the dinner with a lot of political questions. The conversation flows around babies and travel, art and movies. But later I look up some of Marina's newspaper columns, collected in the book *In Liberal Doses*, and find a feisty challenge to the authority of the religious leaders to make rules governing all Malaysians, or even all Malays.

In one column she laments 'the gatekeeper syndrome among our religious establishment where they, and only they, control the meaning of God's word. Sounds like the bad old days of medieval European times when the religious authorities ruled over an uneducated and all-believing laity. Keep everyone ignorant and they won't question whatever we tell them, even when it's blatantly unjust. All in the name of God, the Merciful and the Beneficent. Let us apply that old political adage here too: power corrupts and absolute power corrupts absolutely.'

In the same column she criticises what she sees as the hypocrisy of many religious people towards the suffering especially of AIDS victims, recalling 'some extraordinary encounters with so-called religious people who can be exceptionally callous and mean-spirited' and further comments: 'Working as I do in a field that requires great reservoirs of compassion, I have often been dismayed by religious types who blithely say things like since there is no cure for AIDS, let's just concentrate on prevention and let those already infected die.'

This is all tough and fiery stuff but there is a sense in which Marina represents much more than just her own efforts, and that is the challenge to fundamentalism, even to excessive conservatism, mounted by Malaysia's formidable feminists.

Another challenge is simple indifference.

Malaysia's press is pretty tame, racier in KL than elsewhere in the country but overall pretty tame. But it is highly competitive and has to survive commercially in a competitive environment. Its concerns give a reasonable idea of what concerns KL'ers.

In KL, notwithstanding the tight advertising budgets and high newsprint costs, there has been, for example, a flowering of lifestyle magazines. None of them is remotely fundamentalist, some of them are quite raunchy, titles such as *Men's Review* or a host of women's magazines. *Men's Review*'s bikini-clad centrefolds and pin-ups are right at the edge for an overtly Muslim society but most of the magazine's contents are mainstream lifestyle journalism with book and film reviews and just a touch of politics. These magazines circulate primarily in the big cities, mainly really in KL itself.

While in KL I devour all these journals and look, each day, at three newspapers: the establishment broadsheet, *The New Straits Times*, *The Star*, a conventional tabloid, and *The Malay Mail*, by far the raciest of the English-language tabloids.

The NST is pretty staid but two things strike me about it—the range of its international coverage and the deeply middle-class concerns of its readers. As V.S. Naipaul has noted, foreign coverage in the newspapers of a lot of Muslim countries is mainly about other Muslim countries, just as foreign coverage in the old communist countries used to be mainly about other communist countries. That is not so in the NST. There is a strong regional coverage of Southeast Asia. Indeed one moderating influence on Islamic fundamentalism in both Malaysia and Indonesia is the broader Southeast Asian context, embracing countries like Buddhist Thailand and Catholic Philippines. The Association of Southeast Asian Nations is the main international institution and KL looks there rather than to the Middle East for its primary foreign policy interests.

Similarly the NST doesn't try to pretend that the US is not the world's most important nation or that it doesn't have an interest in Britain as a legacy of colonial times. There is, especially in the op-ed pages, a sophisticated debate about Islam. The paper reprints frequently from *The New York Times* (which as I say is where it gets at least some of its anti-Americanism) and that includes the NYT's diverse coverage of the Middle East. You can frequently read the columns of *The New York Times'* Tom Friedman in the NST and he criticises both Israel and the Palestinian Authority and is frequently critical of Middle Eastern Islamic states like Saudi Arabia. That sort of coverage is not available in too many Muslim countries. You can follow the world reading the NST.

But you can better see what really concerns KL'ers by the NST's huge real estate supplements, fashion spreads, education advertisements, TV gossip, movies and computer sections. Not much of the exotic East there, but that's the point of successful development. It produces stable, middle-class societies in which people aren't obsessed with the struggle for their daily bread or some threat that politics poses to their normal lives.

In all three newspapers there are a lot of stories about child abuse and neglect, so many that it looks like the newspapers are running a campaign, which is a good thing to do, as well as reporting on a grim reality. Some religious conservatives argue that child abuse and neglect are a consequence of the loss of old, religious traditions. They especially blame married women for working, seeing child abuse, like all social problems, as a consequence of urbanisation and rapid social change. Youngsters move to the city, marry and have kids and are cut off from traditional supportive extended family networks back in the *kampungs*. Then both partners work either just to make ends meet or to try to keep up with KL's rampant consumerism. Quality child care is hard to obtain. Hey presto! kids are neglected. But that's a pat explanation and no excuse.

Child abuse is sadly widespread in many parts of the world and in societies at hugely varied levels of development. One of Malaysia's greatest English-language novelists, K.S. Maniam, describes it terrifyingly in his first and broadly autobiographical novel, *The Return*. It concerns the life of Tamils—small traders and rubber tappers—on a big Malaysian plantation some 50 years ago. The violence of the men towards their children is intermittent but utterly savage, almost random, unpredictable to other members of the family, caused by frustration and pain and habit and drink. Yet the boy at the centre of this novel continues to love his father, and you wouldn't even say that child abuse is the novel's primary subject. Maniam, a thoughtful, gentle and infinitely interesting man, once told me that novels are a 'private newspaper'. Their subject is the truths which lie behind the public sphere. Their subjects are private and they are read in private. That KL's newspapers are trying to penetrate that private sphere to shed light on the evil of child abuse shows them acting like real newspapers, doing their jobs. Child abuse is a big problem in Malaysia and it has been for a long time. It's a shameful thing for Malaysia and the newpapers are right to shame the society into changing the practices that give rise to it.

Of course KL's newspapers have some pretty obvious limitations. They don't give the political Opposition a fair go—they're basically pro-Government—but they're quick to highlight services that aren't up to scratch and they act as an informal people's complaints bureau.

The Malay Mail is mild by London tabloid standards but it's certainly the raciest newspaper in KL. On a typical day Whitney Houston and her drug problems and Liz Hurley and her paternity problems are on the front page. They share this honour with a strikingly graphic photograph, a real old-fashioned news hound's pic, of a drug trafficker/addict floating down the Klang River with a bag of rubbish on his head apparently in an attempt to escape the police by disguising himself as rubbish. In other words, the papers and magazines disclose a busy, middle-class city, with all its pleasures and pains, going about its business.

Every now and again, however, the religious authorities overstep themselves and inconvenience normal people going about their normal lives. Some time before I am in KL some twenty-five Malay Muslims were arrested for being in a restaurant that served alcohol. This was an incredible arrest. KL has hundreds, thousands, of restaurants that serve alcohol and Malays frequent them all. Theoretically Malays are not supposed to drink alcohol and though this is often honoured discreetly in the breach, most of the time Malays don't drink booze but aren't fussed if other people do. Every big hotel serves alocohol in its restaurants and I have had meals in these restaurants with PAS activists and other Islamic fundamentalists. By no stretch of the imagination could the mere presence of a Malay in a restaurant that seves alcohol be regarded as strange.

The purpose of the arrests therefore is a little obscure. Is it bravado? Is it aggression, a desire to polarise people around this issue, to stake out new ground as the most authentic Muslim? And of course while the ruling party, UMNO, is avowedly moderate there are Islamic fundamentalists within it, and a larger number of conservatives it would not be quite fair to call fundamentalists. One of the ways UMNO responds to PAS's challenge is to burnish its own Islamic credentials, often with symbolism.

The charges were subsequently dropped and the religious authorities admitted they had overstepped themselves. But it's this sort of incident, which seems to happen about once a year, that fertilises a theme of unease in KL about the ultimate purposes of the Islamic fundamentalists. One of the PAS leaders, Nik Aziz Nik Mat, the chief minister of Kelantan, responded to the arrests by suggesting Muslims and non-Muslims should have separate restaurants, a kind of religious apartheid.

The persistence of these sorts of incidents, and the thinking that lies behind them, convinces many Malays that there needs to be an in-principle response to fundamentalism, a contesting of its ideas on the grounds of spirituality and Koranic interpretation. Materialistic indifference is not enough to meet the challenge the funda- mentalists throw out to the citizens of KL in their desire to get on with normal lives in a normal city.

One of the most formidable groups to answer this challenge is perhaps the most courageous assemblage of feminists in Malaysia— Sisters In Islam.

Zainah Anwar runs Sisters In Islam. I meet her at the Sisters' office, a small converted cottage in a little compound they share with several other non-government organisations. Her desk is busy with papers, she wears a white smock and maroon slacks, and her freckled face is uncovered by veil or *tudong*.

Before she set up the Sisters full-time in 1998 she had a distinguished career in journalism and international relations, working for *The New Straits Times*, later for a strategic think-tank and for several years for the Commonwealth secretariat in London. She went first to a Malaysian university then later to Boston University where she majored in journalism and international relations. She has remained single and says this is not inconsistent with a devout approach to Islam.

As with many Malaysians who have studied abroad, her time in the US was a formative experience: 'I very much enjoyed my time in the US. The biggest culture shock I had there was when my professors actually welcomed my criticisms and opinions.'

One of the reasons the Islamic fundamentalists dislike the Sisters so intensely is that they don't challenge the fundamentalists from a secular perspective, a challenge which the fundamentalists feel fully confident, at least rhetorically, in answering, but rather from within the Islamic tradition itself. Zainah explains: 'It's hard for us as believers to believe that God and our religion would discriminate against half the human race. The God we know is merciful and just. So we went back to the Koran to see if the words of God's teachings really discriminated against us. That was really spiritually uplifting. We found no discrimination there. We found that men had interpreted the Koran to reinforce their power. Now that women are becoming educated they are challenging the traditionalist interpretations. It's the strength of our faith that allows us to do that.'

Zainah says Islam is important to her life, that she never wants to be without her faith: 'Personally, I enjoy the experience of Islam, especially in times of crisis like when my parents died. You don't feel lost, you know what to do, it gives you a sense of rootedness. The rituals are very reassuring.'

Zainah comes across as honest, a completely straightforward woman. She neither dramatises her 'struggle' nor does she downplay its importance or the threats inherent in the rise of the fundamentalists. As a woman challenging the religious authority of the most conservative men, and challenging them on their own ground, she has come in for a lot of abuse.

'Your critics label you a Western feminist, but that's just a bankrupt assertion. They can't challenge our arguments so they just attack our right to make any argument at all. My grandfather was a *shariah* lawyer, my father was a founder of UMNO. I'm very rooted in my tradition and in Islamic scholarship.'

She finds PAS's argument that it is campaigning for democracy and civil liberties against a repressive government wholly unconvincing: 'As a journalist I covered the rivalry between UMNO and PAS and I'm very familiar with PAS people and the bullshit they're spouting now and what they really stand for and it's not democracy and human rights. The obscurantists dominate and hold extreme views not just on women's rights but on other people's rights to express a view on Islam. But if you use Islam as a base for public policy then everyone has a right to comment on it.'

In practice, Zainah says, the *shariah* courts discriminate heavily against women: 'The *shariah* courts have on occasion ruled against men but it's the exception. For example in the polygamy rule the man who wants to take a second wife [Islam allows up to four wives] is supposed to satisfy four conditions—financial ability, a fair and just reason, he must treat all his families equally, and taking another wife must not cause spiritual or mental harm to the existing wife. But the courts very often don't look at any of these questions because they feel that polygamy is a right, or they just look at the financial question, or there is another loophole that if you marry without permission then you only have to pay a small fine and the marriage is registered.

'Many Muslim wives live in constant fear that their husband will take a second wife and many husbands threaten their wives that if they are not obedient that's what they'll do. It makes marriage very unstable for Muslims. The divorce rate for Muslims is the highest for any race in Malaysia.'

The courts, she says, make it vastly easier for a man to secure a divorce than for a woman, no matter what the history of beatings or other abuse.

'We had to campaign like hell to get a domestic violence law. We had to wait for two years after the law was passed before it was gazetted. Some *ulama* [religious scholars] said men have a right to beat their wives, others said it should not be part of the criminal law.

'There is a contradiction between the social reality in this country and what religious authorities want. The reality is that the status and situation of women have advanced. There are more women than men at universities. Women have the freedom to work and don't have the restrictions that women in the Middle East and South Asia face. But the religious authorities want the reverse of that.'

Nonetheless the fundamentalists and the religious conservatives generate a lot of social pressure on women: 'Many women in Malaysia are covered up not because they want to be but because of peer pressure or pressure from bosses. They don't get promoted unless they cover up. Of course some do it as an act of choice and I respect that. Faith shouldn't be coerced but come from within.

'There is a lot of support for us but we get a lot of criticism from PAS and Islamist movements in the country, from men in power who fear we are challenging their authority. We criticise the Government *ulama* as well as the PAS *ulama*. They all went to the same schools. There are *ulama* who support us but they don't have the courage to speak out. The obscurantists are very aggressive. We get hate mail and attacks on us in newspapers. We get condemned at PAS general assemblies. *Harrukah*, the PAS newspaper, asked for us to be banned, for the Government to issue a *fatwa* against us. These people who say they're in favour of freedom of speech and democracy for people who believe in their ideas—all their talk of democracy is bullshit.'

I gotta be straight with you. I admire Zainah. Her arguments have won me. They seem to me to combine authentic religious feeling with sheer common sense. But the approval of people like me means almost nothing in Malaysia. What would Western journalists, who aren't even Muslims, know about it anyway?

On one occasion Zainah faced serious danger. She and several other writers were accused by the religious authorities of insulting

Islam, even though they write respectfully and soberly and extensively quote the Koran to support their arguments. This could have been a serious matter before the courts, with potentially a sentence of three years' imprisonment. The PAS newspaper's website ran polls as to what Zainah and the others' punishment should be and the most popular answer was 'war to the finish'. Zainah wrote to the Prime Minister, Dr Mahathir, saying that some of her group had been subjected to hate mail, abuse and threats of death and rape. There was a proposal that the Religious Affairs Department ban people 'with no in-depth knowledge on Islam' from speaking publicly on Islamic issues. This would really be a step towards a theocratic dictatorship and would have the circular logic of all dictatorships—Islam is true, therefore Islam should be the basis of public policy, but the only people qualified to speak on Islam are the Islamic scholars approved by the established religious authorities, therefore all other citizens must do as these authorities tell them and are not allowed to question or debate the matter. Thus the circularity of dictatorship: authority is true therefore you must obey it. How do we know it's true? Because of its authority.

It's important to note that in the end nothing came of these prosecutions. Dr Mahathir refused to support them and they lapsed. They outraged many prominent Malaysians and a number, even some senior UMNO figures, signed petitions condemning the moves. But the fact that they could occur at all, that there was not universal condemnation of them, upsets many Malaysians.

People like Zainah in their darkest moments fear that if everything went absolutely as badly as it could possibly go, Malaysia could endure a fate something like Iran's, that people get fed up with the Government and cooperate with the fundamentalists because they are its strongest opponents, that people take their personal freedoms and affluence too much for granted and make fatal common cause with the long-term enemies of liberty.

There are many reasons for thinking Malaysia won't go this way. The single brilliant jewel of KL itself is one of these.

Terror Targets in the Golden Triangle

What with all this serious inquiry into Islam, Jessie and I feel like a night on the town. We leave the boys at Balwinder's apartment and take a taxi into KL's entertainment district, its famous Golden Triangle. Once again, we get the nosiest cab driver. He is a big Sikh guy, tall and heavy, a mixture of fat and muscle in equal parts, with a strong, full beard and a proud, red turban on his head.

'Where are you from, sir?'

'Australia.'

'Would I be right in thinking then that you might be following the cricket?'

'Oh yes I love cricket . . . '

'I was a very fine cricketeeeeeeeer myself here in Kuala Lumpur when I was a young man. And of course I was meeting all the great fellows when they came here to play, have you heard of Wesley Hall, a great fast bowler from the West Indies, and Garfield Sobers . . . '

The conversation goes on in this vein for several minutes. I am perfectly happy to feed him pat questions, slow half volleys outside the off stump, for him to verbal out to the boundary. It is generally safest to keep taxi conversation on inoffensive, neutral ground and, with Indian cab drivers, cricket often serves.

This guy has a basso profundo voice and understandably loves the sound of it—rich, melodious—wasted really in a cab. I'm sure he feels he could have been a great orator in the right circumstances. He's probably right, too. But after a little while his curiosity becomes more powerful than his enjoyment at holding forth and he begins his cross-examination.

'I am detecting a most wondrous fragrance. May I ask, sir, is it yours or your wife's?'

'My wife's.'

'And may I ask, sir, is your wife from India?

'I'm from here,' Jessie answers, accustomed to speaking for herself, affronted, I would expect, by having two men talk about her as though she were not there.

'And what nationality are you?'

When Malaysians ask what nationality another Malaysian is they generally don't want to be told 'Malaysian' but rather your ethnic background.

'Sikh, Punjabi,' Jessie says.

The cab driver immediately bursts into a great volume of Punjabi spoken at high speed. Jessie at first answers in Punjabi but then, in consideration of me, switches back to English. There follows a detailed interrogation—what is my occupation, does Jessie work, how did we meet, how many kids, what are their ages, how are they doing in school. At one point he says: 'I must say, madam, that you look very young for your age. Wouldn't you agree, sir, that we are very lucky to be married to Sikh wives?'

I gallantly concur. But the driver switches subjects. He has calibrated precisely the length of the trip and the time available for each subject he would like to cover.

Here is the new subject: 'I would like to enquire about migrating to Australia. There is no future for the racial minorities here in Malaysia. It just gets worse and worse. How should I go about it?'

'Do you have any relatives in Australia?'

'No, unfortunately, I do not.'

This makes it a little tricky. A cab driver in his fifties or sixties with no relatives in Australia has little or no chance of being accepted as a migrant. I don't want to say exactly that in so many words but I don't want to raise any false hopes either. My main priority is to keep the conversation neutral and amiable.

'The best bet would be to make an enquiry at the Australian High Comission.'

'You think that would be best?'

He heaves a heavy sigh as he says this. The melancholy, resigned tone in his voice suggests that he knows already what his chances are. There's a pro forma quality to his inquries, just in case some miracle should be riding around in his taxi. Alas, I am not his miracle.

In our short journey he has displayed for us an impressive emotional range—bombast, eloquence, flattery, curiosity bordering on the busybody, ambition, acute political analysis, world-weary fatalism and an almost heroic acceptance of the travails of life.

The Sikhs are magnificent.

He drops us at the Starbucks coffee shop next to Sungei Wang shopping centre in the Bukit Bintang district. Bukit Bintang has a red-light quality at night, though it's not as blatant as the red-light districts in big Western cities like Sydney or New York. We go to Starbucks because I like the coffee there. Oddly, for Jessie and me Starbucks, that most perfectly American of all brand names, has distinctly Southeast Asian associations. Starbucks was big in Southeast Asia before it came to Sydney and then other parts of Australia. We went to a Starbucks first in Manila, then in Singapore.

This Starbucks has an indoor section, a balcony, where we sit, and below that a vast alfresco area of the extended footpath. It is surrounded by other al fresco cafes. KL has taken to alfresco in the biggest way. All the cafes here, and in many other parts of town, use huge fans not only to cool patrons down but to spray them with a fine mist of water.

This is certainly a sensible measure because the word for the Starbucks corner that night is hot. There are 'babes' everywhere. Mainly it's the Chinese babes who are wearing the tiny mini-skirts, or the slightly longer skirts with the slits that go forever and the barely-there tops. It's scenes like this that *Harrukah* newspaper uses to show how decadent and wicked the Chinese have become. But there are plenty of Malay and Indian babes there too, only marginally less revealingly dressed. While the young guys look cool their costume is more extensive and far less revealing. It's just a fact of life that to look cool guys don't have to expose as much of themselves as girls do.

It's a weird juxtaposition in KL. A sizeable minority of the population wants to reinstitute feudal dress and feudal social codes while a sizebale proportion of KL's youngsters are as hip and foxy as any youngsters anywhere. I start to wonder whether both sides of this civilisational dialogue haven't lost touch with common sense a bit. Surely there's something between the Taliban on one side and *Sex and the City* on the other. Of course pretty much the knock-down, drag-'em-out argument for the hot and spicy crowd is that if you don't care for too much flesh in the face, you don't have to go to the Starbucks corner on a Saturday night.

We finish our coffee and walk down the street, past Planet Hollywood and other trendy eateries. Young KL'ers are out having a good time in large numbers tonight. We walk past the Lot 10 shopping centre corner and down into Jalan Sultan Ismail, the heart of the Golden Triangle. At the bottom of this street is the Hard Rock Cafe, which is always packed at night, and along the street are a string of four- and five-star hotels which each radiate their own buzz of night-life—the Istana, the Regent, the Hilton, the Shangri-La, the Equatorial, the Concorde. Most of the people who stay at these hotels are visitors to KL, but they don't form a foreigners' ghetto because lots of them are visitors from other parts of Malaysia. And as I've observed before most of the folks dining at the big hotel restaurants and using their bars and function rooms are locals. This gives the Golden Triangle a wonderfully mixed feel.

Jessie and I dine at a Thai restaurant, sitting under a fan taking advantage of its spray of misty cooled water. We then go hunting for a disco. Unfortunately the disco in the basement of the Istana is shut for Ramadan. But this proves a blessing as we find a much more interesting place in Jalan P. Ramlee, the street named after Malaysia's most famous movie star. P. Ramlee was the Jack Benny and Bob Hope of early Malay cinema.

I've seen a few of his old black-and-white comedies with English sub-titles. They are like the old Bing Crosby–Bob Hope road movies only funnier and more charming, and so much cleverer and more enjoyable than most Malay movies of today. For one thing, they're not dully earnest. Ramlee was a fine actor and in his movies convinces you of the truth of his characters. The films I saw were certianly not slap-stick. But while respectful enough of Islam everything is handled in these old movies with a light touch. And there's an infinitely more relaxed atmosphere about sex and relations between the sexes in the old P. Ramlee films. In one, Ramlee has two rich but stingy brothers. They marry two beautiful sisters (indicidentally not weaing *tudongs* or other headgear). These two are daughters of a rich but even more stingy local potentate. The girls' father bets the brothers his entire fortune against theirs that they will lose their tempers within a day of marriage.

They readily take the bet. But come the wedding nights and the same pattern is followed by each. First the new groom is not given any food at the table. He can put up with this because bedtime is approaching and the girl is very comely. But, the father informs them, the law of the house is that the new husband sleeps in the stable and the wife sleeps in her own room. Naturally, the brothers lose their tempers, and thereby their fortunes.

P. Ramlee saves his odious brothers by marrying the third sister, with whom he's had a Spencer Tracy-Katharine Hepburn sparring relationship all film. When the time comes he happily goes off to the stable, driving daughter and father gradually bonkers. Eventually he wins the bet, restores his brothers, declares he doesn't want his father-in-law's fortune but settles down instead to a love match with his fiery bride. The plot of course is absurd but it's done with such brio, such conviction and such charm as to be irresistible. I can never walk down Jalan P. Ramlee without thinking how much pleasure he's given.

Now, in furnishing a disco for us, up a few flights of stairs, P. Ramlee does another service. I have to tell you I don't go much for discos myself. But Jessie likes them. There is no cover charge at this hip, trendy place and women get their drinks free.

A disco is not my natural habitat. Like all generously proportioned Western men of a certain age, I tend to look desperate, pathetic, ridiculous or some combination of all three in discos, especially Asian discos, which is one of many reasons I don't go to them.

But in this instance I'm in the company of Jessie, who has been called a disco 'kaki' (if you don't speak Malay I should explain a kaki is, no . . . I'll let the onomatopoeia of the expression speak for itself). In any event the point is I'm automatically exempt from ridicule arising from a whole range of silliness if wholesomely in the company of my wife. This disco is very chic. The strobe lighting flashes, the Back Street Boys boom and beautiful people of all races, including two huge African-American guys who dominate the dance floor, bump, grind, groove, jiggle and generally disport themselves in accordance with international disco protocol.

With one exception. None of the Malays is drinking alcohol, as of course they're not supposed to. I espy one young Malay man with that indefinable but unmistakable swagger of the junior business executive on the way up, sitting in the middle of the disco, wearing a devout goatee, looking in the face rather like the deposed former Deputy Prime Minister, Anwar Ibrahim, greatly enjoying the music and drinking . . . black coffee. There is also a young Malay woman actually wearing the *tudong*, the only one I see that evening. And it has to be admitted that even with every cultural sensitivity in the world, the *tudong* does look out of place in a disco. She is sipping a soft drink.

Over the couple of hours we are I there I work out the new Malaysian disco guide to politics. We already know about UMNO and PAS. To follow this guide you also need to know that Keadilan (Justice), the political party founded by Anwar's wife, Wan Aziza

Wan Ismail, generally appeals to a small group of urban liberal Malays who are also religious. The liberal, mainly Chinese, though notionally non-sectarian, Democratic Action Party competes for the Chinese vote with the government coalition party, the Malaysian Chinese Association, which is close to business. The Malaysian Indian Congress, also part of the ruling coalition, commands majority Indian support.

Anyway, here is the all-time disco guide to Malaysian politics and sociology. PAS members don't go to discos, ever. Keadilan goes but doesn't drink alcohol. The DAP works hard all day, goes to the disco at night and gets drunk. The MIC works in the disco. The MCA owns the disco. UMNO owns the building the disco is in.

After a couple of hours we leave this lively place and wander across the road. A short stroll brings us to the Beach Bar, a big, fake-thatched roof bar and outdoor drinking area with open walls to let the breeze flow. It's a goodly mix of locals and expats, with plenty of Aussies. Malaysia and Australia have recently been having one of their tiffs but you'd never guess it from the Beach Bar.

The Beach Bar looks and sounds like Bali in the City. 'I come from a land down under' blairs out from the speakers. Baby sharks swim in the fish tank. A large crowd is bopping. After a drink we move on and just next door the weirdest thing happens. A girl approaches the two of us and shouts: 'Do you want to come to our party? Everybody's welcome, free drinks. We'd love you to come.'

How can we refuse such a gracious invitation? We are given coupons for drinks, alcoholic or non-alcoholic according to our choice, and enter a cavernous bar in which a lean, long, white crane is swizzling around the dance floor with a camera on it. At first I think this just the latest craze in disco entertainment but someone says they are shooting a scene for a movie and need a crowd in the backgrouond. The female bar staff are in short black skirts or even shorter shorts. This is all the more surprising when I'm told that the filming is not for a movie but for a tourist commercial being made by the Malaysian Tourist Authority. It all seems a bit cheeky for an official Malaysian Government production.

We finish the evening at the lounge of the Shangri-La Hotel. The Shang lobby has been superbly renovated in art deco style. The coffee house flows into the lounge bar which has cloud-like ceilings, two huge marble pillars, a wall-high glass picture window opening on to illuminated gardens and fountains. An Australian jazz combo, male and female, vocal and keyboards, perform from a stage, or really a bare platform, set above an island bar. The crowd is affluent and cool and comprised of all races.

While we are in KL this time everyone, especially Western embassies, is obsessed with the terrorist threat, with identifying possible targets. The US Embassy is guarded by armed soldiers and set behind high walls a long way back from the street. Too many US diplomats have died in too many places, no one can blame them for taking any precaution they can.

But for the rest of us it's hard to identify what's a likely terrorist target. There is nowhere in Malaysia equivalent to Bali, where Westerners go in larger numbers than locals. A lot of people say that the Golden Triangle or some similar entertainment hub somewhere else in the country could be a target. But even in the Golden Triangle there are many more locals than foreigners, which is not to say the terrorists wouldn't strike it. Their viciousness and cruelty are boundless.

The Malaysians say they are as safe as anywhere else and I'm inclined to believe them. They are tough and swift in clamping down on any domestic political violence, tough in rooting out any al-Qaeda connections they find. Nowhere in the world is completely safe, nowhere is certain to be hit. If walking around the Golden Triangle raises by some infinitesimal fraction the already tiny risk that we could directly witness some terrorist act, so be it. It would be madness, and offer a monstrous victory to the terrorists, to stay away from such innocent and enjoyable places.

We walk down to one of the other hotels where there is a big line of cabs waiting. We tell the driver our destination and he says that as he's a 'stand-by' cab he won't use the meter and the fare will be ten ringgit. It's not much money but it's more than twice what the fare should be so, as we haven't boarded the cab yet, we decline and walk a bit further down the road. We flag a passing cab and he takes us back to our hotel for a fare of three ringgit and 50 cents. I give him five ringgit and tell him to keep the change and he's delighted. Everyone has had a perfect night. Terrorists, Islamic extremists—it's hard to believe on a night like this that KL has any political problems at all.

Even if the Golden Triangle is admitted to be quite unrepresentative, it's clear the majority of KL'ers are moderates. Part of the trick is getting them to pay attention and speak out against the extremists.

Desperately Seeking Moderate Muslims

A few days later I meet a prince of the city in Kuala Lumpur. I don't mean literally a prince of the old, fading Malay nobility, but a democratic prince, a prince on the new grids of power, influence, access, money, prestige. Khairy Jamaluddin is chief of staff to the Deputy Prime Minister, Abdullah Badawi. He has recently married his boss's daughter. He's a coming man in KL, a coming man in UMNO. In his twenties, tall, with movie star good looks, impossibly well turned out in perfect black suit, stylish goatee and moustache, mobile phone ever at the ready, dark glasses, hair perfectly gelled, Khairy could easily be mistaken for a Bollywood sex symbol.

Instead he is the archetype of the new Malay, just exactly, one suspects, the sort of character Dr Mahathir was trying to create with his policies of affirmative action and his endless exhortations to Malays to work hard and achieve high. Khairy studied at Oxford and has no end of international associations.

If the Islamic fundamentalists are to be decisively routed it will be by Khairy and his cohorts, the new generation of Malay leaders who have had all the advantages, all the education, who know what the stakes are and how the battle must be fought.

Since the terrorist outrages of September 11, 2001, much of the leadership of the West, in Washington especially, has been dismayed at how timid and how silent are the voices of moderate Muslims. These voices are needed to condemn the terrorists and all their works unequivocally, but also to provide an alternative vision of Islam and Islamic politics. Although Dr Mahathir and his Government and much of UMNO have no end of criticisms of and specific disagreements with Washington, they are unquestionably moderate Muslims.

Operationally they cooperate closely with the US in the war on terror. More important, they clearly offer a vision of Islam which explicitly contradicts and confounds the terrorists.

September 11 changed the dynamics of politics in Malaysia. It reminded people what they don't like about extremists. The confused and morally ambiguous response of PAS showed people the connection between fundamentalism and terrorism. People started to remember what they like about the Malaysian compromise and its social stability and economic growth. Malaysian TV ran a lot of programs about Afghanistan under the Taliban. The subtext was pretty clear—is this how you want to live? Whatever you think of UMNO, would you really prefer the Taliban?

The day I meet him Khairy is alive with a new political energy. To suit my convenience he comes in to see me at the Mandarin Oriental Hotel, just next to the twin towers. We meet in the sumptuous luxury of its lounge. I'm not a small person but I feel I am in danger of sinking from view in the leather sofa, it is so deep, so cushy and yielding and luxurious. We talk over foaming cappuccinos (at least *I'm* drinking cappuccino, Khairy abstains because it's Ramadan). He politely switches off his mobile phone, which otherwise rings constantly, for the duration of our conversation.

Khairy and many of his generation believe that revulsion against terrorism and extremism gives them an opportunity to entrench the Malaysian compromise.

'Some would call it the new Malay dilemma,' Khairy says, drawing on the title of Dr Mahathir's first book, published way back in 1969.

'For Malaysia we are at a crossroads in how we define our way of life. The new Malay dilemma is whether we remain moderate or go the PAS way. We're in the middle. We're not a secular state like Turkey. We're not a full-blown Wahabi Islamic state like Saudi Arabia. When Dr Mahathir took office in 1981 he embarked on a program of greater Islamisation. The question is: does that start you on a slippery slope in which Islamist claims have ever greater legitimacy? Dr Mahathir has declared Malaysia a modern Islamic state as a statement of fact, not a statement of intent. But should UMNO out-PAS PAS? Some think so. But the truth is we will never win such a fight. Whether Malaysia can define and defend our Islam is the big question. It's an internal debate (within the Malay community). We have to say to our internal constituency there's nothing more we can do to make Malaysia more Islamic. We have to address political Islam. We're up against PAS, which uses Islam as a political device. When PAS accuses us of not implementing *hudud* [Islamic law and punishments] there is a tendency for the Government to say "We've got a lot of non-Muslims, so we can't implement those laws." But that's an argument by default. We have to argue on grounds of principle, on jurisprudential grounds. Now, with UMNO's new strength, it's the most positive time for UMNO to define its Islam.'

In Malaysia there is a saying for a politician who is too slick and doesn't go down well with the ordinary folk—that he's not a good *kampung* campaigner. In Australia the same idea is embodied in the expression that a politician has lost touch with the mainstream, while the Chinese say a leader has become cut off from the masses. The Americans capture the same feeling, that a politician or an idea may be too high-falutin' to appeal to the average person, with the question: will it play in Peoria? Every political culture recognises the trap for a pol who is just too smooth, just a bit too far above his constituency. There is surely a danger that Khairy and his pals will fall into this trap.

Khairy is a very impressive individual, but he provokes these thoughts in me. You can imagine any mother wishing her daughter would bring home a Khairy. But, I ask a friend after meeting Khairy, is there a danger he's *too* slick, just *too* perfectly polished to go down well in the *kampung*?

My friend doesn't think so: 'It depends how he handles it. If he handles it right Khairy could get the reaction in the *kampungs*: "Ah, that fella, he's pretty smart isn't he, knows what he's talking about, better go along with him." If Khairy and his generation can't win this debate about Islam we are really doomed.'

Khairy believes there is no effective alternative to Malaysia's model of communal politics and power sharing. It doesn't sit perfectly with Western liberalism which would rather see citizens entirely as individuals and not at all constrained by ethnicity. But Khairy believes a serious attempt to break the communal model of Malaysian politics would lead to demagoguery, polarisation and extremism.

Certainly the danger Khairy nominates of UMNO trying to out-PAS PAS is a real one. Governments all over the world, across the spectrum from democratic to authoritarian, often try to deal with an extremist challenge in part by co-opting its less extreme supporters. When it's a democratic government confronted with, say, a movement of social and even racial reaction emanating from rural constituencies, this can take the only mildly corrupt form of simply buying off the farm vote, not giving anything on race but giving lots of dollars instead. The process is unedifying, it can be expensive, but it's all part of the genius of democracy. Authoritarian governments which take public opinion seriously can often pull off a similar trick. But this is a dangerous game to play with Islamic fundamentalists. If most Malaysians are Muslim, and modestly observant, it is natural that a lot of Malaysian life, even political life, will be carried out in as a Muslim idiom. But once you start making concessions to the fundamentalists you have to be careful where you draw the line, and you have to be pretty firm once the line is drawn. It's too easy to create the syndrome that more Islam equates to better Islam, therefore every aspect of life should come under strict Muslim rule. And who better to provide these rules than the *ulama*?

Moderate Muslims believe that this is not only simplistic and impractical but distorts Islam. It is a necessity to make these arguments as principled religious arguments or there will be a great danger of the moderates looking as though they are less religious and therefore less virtuous than the fundamentalists. If the message is that you're going to Islamise society anyway, that this is the right thing to do, people will be tempted to follow the groups who look wholehearted about it.

The Malaysian Government has made repeated efforts to set up institutions which promote moderate Islam. But friends in KL tell me that in the end these are often captured by very conservative elements, if not outright fundamentalists. And as Sisters In Islam have found, few Malaysian religious scholars are forthcoming about taking the fundamentalists on. The fundamentalists have been successful in establishing the idea that they are the most sincere Muslims.

I discuss these matters with a political opponent of the Government who doesn't come from a predominantly religious point of view. Dr Rustam Sani, once a political scientist and academic, is now the Deputy President of Parti Rakyat, a small, old socialist party which is now in coalition with Keadilan and PAS. Rustam and I were once commissioned to do a joint biography of Dr Mahathir, but we both walked away from the project for different reasons.

A small, dapper man, he is unusually analytical for an activist. He has prominent upper teeth and looks something like a slimmed-down Malay version of the American actor, James Earl Jones. He comes into the MiCasa to meet me and we sit by the pool and talk. He readily admits that two decades ago many Malays ate lunch during Ramadan but since that time there has been a great upsurge in religious observance in Malaysia.

He confesses to unease about PAS's advocacy of a Muslim state. His own party's formula is a neat compromise, that a state run along lines of justice and decency will come to embody Islamic values and need not be formally called an Islamic state or run by the *ulama*.

Nonetheless he seems to recognise that this is a pretty ineffectual compromise. But his analysis of the dilemmas and limitations of moderate Islam is enlightening: 'The idea of an Islamic state goes down OK in Malay heartland electorates, but in mixed electorates it is quite difficult. PAS has this long-term view of an Islamic state which it hasn't really articulated yet. PAS has not been careful in articulating this idea against the background of Saudi Arabia, Iran, Libya. We [Parti Rakyat] present the idea of a state pursuing social justice which will embody Islam even if that's not its name.'

Surely, I ask him, no one could look at Iran or Saudi Arabia and want anything like that for Malaysia. His reply is instructive: 'It would be difficult to make a rational decision like that but if you're a Malay Muslim and a true believer you don't think like that. They're trying to put the idea that the Muslim state is good for your soul. In referring to Iran or Saudi Arabia they say that is not true Islam. For millions who blindly believe that the idea of an Islamic state is good, they believe that it is something God has given us. This is the way some PAS leaders present it, it's more a question of belief, identity, spirituality than anything practical.

'In Indonesia there was a more rational idea of Islam but even there it's becoming less so. In Malaysia those people who've tried to promote moderate Islam have not been convincing. They're seen as ignorant of Islam. The Government Islamic bodies either don't seem independent or if they do have freedom of expression their conservatism makes them sound like PAS. Also they don't speak with authority, with *ulama* credentials.

'There are other positions you can take but we don't have credible spokesmen for these positions. We have some intellectuals like Karim Raslan but they are so uprooted and detached from their own societies.

'The Sisters In Islam got into trouble with the Ulama Council. I sympathise a lot with their outlook but they don't come with the right credentials. They appeal only to the middle class. They don't penetrate to the people they should. This is where the whole progressive, moderate Islamic movement is lacking all over the world.'

One Government attempt to bolster moderate Islam is IKIM, the Institute of Islamic Understanding. It certainly hasn't been captured by fundamentalists. From the look of its buildings, it's lavishly funded. Its KL headquarters looks like a modest palace, with bright yellow buildings with orange terracotta tile roofs. The four main buildings are set around a tiled courtyard. The whole complex is surrounded by lavish gardens. There are pavilions and gazebos seemingly wherever you look.

The two staff members I chat to the day I visit are sensible and mainstream and certainly moderate. But what really strikes me is the empty, lifeless quality of the buildings. The two men I speak to appear to be the only people there. My visit may have been at an unrepresentative time, but IKIM has the feel of a lushly funded, elaborate and empty shell, a monument to moderation with a less than moderate following.

This is the perennial paradox of common sense in politics, and one of its greatest difficulties. Common sense doesn't fire the passions, it leads to few inspiring campaigns, few committed campaigners. The extremist is the natural demagogue, the natural leader. The extremist's cause is easy to explain: No to secular sinfulness, yes to purity and God's way! The advocate of common sense has much less appealing slogans: let's not encourage sinfulness but on the other hand let's keep discouragement within moderate bounds so that stability is maintained and overall amenity reasonably maximised. Doesn't exactly get the blood racing, does it?

In Malaysian history, the most passionate advocate for moderation in religious matters, if not necessarily in everything else, has been its longest-serving Prime Minister, Dr Mahathir Mohamad.

The Manic Moderate

An Appointment with the Doctor

You get up early when you're going to see the doctor in Malaysia, at least Jessie and I do the day we are scheduled to see Dr Mahathir. I've interviewed him a lot over the years and among his many endearing qualities the one which journalists love the most is that he always gives you a story. There are political leaders who can talk for an hour and give you nothing. Believe me, it's happened to me. Trying to explain to an editor why you've flown 10 000 kilometres (or whatever the distance is) to talk to some guy who's told you nothing is one of the less glorious experiences of journalism. With Dr M, that never, ever happens.

Another thing is odd about Dr Mahathir. The interview always starts on time. Most leaders are manic in their busyness, everyone wants a bite of their time, unexpected problems crop up and their schedule tends to start slipping mid-morning and fall further behind as the day goes by. Politicians, especially those less senior than national leaders, also I suspect quite like the idea of keeping the reporter waiting. It shows who's boss. But with Dr Mahathir the interview always starts bang on schedule, which means it's a good thing to be early.

So Jessie and I are in the Tapas Bar by 7.30 a.m., washed and scrubbed, bright-eyed and bushy-tailed, seated and having a cut-down version of the MiCasa buffet breakfast. We have a car ordered for 7.45 even though our appointment is at 9.00. PutraJaya, the administrative capital, is about an hour's drive out of KL, depending on the traffic. Luckily our hotel is on the right side of the city for the trip.

The Government has moved a lot of ministries out from the centre of KL to PutraJaya, which is on the way to the airport and next to CyberJaya, the supposed IT hub at the heart of the Multi-Media Super Corridor. Some ministries, like Defence, presumably because of all kinds of hard-wired defence intelligence gismos, plan to stay in KL central.

For some reason traffic is light this morning, the taxi driver zooms along and we are out in the vicinity of CyberJaya in a trice. As there's plenty of time I ask him to drive into CyberJaya itself, which is just off the main highway. I don't know whether to be impressed or disappointed by CyberJaya. There's a bit of building going on, a lot of land has been cleared and the new buildings are impressive enough—modern, state-of-the-art stuff in white and other pale colours suitable for the tropics. But there's no doubt it's smaller than the Government would have wanted by now. CyberJaya was meant to take Malaysia roaring into the IT age. The problem is the IT age never eventuated as its countless prophets and promoters forecast it would in the 1990s. The collapse of the dot coms—their transformation into the dot bombs—saw to that.

At the same time China became a giant magnet for foreign investment, drawing to itself much of the investors' money that was supposed to fuel projects such as CyberJaya all over Southeast Asia. One of the strongest criticisms made of Mahathir is his fondness for giant projects like KLIA and CyberJaya. It's true that some of them don't work out, or don't work out as well as he hopes. But enough of them seem to work well enough for Malaysia still to record good economic growth. KL is undeniably a middle-class city and it wasn't anything like that forty years ago.

From CyberJaya it's a short drive to PutraJaya itself. A lot of ministries, and a lot of civil servants, are housed here. The land is rich and dramatic, with vast swathes of palm oil trees surviving from the plantation days. The density and fecundity of the Malaysian jungle never cease to amaze me. The housing is good quality, a mixture of freestanding bungalows, connected townhouses (two normally sharing a common wall) and apartment buildings. The accommodation looks as good as, or because it's newer perhaps even better than, most of what's on offer in KL. Locals tell me it's a good bit cheaper as the Government wants to encourage more people to live there. If you had a car, and many KL families do, it would offer a lot and it's set to keep growing and spouting more amenities. The appeal of a spacious home, a fan in the ceiling, three good meals a day, a colour TV and a refrigerator, a motor car, a doctor when someone gets sick, a decent government school nearby—it's easy to underestimate their importance unless you haven't had them. I have seen these elements of the good life— they are not everything of the good life but they are its bedrock foundation—spread further and further across KL and I feel I can forgive Mahathir a great deal as a result.

Even after our various peregrinations we arrive at the Prime Minister's PutraJaya office at 8.30. At the gate we are told to drive back out to the street and through a nearby carpark to the reception office and get a pass. The reception office does indeed have us on its list. There is no smiling bureaucratic Malay indifference here. The PM's office operates efficiently. Jessie and I exchange our passports for passes and are instructed to get back in our car and drive back to the main gate. Passes inspected, lists ticked off, we are then allowed to drive on up to the main entrance. This turns out to be about a three-minute walk from where we just got our passes, it would have been quicker to walk, but we are not complaining.

The Prime Minister's office is a huge building in PutraJaya, rightly regarded as a tourist attraction in its own right, along with the equally monolithic national mosque next door. Sitting atop a small hill, it is toned in brown and green and a huge green minaret sits on its top, between two smaller minarets.

All this grandeur is meant to serve a political purpose, of course: to instil in Malaysians, especially Malays, a sense of civic pride and achievement. If KL was originally a Chinese town, PutraJaya is wholly Malay.

At the base of the PM's office the huge building blocks and massive, unadorned face of the building have the look of a Chicago bank in the 1950s, civic and square and solid and impassive. The front door is marked by a cluster of green pot plants on either side and a square of blue carpet at the front. Two sets of sliding glass doors bring us into air-conditioned comfort. Behind a tall counter a bevy of Malay women, all wearing *tudongs*, usher us through an electronic security gate, opened by our passes. One of these women takes us up to the second floor and we walk down a series of long corridors. We emerge out of one corridor into a more open space. A full-length glass window displays a lush, internal courtyard of the most precisely manicured plants. We walk on deep pile carpet underneath huge chandeliers, past the most sumptuous, cloth-covered sofas. Does anyone ever sit on these sofas?

My pass is exchanged for one which will actually allow me into the presence of the Prime Minister. Jessie keeps her inferior pass. We are taken into what appears to be a sealed room (after the door is shut behind us it seems like just another wall panel and I couldn't with any certainty have found my way back out of the room) and instructed to take a lift to the seventh floor. We emerge into another sealed room and open at random one of three panel/doors marked 'Must be kept closed at all times'. A security man has magically guessed which one of these panels we will emerge through and takes us to another waiting room, with brocaded sofas and general French empire effect, where we are later greeted by two civilian officials, one of them my old friend, Datuk Hisham Makaruddin, one of the PM's senior advisers. I have been dealing with Datuk Hisham for many years. We have never become close, we have never become distant. He is the embodiment of professionalism, always courteous, always the soul of friendly helpfulness, never venturing a centimetre further than seems appropriate in the relationship between the PM's office and a foreign writer.

I suspect this *Man From Uncle* routine of serial passes and sealed rooms and all the associated falderol of getting into the PM's office doesn't actually have all that much to do with security. As Mahathir himself points out to me he often does his own shopping at weekends around KL. He's generally relaxed about security. He's always out and about around Malaysia and is generally a highly visible and accessible leader. My guess is it's more to do with Malay love of gadgetry and the sheer fun for the building's managers of being state-of-the-art just for its own sake.

Jessie asks one of the officials whether he thinks Mahathir really should retire from politics as he's promised.

'Oh, no,' the official says. 'I wish he would just go on and on.'

Whatever else Mahathir is, he is certainly a religious moderate. At a famous speech to the World Economic Forum in New York in 2002 he made a stinging attack on Islamic fundamentalism: 'Islam is a religion of peace and moderation. If it does not appear to be so today, it is not because of the teachings of Islam but the interpretations made by those apparently learned in Islam to suit their patrons . . .

'The early *ulamas* were knowledgeable in many disciplines besides Islamic theology. Today political *ulamas* are only knowledgeable about those parts of the teachings of Islam which seemingly support their political views. Many misinterpret and distort Islam.'

Some commentators saw this as an opportunistic grab for cheap applause from an American audience. But Mahathir has made exactly this sort of speech inside Malaysia to domestic audiences many times. Later that same year he hosted an Organisation of Islamic Conference meeting in KL. Strikingly, Mahathir proposed that terrorism be defined as any armed attack on civilians. The OIC didn't go along with his definition. His speech contained all the standard criticisms of Israel, which almost any Islamic political leader feels obliged to make. But it also contained one of the most explicit condemnations of Palestinian suicide bombings from any mainstream leader in the Muslim world. It is little wonder that Tom Friedman of *The New York Times* described Mahathir as 'courageous'. Mahathir's words certainly were direct: 'Muslims everywhere must condemn terrorism once it is clearly defined. Terrorising people is not the way of Islam. Certainly killing innocent people is not Islamic.'

Here was a moderate Muslim voice to make Western hearts sing! It would be wrong to overlook Mahathir's trenchant and repeated criticisms of US foreign policy but here is a leader who will preach moderation to his own people even when their emotions may be running the other way. That's not exactly common in the Muslim world. Certainly neighbouring Indonesia's leaders mostly don't speak directly like this.

The Mahathir story is a strange one. He comes from sleepy Alor Setar, where I went to interview Fadzil Noor. He was the youngest of nine children, his father a school headmaster. Mahathir studied medicine in Singapore, one of the first Malays to do so. He lived through British then Japanese then for a second time British rule of his country. His outlook was formed by colonialism. He was a political activist in the Malay community and while working as a doctor, first for the Government service then in private practice, was active as a journalistic agitator in Malay newspapers. When you look back at that journalism it's intersting how similar it is in style to Mahathir's pronouncements decades later, and how a coherent body of ideas formed the core of his political commitment from the start.

Mahathir was always about ethnic Malay self-assertion and pride. The old colonial structure had the British on top, the Chinese in the middle as traders and the Malays at the bottom. The exception of course was the Malay aristocracy who always had a special political role.

As with a lot of leaders who lived through colonialism, all this seared itself into Mahathir's psyche. He once told me: 'Even as a schoolboy I felt we Malays were looked down on by the British colonisers. I felt Malays should have a part in the wealth of this country. The towns in those days were 100 per cent Chinese.'

So, I asked him, was his motivation partly anger?

'I think I'm entitled to be angry when people look down on me.'

In 1969 he wrote his most extraordinary book, *The Malay Dilemma*, which got him expelled from UMNO. It was among other things a tough attack on the Malay Government for not doing more to redistribute wealth and opportunity to the Malays. It was a heartfelt plea that the Malay race were about to lose control of their homeland. All this is the standard sort of stuff that ethnic leaders in recently decolonised societies come up with. What was novel about *The Malay Dilemma* was the stern, scolding tone it took to its own Malay readership, lambasting them for their lack of enterprise and drive.

This has always been a key element of Mahathir, one of the things that marks him out as an altogether unusual leader. He doesn't just give his people someone to blame. He constantly challenges them to do better, in effect to blame themselves, to take responsibility for their own situation and to take responsibility for improving it. Here is another distinction between Mahathir and almost every other leader of a defined ethnic group, he never saw the means of improvement as purely political. In other words the solution was not just for Malays to control the Government and distribute more of the goodies to the Malay community. The whole Malay psyche had to change, not primarily in terms of politics but of economic and cultural outlook—a willingness to compete, a stress on technical education and modern economics.

There is also in *The Malay Dilemma* a little bit of strange genetic theorising and speculation, which would be regarded as wildly politically incorrect these days, about how Malay inbreeding had weakened the stock.

A typical passage from *The Malay Dilemma*, of Mahathir reading a tough love lesson to his fellow Malays, goes: 'The Malays, whose own hereditary and environmental influence had been so debilitating, could do nothing but retreat before the onslaught of the Chinese immigrants. Whatever the Malays could do, the Chinese could do better and more cheaply. Before long the industrious and determined immigrants had displaced the Malays in petty trading and all branches of skilled work. As their wealth increased so did their circle of contacts. Calling on their previous experience with officialdom in their own homeland, the Chinese imigrants were soon establishing the type of relationship between officials and traders which existed in China.'

The other interesting thing about the passage is its tone of voice. Mahathir is a natural newspaper columnist. All his books, and this is not true of his speeches, are written in the same kind of middle-brow newspaper op-ed style, which suggests that they're all written by him. The speeches are more formal and sometimes grandiloquent—they carry his ideas well enough but my impression is staffers have more of a role with the speeches. But the books are pure Mahathir—by the way how many political leaders really write their own books?—at their best they deploy a sturdy common sense backed up by a real knowledge of how the world works. At their worst they lack the scholarly depth of reading their subject matter could do with and sometimes suffer from a lack of balance. But his books have provided a rich mother lode for biographers.

Nineteen sixty-nine was the year of terrible race riots in KL, in which hundreds of Chinese were killed. The Government was shattered and decided it had to take drastic affirmative action measures to give Malays a stake in the economy. These measures undeniably constitute discrimination. On the other hand they have also undeniably had a role in producing a Malaysia in which all the races can prosper. And since 1969 there have been no politically motivated racial killings.

Mahathir was brought back into UMNO because he had championed ideas which the Government now wanted to adopt. He was quickly elevated to parliament, a deputy ministry, a full ministry, the deputy leadership and in 1981 the Prime Ministership. It has been a stormy ride ever since. There was the recession in the mid-1980s and a near-run leadership challenge in 1987, then in 1997 the Asian economic crisis and the next year the spectacular falling out with and jailing of Anwar Ibrahim, the former Deputy Prime Minister.

Like many successful political leaders Mahathir has somehow managed to make a national theatre out of the politics of which he is always the centre, while keeping a broad stability and predictability about policy. Of course there have been lots of course corrections over the years but there is a solidity to Malaysian policy, it's not whimsically changed by a whimsical leader.

At last nine o'clock rolls around and, right on time, I am ushered into Mahathir's presence. His office is huge. It's divided into two areas by a large, wooden screen of traditional Malay design. One area has a couple of sofas and is probably used when small groups visit the PM. But in one-on-one discussions Mahathir eschews the phony bonhomie of a casual lounge chat and stays at his desk.

He is in his late seventies now, there are a couple of sun spots on his face, otherwise he doesn't look much different from any time in the last decade or more. He doesn't look athletic or especially vigorous, but there is a leathery, durable look about him—'as tough as old army boots' as one Western diplomat once described him to me. He is seated at his big desk, six or eight briefcases of papers to one side, presumably requiring attention some time that day. He is reading *The New Straits Times*. The attitude of his body is passive— *OK, what are you going to bowl up to me?* is the general impression.

In person Mahathir is always softly spoken (sometimes too softly even for the tape to pick up properly), courteous and solicitous. He is certainly not gushing but even if he is saying trenchant things to you he says them in a low key manner. I should think that in neogitations he would be exceptionally difficult to read.

Our discussion starts with the issues of the day. He castigates the US for the way it's handling the war on terror. He castigates Australia for being too pro-American. He doesn't like the travel advisories several Western governments have issued to their citizens regarding the supposed dangers of travelling to Southeast Asia, including Malaysia. These are standard Mahathir positions and in due course they generate the standard headlines back home.

But I am more interested today to ask him about some of his own motivations in politics. The Japanese occupation of Malaya in World War II, for example, brutal as it was, gravely weakened the British position for independence-generation leaders like Mahathir.

'Having seen the Japanese push the British out of the country we knew the British were not invincible as they had tried to convince us. We felt when they came back [after World War II] we were still prepared to be part of the great British Empire but the British were greedy. Instead of returning to the status quo where we were protected Malay states the British tried to make us full colonies. At that stage the Malays rose and I was part of that.'

Unlike a lot of leaders who always thought they were going to get to the top Mahathir thought the opposite and the reckless honesty and brutal defiance of his pronouncements at the time don't suggest someone who had an eye to his political future.

Did he ever think he would be Prime Minister? 'Oh no, I couldn't even imagine being a member of the Government. I thought I would be playing at the periphery, maybe achieving local leadership. The whole idea at that time was too big for me. Most people at that time couldn't imagine Malays becoming Prime Minister or even becoming chief minister. It was a complete change [in mentality].

'I knew Malays in colonial times—how they looked up to the British, how they tried to become very English in some ways. It didn't get them anywhere. I rather felt I wasn't attracted by that attitude.'

The fact that he wasn't a member of a Malay royal family was also important: 'I'm quite sure if I'd been a member of royalty and given all kinds of privileges I wouldn't have thought being under colonial rule by the British was so bad.'

I ask him about his liberal, verging on radical, daughter Marina: 'She's quite critical of the Government sometimes. She has always been very, very independent. Some people say she's very much like me. I am proud of her but I have no control.'

Mahathir is not just blunt about the failings of his own race, the Malays, or about what he sees as the shortcomings of US and Australian foreign policy. He is also, and this again is remarkable for a Muslim leader, corruscatingly honest about the failings of Muslim regimes in the Middle East: 'I have always blamed the Muslims for the situation they're in. Of course others contributed as well but the fact is they are not really following the teachings of Islam and that I have to criticise. I have spoken quite forthrightly against that.'

So do you think Islam, properly understood, is not incompatible with modernisation, I ask.

'Not at all. In fact Islam was a modernising force when it came 1400 years ago. Islam pioneered most of the sciences—medicine, education and other things. Because they were very well educated they changed the world and the Europeans came to learn of the sciences from the Muslims. If we had continued with that we would have been a very progressive nation, at least equal with the rest of the world. Unfortunately halfway through, the Muslim jurists decided to concentrate mostly on legal aspects, punishments for whatever, and forget about non-Islamic knowledge. That is when the Muslim civilisation began to relapse.'

This is a crucial connection for Mahathir. It was the feminist insight of the 1970s that sex is not destiny. I cannot believe either that culture is destiny, that some cultures succeed and some cultures fail and that's all there is to it. This belief is constantly disproved by history. After all, after World War II, and then after the Korean War, it was thought that first the Japanese then the Koreans could not succeed at modernisation because Confucianism was culturally opposed to modernisation. The Mandarin gentleman with his long fingernails could not manipulate machinery. The stress on hierarchy and deference to elders was hostile to modern citizenship and modern technology. In the event good policy and good leadership meant that these two most Confucian societies became highly successful at modernisation, even while retaining strong elements of Confucianism too.

Surely, too, religion is not destiny. Most, virtually all, religions are amenable to modernisation if there is good leadership and good policy. Islam will be in practice what Muslims make of it. The most fascinating theme in Mahathir's career has been his long attempt to link the traditional virtues of Islam with the embrace of modernisation, to make Islam itself a force for modernisation.

It's no point Western leaders telling Muslim societies to ignore their Islam and become modern instead. The trickier but infinitely more promising path is to practise modernisation in a way that is compatible with Islam and to practise Islam in a way that is compatible with modernisation. It can be done. Mahathir has done it.

Anyway, back to the interview. You get the impression the young Mahathir was a fiery and intense kid, proud of his dad, proud of his race, determined that no one was going to push him around. I ask him which leaders were his childhood heroes.

'I read a lot about history, about leaders who changed their countries and peoples, how they dragged them into a modern world. And of course I was always interested in the struggles of the Prophet of Islam—how he was able to get the warring Arab tribes to make peace among themselves and develop a culture and civilisation which resulted in the Muslim world. He changed a very primitive people.

'There were others (i.e. other leaders) who changed their people—Genghis Khan, for example. He didn't last for very long. Peter the Great. Napoleon. These are great leaders. One cannot help but be attracted by their achievements.'

And who among the world's leaders does he admire today?

'In the last twenty years I don't see many leaders.'

Sometimes Mahathir has expressed frustration that the Malays have not moved faster, that economically they are still so far behind the Chinese. Looking back on his career, he acknowledges this: 'We have succeeded to some extent. We now see some Malays involved in business, in big business, and some of them are successful. Of course many fail. But we see few Malays involved in small business, in retail business. And some of the towns are becoming very Chinese. This is a separation we don't like. We would like Malays to get involved at every level of business.'

Asked to nominate his greatest achievement in office he goes immediately, tellingly, to race, to the maintenance of racial harmony. Even during the recession of 1997/98 there were no race riots and that is hugely important.

'When I was announced as Deputy Prime Minister, which means I would succeed as Prime Minister, there were fears among the Chinese that I would be very anti-Chinese. But of course in my career the Chinese have been very supportive and realised I am not what they made me out to be. And because of that I think we have achieved racial harmony in this country to a higher degree than was thought possible.'

For a moment we look out the window together at this incredible, green and prosperous land with all the riches of all its races.

You must be proud of your country, Dr Mahathir?

'Yes, I am. Proud and satisfied.'

Sadness, Children and Jihad

Our next appointment that morning is less cheerful. It seems an odd coincidence of timing that straight after seeing Mahathir Jessie and I drive into Demansara, an upmarket suburb close in to central KL, in a part of town used a lot by government officials and other panjandrums.

We are going to see Wan Aziza Wan Ismail, the wife of former Deputy Prime Minister, Anwar Ibrahim. Anwar fell out badly with his boss over economic policy. Anwar wanted to follow IMF orthodoxy during the 1997/98 economic crisis. The International Monetary Fund, with its one-size-fits-all economic remedies, had a lot of victims and to some extent Anwar was one. At the time progressive, liberal international opinion hailed Anwar's courage and policy foresight. Everyone agreed with the IMF–Anwar prescriptions—high interest rates, no grand projects, expenditure cuts, no exchange controls.

It's history now that Mahathir took the opposite course, imposing limited currency and capital controls, to take the ringgit out of the hands of speculators, to cool the whole manic process of hot money pouring in and out of countries and melting their economies in the process. It's also history that Mahathir's approach, in economic policy terms, was fully vindicated and Malaysia survived the economic crisis better than any nation in Southeast Asia except Singapore.

Mahathir assures me that their policy differences had nothing to do with Anwar's jailing. All I did, Mahathir says, was dismiss him from office. After that it was up to the police. Mahathir further points out that Anwar was still a member of the Government when the key economic policy decisions were made. The point of that is that Anwar's presence in the Government did not paralyse it or prevent Mahathir from implementing his policies.

Subsequently Anwar was charged with obstruction of justice, corruption related to obstruction of justice and sodomy, and jailed for a lengthy sentence. Anwar and his family have always maintained his innocence.

Whatever the truth is about Anwar, his wife is an admirable woman. Today we approach her home at the end of a long and winding cul de sac. It's a pretty suburban KL home, a two-storey bungalow Malaysians would call it, comfortable, affluent, without being at all lavish. Although the house itself is not remarkable it's easy to spot for it's plastered with pro-Anwar posters. It's a brave gesture.

I visited the house before, not very long after Anwar went to jail. Wan Aziza, in the wake of her husband's imprisonment, founded the Keadilan Party which looked for a brief moment as though it might become a force in Malaysian politics. Now it has a handful of parliamentary members, it has not fulfilled its multiracial promise and is dominated by Malays. Far from being the liberal conscience of Malaysian politics it has come to contain some extremely conservative Islamist voices and is best seen as a small breakaway group from UMNO.

When I visited the house before it was a hive of activity, with party workers all over the place and a swing door from the living room into the kitchen carrying a sign: 'Family Only'.

This day the house is not like that at all. It has been remarkably easy to secure an interview with Wan Aziza. There seems almost no protective carapace of party structure and loyalist support around her. It was just a question of ringing her mobile and making a time.

She is leaving next day for a conference in Bangkok so the appointment has to be today.

The house is hushed, there is the faintest echo of a child's voice somewhere. In the living room there is a piano, a cluster of sofas, a dining table and a wall cabinet, ceiling fans rather than air-con. Apart from the scrolls in Arabic—presumably Koranic verses—it could be the living room of any average well-to-do family in any of dozens of countries.

Only one thing really stands out about the house. The panel in the front door that was broken down by the police when they came to arrest Anwar has been left unrepaired—it functions in its way as a small shrine.

Wan Aziza apologises for not serving us coffee. It's Ramadan, the fasting month.

'You know it's our custom not to serve during Ramadan,' she says.

Actually in the past week I've met every different possible response to the problem of hospitality for non-Muslims in Malay homes and offices during Ramadan. On one occasion I was served coffee while my host didn't take anything. Another time I was not served coffee and my host apologised. I replied that I understood it was Ramadan but he said no, we are supposed to give hospitality to strangers during Ramadan but I was not prepared for your visit. And then there are occasions when, quite sensibly, the matter is simply not raised at all. I've been at conferences in KL during Ramadan in which the Malays disappear for a rest at lunchtime and the non-Malays eat to their heart's content. You are generally subject to so much and such attentive Malay hospitality that a rest from consuming for a couple of hours during Ramadan seems a good idea.

Wan Aziza wears the *tudong*, as she has for many years. She was an opthalmologist and did some of her training at Trinity College, Dublin. Today she makes some effort to talk about politics but really she's most animated talking about Anwar's health.

I try to question her about policy but my heart isn't in it and neither is hers. Keadilan is in a coalition with PAS and I ask her about some of the offensive things PAS says—everything from that women should not be parliamentary candidates to wanting to institute an Islamic state, to all its mad conspiracy theories. Her response, to be honest with you, is less than wholly convincing: 'If you know the PAS heartland, PAS has to have that rhetoric.'

What about all the *jihad* stuff, what does *jihad* actually mean?

'*Jihad* as suicide bombing is wrong. *Jihad* is helping the poor, giving up something of yourself, but also if your life is threatened to fight back in self-defence. The image of the sword-wielding Muslim screaming death to the infidel is totally wrong.'

Well of course if the world were ruled by people as gentle as Wan Aziza perhaps that's what *jihad* would mean. But when the PAS leader called for *jihad* against the United States I don't think that's exactly what he had in mind.

I ask her about the US military action in Afghanistan, which she opposes. It is certainly reasonable to oppose this US policy but she simultaneously thinks it's right that the former al-Qaeda terrorist camps in Afghanistan should be destroyed by the Americans.

'If they [the US] go against Afghanistan what do they have? Collateral damage is also human beings. Of course I also abhor [the terrorism of] 9/11 and the loss of life. Of course you have to destroy the terrorist camps but if I'm an Afghan what have *I* done? It's bully tactics the US is using. I'm sure there are other ways of doing it.'

So *jihad* means giving to the poor and the US should destroy al-Qaeda's terrorist camps nicely. I don't begrudge Wan Aziza her gentle equivocations. These are insoluble dilemmas she faces, impossible choices.

She becomes more animated when talking about her six children. The eldest daughter, studying electrical engineering at university, has made the dean's list. That's a wonderful thing. Another child is at school in Australia. Marina Mahathir has a child at school in Australia too. I wonder if they've ever met.

Wan Aziza acknowledges some of Mahathir's success in promoting Malaysian development but understandably claims it as Anwar's success. Yet this too leads to a contradiction—how can the

Government be so bad if for so long Anwar was so key a part of its success?

I leave Wan Aziza's home full of melancholy. I was so buoyant about Malaysia just a couple of hours ago, now I am downcast.

Lunch, Breakfast and Dinner

Jessie and I decide to cheer ourselves up by going to a little cafe for lunch not far from the hotel, which serves some of our favourite food, to wit, chicken rice.

Hainanese chicken rice is a staple in many parts of Southeast Asia. It's a simple dish, done just right it's irresistible. The key is that everything has to be fresh and the condiments must be mixed in precisely the right proportions. There is a small ball of rice, a serve of chopped chicken, either steamed or fried, some thick soy sauce with chillies and ginger. This is a simple cafe, just about empty when we arrive towards the end of lunchtime, and we go to the counter and order and pay.

Some time passes. Our drinks arrive. Some more time passes. I go back to the counter—is our chicken rice on the way?

'Have you ordered it?'

'Yes, I ordered it here when I paid for it.'

'Have you ordered it outside?'

'What do you mean "outside"?'

'You pay for it here, you order it outside from the chicken rice counter.'

We'd been to that restaurant before and this is a completely new procedure to us. But what is noteworthy about it all is that at no stage had we ever been more than two metres from the girl at the counter. We had been in her line of sight all the time. We hadn't left our table. We were in fact the only customers in the cafe. She must have seen that we hadn't ordered outside and didn't know we needed to. It is the majestic serenity of the Malay indifference in the service industry which is impressive. She had been instructed to take orders and take payments. Most of the orders were provided from behind the counter. But the chicken rice was supplied from a stall outside. She hadn't been instructed to pass the order to the stall outside, or to tell us to do so, so she didn't do it. Logic, initiative, mere common sense don't enter the equation. And of course she was perfectly polite about everything.

Once when we foolishly defected from the MiCasa to try another hotel, Jessie and I encountered the saga of the skim milk. I love the unpredictability of travel but I also love its little routines. When I travel I always start breakfast with cereal and skim milk. If I'm being virtuous I finish breakfast at that point. I realise it's pretty illogical to have skim milk with your cereal if you're then going to eat a full buffet breakfast, but I'm not always logical or virtuous. And if I'm carrying a few extra kilos it's certainly not because of the occasional unavailability of low-fat milk.

But, hey, we all have our foibles.

We came down for breakfast first day at this hotel and there was no low-fat milk. This isn't really the deprivation of a basic human right but still I thought I'd ask the headwaiter about it.

'Oh, sorry sir. Today we are out of stock but will have low-fat milk tomorrow.'

Next day, still no skim milk so I ask the waiter the same question and get the same answer: 'Oh, sorry sir. Today we are out of stock but will have low-fat milk tomorrow.'

This goes on for four or five days, every day the same question, every day the same response, and finally, just to be perverse really, I ask him: 'Why do you keep saying it will be here tomorrow but it never shows up tomorrow?'

'Actually we find the guests have no demand for it so we don't stock it any more.'

That would have been a perfectly reasonable answer on day one. I can only assume a form of Malay politeness which hates to say no has led him to avoid even that mild confrontation by simply putting it off until tomorrow.

Now, showing not the slightest zot of cultural sensitivity, and breaking every rule there is in good cross-cultural relations, just to be super-perverse I ask him why then has he told me every day that it would be there tomorrow.

'No, I never said it would be here tomorrow.'

'You did, you just said it two minutes ago.'

'No, I never said that.'

The next day, coincidentally our last at that hotel, there was a container of cold, skim milk on the counter.

Fathoming Malay social customs can be tricky, even if, like me, you spend a lot of time in KL.

A big business type invites me for dinner. Jessie has a family commitment and can't go. The big business type has a new house he is very proud of and sends a car to fetch me. The house is on the edge of a golf course and seems to be composed entirely of glass. This is surely worth a new proverb: people in glass houses shouldn't live on golf courses. My host tells me the glass is super-reinforced, the builder has guaranteed its unsmashability and the golf course is committed to big payments if a ball does break the glass. Nonetheless it feels like a risk to me. I'd be uncomfortable living in that house: you'd feel pretty silly if a ball came whistling through an open window and landed in your soup.

But of course there are no open windows because the house is so comprehensively air-conned. The guests are a mixture of the business type's senior work colleagues and a few outsiders. There are men and women, Malays, Indians and Chinese. One of the guests, a Chinese, is a rising man in the Opposition DAP. I think it's rather liberal of the business type to have him as a guest, especially with a foreign reporter present.

A few things confuse me. I have heard the business guy has two wives, two households, two sets of servants. When the wife comes in to say hello I am struck dumb, not knowing whether she is wife number one or wife number two and what I should call her. This is highly illogical on my part but it doesn't matter because she stays literally just for a second and then is gone. We don't see her again, although we are given to understand that she has had some hand at least in supervising the preparation of the food.

The normal thirty-seven courses come through and we eat to the point of exhaustion. But then the real feast starts, a whole series of Malaysian fruits it would be grossly impolite to refuse. Our old friend the durian—cut, smelled, relished, eaten and cleared away in quick fashion so that its odour is not overpowering. Then there's rambutan, which doesn't smell but looks as unappetising as the durian. Mangosteen. Papaya. Honeydew melon. Pineapple. Sugar bananas. Watermelon. And on and on it goes.

There is no booze but the evening passes in great hilarity. There isn't much small talk, in the conventional, Western, dinner-party sense of the term, and not much Big Talk, in the sense of Serious Discussion of Weighty Topics. There is just an endless series of jokes and funny stories, most only mildly ribald and some not ribald at all, about public figures, semi-public figures and absent work colleagues. I don't know all the people in all the stories but the laughter itself is intoxicating and contagious. After a while I am roaring as much as any of them and adding my own contribution of matching Australian jokes on the powerful, in response to which the other dinner guests all guffaw with as much enthusiasm as they do about the local stories. People's own jokes induce positively uncontrollable hilarity in themselves, so that they frequently struggle just to get the story out.

And no matter how lame the punch line we all burst into hysterical fits of laughter. Even the suggestion that a punch line is about to be delivered sets us off. People interpose alternative punch lines and finish each other's stories. I have never encountered anything quite like it. For the period that the meal lasts we are in a conspiracy of laughter, a special fellowship of mirth, a golden circle of camaraderie and good feeling. Of course, in this life all such things are temporary.

In due course the evening ends and we all go home. I am grateful to my host for his generous hospitality and completely at a loss to explain the evening I've just had.

Long Blacks, Idola and Friends

We are coming to the end of our time in KL and I have the chance to catch up with an old friend, Abdul, a big man in a middling business, no tycoon but an older man of long experience and reasonable success, and a thoughtful intellectual to boot. We meet at one of the alfresco coffee shops at KLCC. Ramadan has finished and Abdul orders a long black.

Abdul is a senior man. He's been a political activist, though never held ofice. I've known him a long time and he seems in an uncharacteristically sombre mood. I am a cappuccino addict but I would feel frivolous ordering a cappuccino against Abdul's purposeful long black. As a respectful younger man should, I follow his lead and order a long black too.

Abdul is concerned at the trend of developments in the Islamic world. He is concerned too about the way the US in his view is losing the battle for Islamic opinion. He is concerned about the onward march of the fundamentalists all over the Islamic world. The trends are hard to pick. He doesn't pretend to know the future. But I've seldom found him in such a pessimistic frame of mind, so little seeing the funny side of anything.

Most of all, he is concerned for the future of his own country. He's not sure the political system is sturdy enough to last but he doesn't see any remotely acceptable alternative.

He doesn't see any easy answers in Western liberalism, nor in any of the normal prescriptions outsiders offer for his country— more democracy, greater transparency in corporate governance, all the rest. It's not that he's against these things. It's more that he sees every group within Malaysia acting from self-interest which is disguised alternately with religious or democratic rhetoric.

'All these so-called liberal Malays who talk about liberalism and transparency and democracy, they're all telling you lies. They don't want liberalism and transparency in their own lives. There's no such thing as Malay democracy. There's not a Malay in this country who doesn't want his son to get a preferred place in the university. There's not one who wants his son to have to compete honestly with the Chinese son next door. They all want the special privileges and special assistance. And what does special opportunity mean for one except denying that opportunity for the other? The whole of Malay life is based on the opposite of transparency. Which Malay is prepared to really take responsibility for his own life and his family's life and ask for nothing more from the Government than fair treatment and equal opportunity?'

It is important to note that in this one respect at least, Abdul's pessimism was unjustified. Since that conversation the Government has introduced a far more meritocratic system for university entry.

'And the alternative is PAS. PAS offers nothing. It's not only its extremism that I'm worried about. It knows nothing about a modern economy. Its ignorance is frightening. It's at war with the idea of a modern economy. Support for PAS means Malays rejecting the modern world. It's a complete dead end for Malay identity. So where does the modern Malay go, the person who is willing to take responsibility for himself, who doesn't want any special favours from the Government?'

He pauses for a while, perhaps feels some necessity to answer his own question: 'Maybe our unique compromise can hold together.' But there is irony and bitterness in his voice.

We sit there together a long time, staring into greenery made almost psychedelic by the fierce tropical sun. Some of the time we sit in silence. It isn't necessary for me to prompt Abdul with too many questions. The words are coming from some place deep inside his heart. Ultimately they are words of love, love of his nation, love of our friendship. I'm grateful for his honesty, and his trust, and know that it would be ridiculous to offer any facile words of comfort.

Perhaps few countries' politics could withstand the fierce metaphysical contemplation Abdul is giving to Malaysia's that day. In the long run, as Keynes said, we are all dead. Most politics, and certainly democratic politics even at something like its best, is all messy compromise and awkward improvisation. Few lines run straight in any nation's politics. Pure principle informs utopias of the mind which become hell on Earth if they're enacted. Even as I sit with Abdul, and am nearly overwhelmed by his dark vision, I cling to the idea that Malaysia's political class, taking everything into account, hasn't done too badly.

Then, too, we are all subject to moods, even in our deepest reflections. The soul too has its seasons. I don't think Abdul's pessimism that day is the whole story, even the whole story of his own thinking. He, more than anyone, is not blind to the real success of Malaysia. But like the best patriots everywhere, he wants his nation to be much better than it is.

One thing that's improving a little is Malay cinema. It has nowhere near the vitality it had in P. Ramlee's day. But one facet of globalisation is that virtually any modestly wealthy society can attain a level of solid technical competence in film-making, which allows the nation to tell some of its own stories to its own people. Even if most national cinemas are swamped by Hollywood (India's Bollywood is a noble exception) even a few local films a year can be both an important window into a culture and a means for the society to talk to itself.

I have seen some incredibly bad Malay films but on this visit I see a video of one that is quite passable, which on the surface seems unremarkable but contains one or two features that on consideration are astounding.

Idola is a fairly standard romance. Idola is a pretty, successful, career woman who lives with her younger sister who is still at school. Idola wears a *tudong* outside, in the presence of men, but not indoors with just her sister at home. Idola is a lawyer or some such, full of serious intent and high purpose, a Malay Meryl Streep. Idola's younger sister, though chafing at times at older sister's rules and regulations, does more or less as she's told and is a good girl.

Idola meets an attractive, moustachioed record producer who also lives with his younger sister. His younger sister is an emerging pop star and, although he tells her friends when to leave the house so his sister can get some sleep, she is more rebellious and a bit of a naughty girl, though this naughtiness is pretty mild and only hinted at rather than shown.

The chap also has a couple of kids from a failed marriage but they live with their mother. He is a kind of Malay Ben Stiller nice guy, easily misunderstood, who mostly doesn't get the breaks until the end of the film. He and Idola have a spirited disagreement throughout the film about whether his record producing is really socially useful work. This is a Malay version of the Billy Crystal/ Meg Ryan gender disagreements.

Attraction between Idola and the chap soon blossoms (well, why else would you make the film?). They arrange in a most modest and chaste way to spend a weekend at a resort together. The chap takes his kids and Idola takes her sister and they stay, naturally, in separate bungalows.

All is going swimmingly until the chap's wife, from whom he is not yet formally divorced, turns up in his bed. She isn't really making a pitch to resume the marriage, she's just interested in seeing his new girlfriend.

Yikes!, or some Malay equivalent, says the guy, you can't stay here, certainly not in my bed!

Why not, says his ex, it's nothing new for us to share a bed.

He sleeps on the sofa, his ex stays in the bed.

Next morning the ex is wandering around in nothing more than the baggy T-shirt she has worn to bed. In a very daring and saucy touch by Malay standards the ex keeps lifting the back of her T-shirt up to scratch her bum. The viewer doesn't quite get an eyefull of the bum as it's in shadow and the moment is fleeting but this must be a very suggestive and provocative moment in Malay cinema.

Idola catches one glimpse of the ex, jumps naturally to the wrong conclusions, bundles her sister into the car and rushes back to KL. In due course, after the obligatory sadness and estrangement, Idola and the guy meet again, all is explained, love blossoms once more and the film ends with marriage beckoning.

It's all a perfectly professional production if not very remarkable, except, as I say, for two features.

One is that I cannot really work out the film's point of view. Idola is the hero and is meant to embody Malay virtues. That's fair enough. Central to her identity is covering up her hair from male view, which she goes to great lengths to do. But all the scenes at home are of her hair uncovered. So isn't the film really transgressing the values it claims to be promoting?

If this were a Western film about Malays that would be fair enough. But I don't see how it really works as a film within the Malay Muslim tradition. This is of course a hundred times more so the case with the scenes of the ex-wife's backside. I suppose Hollywood was guilty of similar hypocrisy in the 1950s. Is that hypocrisy sustainable? Will it lead inevitably either to full liberalisation or a conservative backlash?

Maybe it is sustainable. I hope it is. As I say, there's got to be some alternative for a society apart from either the Taliban on one hand or *Sex and the City* on the other. For all its didactic elements, *Idola* is reasonably well made and works as cinema because its primary concern is the story of the relationships rather than preaching about values. It just, perhaps only just, manages to succeed in making the values implicit in believable characters rather than making the characters mere mechanistic puppets to display the values.

However, there is one aspect of the film which really is incredible though KL friends tell me it's typical. There is not one non-Malay face in the entire film. I was watching it with sub-titles so I may have missed something but as far as I could tell the city it was set in was KL itself. If KL is a majority Malay city it's only a bare majority. There are huge Chinese and Indian populations. I have seldom been in a social setting in KL in which Chinese and Indians, as well as Malays, are not present. It's almost inconceivable that you could go into shops and restaurants and resorts and find only Malays.

Yet that is the fantasy world that *Idola* shows. Idola is a gentle and self-consciously wholesome movie but this exclusion of the non-Malays strikes me as truly pernicious. It undermines one of the basic social tasks of a national cinema—to show a nation to itself. Is it going too far to suggest that the exclusion of the non-Malays from this ideal world is an indication that that's how some Malays wish their society was, free of non-Malay races? It reminds me of those American sitcoms of the 1950s and early 1960s—*Leave it to Beaver, The Nelsons, My Three Sons*. In some ways they too were wholesome and full of good values. But when you think back to them, can you ever remember seeing a single black in them at all? This was a pure whitebread fantasy America which simply didn't exist, which never existed. The exclusion of blacks from shows like that was a powerful indicator of what white society thought of blacks, what it wished it could be. Even today many American sitcoms exclude blacks as primary characters but nowadays they virtually never exclude them totally even from the ambient society.

Not all Malaysian films and TV shows are like *Idola*. Jessie and I every week watch a sitcom called *Kopitiam*, about a coffee shop. It is entirely the opposite of *Idola* in having all three races in every episode. It's a madcap show and quite amusing. Jessie and I never saw the original episodes in which the relationships of all the principals are no doubt explained. The Kopitiam coffee shop is so multi-racial it's a bit hard to fathom just what the relationships between the family members and friends who run the coffee shop might be.

Mind you some Malaysian familes are quite like that in reality, especially in big cities like KL. A lot of Chinese orphans were adopted by Malay families. I have a friend whose family is an equal mix of Chinese and Indian. The relatives at any large gathering of their family form three distinct racial types—Chinese, Indians and mixed. *Kopitiam* doesn't go on about its multi-racialism. That is not its point. It's not didactic, though like a lot of sitcoms, especially Asian sitcoms, it is at times quite sentimental. It is well made and good fun for an idle half-hour. Its multi-racialism, while idealised, is infinitely closer to reality than *Idola*'s bizarre mono-Malayism.

On our last night in KL Jessie and I go to Bangsar Baru for dinner. Bangsar Baru is the most stylish area of KL. It's the Chelsea, the Greenwich Village, the Double Bay of KL. It's a few blocks of expensive, high-class restaurants, bars, boutique retail outlets, art galleries, high-quality bookshops, cyber-cafes and the like. It isn't cheap. It is in no sense a red-light district but some of its bars are a bit raunchy and this leads to intermittent conflict with the big mosque just across the road. Bangsar Baru also has a big night market which is not cheap by market standards but very cheap compared to the formal shops in BB, so it does a brisk trade. It's another place where locals and Westerners can promenade and prattle, display and observe.

Before dinner we go to see an old friend, Dr Noordin Sopiee. Noordin runs the Institute for Strategic and International Studies. He's a former editor-in-chief of *The New Straits Times*. He is one of the most cosmopolitan and sophisticated men I know. He kindly has us for afternoon tea at his home, a multi-level townhouse on the edge of Bangsar Baru. Noordin has a wicked sense of humour, and a perfect command of English, American and Australian vernacular which he deploys to sometimes idiosyncratic effect.

He is an endlessly patient friend, always willing to explain the complexities of Malaysian, regional or global politics. We talk that day about the changes in Malaysia under Mahathir: 'The economy is completely transformed. When Mahathir came to power we were based on farming and mining. Now on some measures we're the third or fourth most industrialised country. We were farmers and fishermen, now we're factory workers, next we'll be service providers.'

Sometimes Mahathir has lamented that he hasn't achieved more. I ask Noordin about the shortcomings: 'He would say that he's failed to create Malays who can compete fully with the overseas Chinese. I think this is a bit unfair because even the Chinese in China can't compete with the overseas Chinese. Maybe only the overseas Jews can compete with the overseas Chinese, the Jews in Israel can't compete with the overseas Jews. The overseas Chinese are a remarkable people. The overseas Chinese will work from 9 a.m. to 10 p.m. and think nothing of it.'

Noordin, though less driven than Mahathir, does talk too of the remaking of the Malay person, the Malay mind, the Malay culture.

Although he is generally upbeat about his country he acknowledges a particular problem for the Malay male.

'More than 60 per cent of the students at universities are female, and this is only because of discrimination in favour of males, otherwise it would be 70/30 or worse.'

This is not just a crisis for the Malay male. It's a worldwide phenomenon. Knowledge has been feminised. Computers are really about verbal skills and girls traditionally do better at that than boys. Boys are more physically active and like to learn more by doing. Girls are more willing to be physically passive and learn by reading and talking and speculating.

In Malaysia the phenomenon has a few special wrinkles. Because of the religious traditions the male is still supposed to be the source of authority in the Malay household. Religion itself is another source of authority. Religious knowledge, and certainly religious authority, are traditionally the preserves of men. One way for young men to escape the competition of young women at university is to study religion.

Meanwhile it's not only women these young Malay men are having to compete with. Chinese families are scraping every penny together to send their kids to universities abroad to study electronics or law or medicine or business. If they come back to Malaysia who is better equipped to compete in the global economy—the Chinese kid with the American degree in business studies or computing, a degree studied in the English language, the Malay girl who has graduated in medicine, who also, because sophisticated science can't really be taught in Malay, has learned mainly in English, or the Malay boy who has majored in religious studies, all of it studied in Malay? Naturally the situation is more complex than those stereotypes but they do capture something of the reality. Numbers of my Malay friends tell me they fear too many Malay males will turn to Islamic fundamentalism simply because too many of them cannot cope with the modern economy.

Noordin offers a countervailing point: 'All over East Asia the urge for stability is very strong.'

In my annual pilgrimages to KL the city has become my second home. I have come to love KL. I'm not an insider but KL has made me a welcome guest, an outsider whose presence is generously tolerated, sometimes even enjoyed. The infinite Malay courtesy, the boundless Chinese energy, the Indian love of conversation, and of the English language which they have taken to places we Anglo-Celts could never have imagined, they all mix together in the most fantastic smorgasbord of a city.

You can sample anything in KL. Of course the city has its seedy side—the used syringes disfiguring the Islamic Cemetry—which city doesn't?

Late in the film *Entrapment*, Sean Connery is stranded in some desperate fix, clinging for dear life to the footbridge between the twin towers. He turns to his beautiful side-kick and says something like: 'If you don't feel alive now, you never will.'

I couldn't agree with him more.

Nonetheless KL has its frustrations as well. Sometimes you wonder whether the Malays are really going to make it, whether all this success isn't substantially just a function of having a big Chinese minority. I go back and forth on these questions in my own mind.

I break off this reverie to attend once more to Noordin's words. Noordin is not only the soul of kindness and helpfulness, he is probably the most urbane man I know, and perhaps the smartest. Sometimes he is too smart for me. I can discuss any issue with him and he will explore it for me from all angles. But his mind is so quicksilver and so slippery there are times when I emerge from a long and deep discussion with him not knowing what he actually thinks, what his own opinion is.

Yet he tells me that when his family gets together, in one particular way he is its least cultivated member. He is the one least able to quote verses from the Koran to bolster whatever position he is arguing. Of course Noordin is a believing Muslim, but this ambivalence between worldly knowledge and religious knowledge is peculiarly Malaysian.

Noordin has two sons planning to get married this year and, good father that he is, he is budgeting for their weddings—1100 guests at the Istana Hotel at 70 ringgit per guest. As a fellow parent I shudder on his behalf.

As Jessie and I are preparing to leave one son comes in. I met him a few years ago and he was a big, solemn boy. Now he has lost the puppy fat and is a handsome young man. He brings his fiancée into the room and introduces her.

Noordin turns to us: 'Beautiful or not?'

He beams with pride at the young couple.

A little scene plays out I can barely imagine in a Western home. The girl goes over to Noordin, bows her head and makes to take his hands in her own. Noordin quickly withdraws his hands in a gesture that they must have repeated many times over.

The son, this strapping young man, comes over to his father and lightly kisses Noordin's bald pate as the father whispers a single word: *sayang*—love.

I have a lot to learn.

Singapore

Feelin' Funky in the Lion City

The journey to Singapore from Kuala Lumpur is longer than you'd think. The best way to make it is by train.

I am catching the train from KL Central to Singapore at 7.40 in the morning so Jessie and I head back to the hotel from Balwinder's, where I have said goodbye to the boys, for an early night. Alas, it is not to prove a peaceful one. We go to bed early but are woken about 3.00 am. The guy next door, whoever it is, has either had a romantic conquest or transacted some commerce with a lady of the night. In any event loud squeals of laughter and gibberish conversation come through the walls, as does the sound of TV up very high.

I know the secret of staying happily in a hotel is to go with the flow, not to be fussed, but the level of noise this guy and his consort are making is unbelievable. Finally the human noises stop but the TV drones on, incredibly loud. At 4 a.m. I ring the front desk to ask them to tell him to turn off his TV, which he's obviously left on before going to sleep.

At 4.30 I call the front desk again to repeat the request. They'd tried calling him but got no answer. Well maybe he's gone out, I say, they should come up and turn the TV off themselves. Another 15 minutes, the TV still blaring, my blood pressure soaring to stratospheric levels, I decide to walk down the hall, bang on the guy's door and ask him to turn the bloody TV off myself. But when I get there I find the night manager from downstairs, accompanied by a security guard, is already doing this. The guy, whom I never see, quietly apologises to the night manager and turns his TV off. I feel like a gale-force wind with no sails to blow into, no ships to capsize, no seas to whip up. I go back to our room in a towering rage, lie on the bed sure that I will get no further sleep and instantly fall into the kind of heavy, frenetic slumber that Dostoevsky and the other Russians are so strong on, waking only when I became conscious of Jessie gently shaking me and telling me it's time to go.

I catch the train with a couple of minutes to spare. The first-class fare, all the way to Singapore, is only 68 ringgit. Travelling first class, when the fare is so little, is a modest extravagance. I don't love trains as much as Paul Theroux does. I tend to feel about airplanes the way he does about trains, I want to get on every one I see.

But trains certainly have their compensations. I am looking forward to this journey. It's a very long train and good-natured anarchy reigns at the station. Somehow out of all this chaos the people who are supposed to be on the train end up on it and the people who aren't don't.

Despite the chaos I have a numbered seat which I find easily enough. The seat itself is comfortable, not luxurious like a business-class airplane seat but much better than an economy-class airplane seat.

The air-con, however. The air-con.

That's another matter altogether.

It is arctic. And here's a trick about trains, even in first class they seldom supply blankets or pillows. So on a long journey if you want to be comfortable you have to imitate a bag lady, with all sorts of bedding and belongings about your person. This day I have of course not brought a blanket or pillow, nor worn a jumper. Why would I? I'm in the tropics, right? In the tropics you ward off the heat. But this icy air-con is going to last for seven hours. Luckily I am wearing long pants and a suit jacket which, turned backwards, presents a feeble defence against the waves of chilled air blasting at my seat.

Even with the cold I am still looking forward to the journey. The countryside is full of interest, mysterious and beguiling. I have brought a book but am in that state of happy near somnolence in which I can feel the tender embrace of sleep approaching. I will watch a little and then doze, then wake to watch some more. That is my plan. All that is needed now is for the train to leave. It moves, drowsiness is welcome, my eyelids are heavy, the gentle chatter of other passengers is soothing, I am drifting away . . .

'Jackie Stewart, the great Scottish racing driver, is the subject of our film profile today!'

A public address system in a nauseating cockney-TV-Brit accent bursts into my head, pounding into a consciousness made tender by the rigours of the night. I open my eyes to see that at either end of the carriage is a big TV set, up high so that everyone can see it. And whereas even the meanest economy-class seat in an airplane has its own headset, in a train these 'entertainments' are compulsorily communal.

I have nothing against Jackie Stewart, I'm sure he's a good fellow, but I never want to hear his name again. Jackie Stewart, though I did not guess this at the time, would be followed by a loud, low-grade, American cartoon, which in its turn would be followed by the film, *Maverick*, and this in turn would be followed by . . . Jackie Stewart again! The whole sequence repeats, all the way to Singapore.

Where is my karmic serenity? After a while I am so tired that I lie back and shut my eyes anyway. But then I enter, albeit only briefly, into a strange borderland consciousness. It is an intimation, I suspect, of paranoid schizophrenia, with terrible voices and sounds, racing cars and cockney commentators, invading a consciousness otherwise blank and weary.

I quickly give up trying to rest and go to the bathroom to splash some water on my face. But the first-class toilets are among the filthiest I've ever seen, which is surprising for such an otherwise technically competent service.

Still, you get used to things. And I have Jackie Stewart to thank for this—he kept me awake to see the most visually stunning train journey I have ever taken. If you were wide awake enough to enjoy it properly, and if the noise were removed, this journey would offer sublime pleasures.

The morning mists are just lifting as we chug through KL. The few hills nearby are ringed in clouds, their modest peaks managing the small triumph of piercing the cloud cover.

At first the train follows a main road and I see the new day begin to stir in KL. The train passes by our old friend, The Palace of the Golden Horses. On the edge of KL some broken-down *kampungs* are to be seen, showing me that not all of KL is middle class by any means. Some of the *kampung* houses are run-down, the old, brown slats of wood dilapidated and decayed, the same for the tin roofs of the even poorer houses. Even the more solid bungalows along the train line appear to be in need of repair and maintenance. They are frequently discoloured, with moss-like growths on the walls. Keeping the paint fresh is obviously a struggle in this dense and humid atmosphere.

All the way down the Malay peninsula the overwhelming impression the rail journey gives is of the strength and aggression of the Malay jungle. It is so green, so densely green, the jungle comes right up to the rail tracks, reluctantly ceding a yard or two to the railway line, rapidly filling any cracks left even in the towns and cities.

All the way down the peninsula the stunning greens are maintained. To Australian eyes there is an almost unbelievable richness to the colours. The jungle seems only unwillingly to have yielded territory to occasional towns and roads. Yet we know this is untrue, vast swathes of jungle have been cleared or logged or developed. Plenty of palm oil and rubber tree plantations are in evidence.

I see through the windows spasmodic towns and again Malaysia's diversity is brought home to me. Here is a Hindu temple, there a mosque, now a Buddhist temple, then a Fajar chain shopping mall.

Despite the arctic air-con and Jackie Stewart's life story it is a grand, beautiful, tropical journey. I have read somewhere that the

Malay peninsula is the most fecund, the most densely alive, stretch of land on Earth and I can well believe it after this journey.

In the seats in front of me is a young Malay family, a young couple and two incredibly cute kids. The little girl, aged about three or four, is poking her head over the top of the seat, smiling and playing. Jessie has packed me some cookies to eat on the journey. I offer them to the kid and she shyly takes two. I realise straight away that I should have asked the parents' permission first. In a Western country it sometimes seems that any contact between an adult male and a kid not related to him is automatically shrouded in suspicion. Let me give you an example. I wear glasses and am blind as a bat without them. Naturally I don't wear them when I swim. Once at a beach in Sydney I called over one of my sons for some reason. At first he was reluctant to come and I shouted at him to get over here. He came slowly and reluctantly. *Quel horreur* when I discovered it wasn't one of my sons at all but some other kid who vaguely resembled them. I was covered in embarrassment and also a kind of fear that people would think I had some evil purpose with the kid.

Anyway none of this applies in the train. The parents thank me for offering their daughter a cookie. Southeast Asian societies still look on kids as such a blessing, families are so much centred on the kids, especially when they're still infants, that it's regarded as natural for strangers to make a fuss of them. Nonetheless when you're a Western male travelling alone it's as good to assume that a well-earned suspicion of possible malevolence hangs around you and it's best not to be too effusive about anything. In the company of your wife it's totally different.

A journey of seven hours involves certain practicalities. There are two bathrooms, Western-style and Malay-style. I revisit the Western one but it's not encouraging. It has no toilet paper and is dank and dark everywhere. The Malay-style toilet is a low squat affair, common throughout Asia, and is entirely covered in water. It has toilet paper but this looks incredibly mouldy and decayed, and the wall bears the encouraging sign: 'If you accidentally soil the toilet please clean it for the comfort of the next passenger.'

Both Malay and Western toilets have flushing mechanisms operated by foot pedals. Neither works.

Outside the astonishing greens, and the muddy browns of the rain-swollen rivers, continue. Sometimes the trees are so close to the rain-splashed windows, and the leaves so strangely shaped and disported, they seem to be intelligent creatures waving at the train, and perhaps they are.

In Johor Baru, the big city at the southern end of the peninsula, just across the causeway from Singapore, we all leave the train to have our passports checked. We then rattle across the causeway and enter Singapore.

The change from Malaysia to Singapore is striking. Viewed from the train every building in Singapore looks more affluent, neat and attractive. KL is a middle-class city. Singapore is a rich city. The paint is fresher, the upkeep better, everything in its place and a place for everything. The buildings are better maintained. Even the elevated pedestrian walkways across busy roads are covered with orderly green vines and plants, precisely cultivated and arranged to soften the look of the concrete.

At Woodlawn, the Singapore rail terminal, the passport business is repeated all over again. Singapore and Malaysia are constantly bickering about border arrangements and all manner of small stuff. Having to do immigration procedures twice is the normal sort of nonsense that comes out of this bickering. For a time, 1963 to 1965, Singapore was actually part of Malaysia. Then in 1965 it was booted out and has been fully independent ever since. Malaysia is predominantly Malay with a large Chinese minority, Singapore is predominantly Chinese with a large Malay minority.

The two nations share most interests but they are like two squabbling siblings, two brothers who inherited the same traits in different proportions constantly elbowing each other aside for prominence and success. Singapore is a good deal richer than Malaysia. Malaysia is many times bigger than Singapore. They remind me of Niles and Frasier Crane in the *Frasier* TV show.

It is raining when I arrive in Singapore, which induces a rare thing, a half-hour wait for a taxi outside the train station. Then it turns out when I get the cab the hotel I've booked into, the Furama, is just around the corner in Chinatown. I could have walked in a trice.

The Furama is bursting with activity. It must have an occupancy rate that night of 99 per cent. Singapore redeveloped too much of its old Chinatown before it realised that tourists enjoyed the old-style buildings and neighbourhoods. Now it has remodelled old shop-houses. They look cute, like everything in Singapore, but they don't look like a real Southeast Asian Chinatown.

After my long train journey I feel the need to move around. So, after checking into the Furama, I decide to walk up to the famous Raffles Hotel for dinner. My walk takes me through Chinatown, still bustling at night, and then across a pretty city park. Naturally you never feel any risk about walking in a city park at night in Singapore.

It's a warm night—every night is warm in Singapore—and lots of folks are out shopping, lots of shops are still open. I walk past a strange-looking establishment called Spartacus. The outside wall is covered with paintings of muscular, naked men in classical Greek setting. The door announces a cover charge of S$15 and there is a small line of muscular young men, some in leather, outside waiting for entry (how hot and uncomfortable must leather be in the Singapore heat, but no doubt inside is air-con).

I don't know what goes on inside Spartacus but I can't imagine in the formerly straight-laced Singapore, say of the 1970s and 1980s, that there were too many establishments like Spartacus.

I walk a little further and come to the footbridge over Singapore River. On the near side is the Boat Quays. I walk along here and see a very flash row of restaurants, bars and discos. The restaurants—Chinese, Indian, Thai, French—are hideously expensive. A spruiker approaches me with the invitation that happy hour is on and I can purchase two beers for S$14.

Fourteen dollars! Yikes.

The crowd at Boat Quays is mixed—Chinese, Indian, Western expat. I walk further up towards Raffles but before I get to the legendary hotel I call in on Raffles City. This is a complex of at least two hotels and a vast, vast shopping centre, built around a huge, central atrium.

Just walking around the shopping centre cheers me. Shopping malls are naturally more family-oriented than restaurant strips and the good burghers of Singapore are out in all their finery, browsing and sluicing, enjoying the air-con, enjoying the merchandise, enjoying each other.

I stroll across to Raffles thinking I will dine there. Raffles is an incredible white palace of luxury. Michael Jackson stays there when he's in Singapore (which is admittedly not all that often). It was built by the Sarki brothers. Raffles does indeed have paying, staying guests but it seems now to be predominantly a food and beverages outlet. There is a long bar and a tiffin (tea, morning or afternoon) room, boutique shops selling whatever, restaurants set around gardens, restaurants serving curries, restaurants serving buffets, tea and coffee shops, upstairs bars and downstairs bars, billiards rooms and lounges.

The grand front entrace is supervised by giant Sikh doormen in red finery and turbans. The outside of the building is brilliant white, the predominant motif inside is wood panelling of different shades and many internal courtyards and pot plants. Doubtless it's mainly for tourists but plenty of locals go there too when they feel like spending money. It's a Singapore landmark.

In any event it's too grand for me this night so I walk back instead to a coffee shop on the first floor of the Raffles city shops. It has a famous chicken pie for about S$6. After the briefest of dinners I return to the Furama and a deep slumber, in which I dream I am being pursued across an ice-covered tropical jungle by a rampant British racing car driver travelling in a long train saying over and over in a thick cockney accent: 'And our subject today is Jackie Stewart.'

The next day, refreshed and free of the curse of Jackie Stewart, I set out to find the funky side of Singapore, little realising to what a preposterous position this will lead me that night. I find myself locked inside a ladies' toilet, while two young women writhe and scream on the floor. Hearing these screams a couple of women open their cubicle doors and are disconcerted first by my presence, second by the writhing, screaming figures on the ground, and third by the fact that the door is barred by a ferocious young woman who won't let anyone pass.

Finding the funky side of Singapore is one thing but this is a bit over the top. It's not quite what I expected. However, it has a wholesome explanation.

I am attending a theatrical performance called 'Circle of Fear'. The program notes describe it as 'site specific'. This is apparently a bit of a trend in nouveau theatre, although to be honest with you not one I've come across before. What it means is that the performance takes place in several different spots beyond the main theatre. So part of the performance is in the theatre itself, part of it in a sort of ante-room, part of it in a storm drain across the road and part of it in the ladies' toilet at the Marine Parade Community Building, next to Starbucks.

The production—again, I'm relying on the program notes because I couldn't quite fathom this from the performance itself—marries an adaptation of Henry James's ghost story, 'Turn of the Screw', with local Chinese ghost legends. The program says the theatre company tries to 'nurture the spirit of exploration and cutting edge discourses in the various disciplines of the performing arts'.

As a piece of theatre it left me cold, except for the extremely disconcerting but blessedly short segment when the audience was ushered into the ladies. That bit felt more like one of those Dame Edna Everage performances where she gets some hapless members of the audience up on the stage, takes a shoe from each on some pretext, and then leaves the poor sods there to suffer excruciating spotlit embarrassment for what seems an age.

Anyway, after this segment I bail out and go back to the hotel. Even though I don't really enjoy it as theatre—very little that describes itself as 'cutting edge' is designed for enjoyment—the performance is instructive about modern Singapore.

For conservative old Singapore has set itself on a course to become a cosmopolitan centre of the arts and the funky, creative, liberated and relaxed capital of Southeast Asia.

Excuse me? I hear you protest.

Singapore? Funky? Liberated?

Singapore, where famously you can't chew chewing gum, the nanny state where you can't smoke in most public places, where long-haired young men from overseas used to be taken on compulsory trips to the barber at the airport.

This city still has the image internationally of being controlled and authoritarian and boring. It's not true and it hasn't been for some time, even before it decided to get funky. It is true that Singapore's not a liberal democracy along Western lines. The Opposition is very weak. But the elections are clean and if the Government lacked fundamental legitimacy with the people they'd throw it out.

I've never found the place boring. Some Western newspapers like *The New York Times* grossly overstate the authoritarianism of Singapore. It has always had quite a lot of key freedoms, like freedom of religion and freedom of movement.

Freedom of movement really means something. Singapore's well-educated young people have the option of going someplace else to live if they don't like Singapore. So too does international capital.

So Singapore wants to be hip and groovy, to keep its people, and to keep foreign money safely ensconced in Singapore.

The Singapore Government apparently understands that it is now running an affluent society. It wants its best people, or at least most of them, to find Singapore's lifestyle sufficiently entertaining and agreeable that they are happy to stay there.

It also wants the best foreign executives to be actively lobbying their companies to set up regional headquarters in Singapore because they enjoy the life there more than in any other Southeast Asian city.

It wants its universities to be able to attract and keep world-class scholars, not just by offering competitive salaries but by offering a comparable quality of life to that found in cities which house great universities. There is now something like an informal international league table of cities. Singapore wants to be in the premier league.

Then there is the desire of Singapore's own population for more mental space, more pleasure, more fulfilment.

There is also something of a feeling that you just can't make the best out of the international economy, with the importance of IT and communications skills, and image and brand and marketing and creativity generally, if the tenor of the society is conformist and regimented. The old Japanese development model, of rote learning at school followed by huge workforce effort measured in countless hours at the office, only works up to a point. Singapore has passed that point.

And then a modern society needs animal spirits.

The Ministry of Information people are helpful when I tell them what I'm trying to discover. Ah, yes, creativity, they reply in knowing fashion. We have a program for that. Very kindly, they allow me to shoe-horn in on an interview the Deputy Prime Minister, Lee Hsien-Loong, is giving to a group of foreign reporters.

Lee Hsien-Loong is the son of the legendary Lee Kuan Yew, Singapore's founding Prime Minister. Lee the younger is sleek, smooth, smart and ruthless. In recent years he has somewhat softened his image preparatory to taking over from the affable Goh Chok Tong as Prime Minister. Although I am not part of the visiting group of journalists I am allowed to gatecrash their interview in the Treasury Building and ask my questions about funky Singapore.

Lee answers in his unhurried, modulated, deep bass voice: 'It's not compulsory to be funky in Singapore but there are certainly plenty of funky people here and you can be funky if you like.'

There are paradoxes in Singapore's drive for greater creativity. Can you direct creativity from the top? As one Asian diplomat puts it to me: 'There is a rigour about Singapore, even when it relaxes.' Can you direct people to lighten up, order them to be loose, socially engineer their coolness?

Well, if *anyone* can I suppose it would be the Singapore Government, though that is not to say it will work. I put some of these paradoxes to Lee.

'We would like to have greater arts activity, partly for our own people,' he says.

'But there is a bit of utilitarianism there too. London is a more interesting place to live than Frankfurt so that's helped it become a bigger financial centre. As to creativity, all you can do is make an environment more conducive to creativity and hope it flowers. Politically we hope it will increase the quality of the debate. It may make a wider debate too and we can manage that.'

He gets a bit testy at the idea that Singapore was totally conformist before: 'Because we emphasise this [creativity] now people say there you are, you used to be very stodgy and everyone just followed like sheep. If that was true we wouldn't have got where we are now.'

Singapore's embrace of the internet is a sign of the explosive effect of modern technology on political and social values. You can't embrace the contemporary economy and seriously try to control the internet at the same time.

'You can't restrict access,' says Lee. 'Pornography is a serious problem. All we do is block 100 sites as a statement of our values. It's only about 100 out of perhaps 10 000 objectionable sites and even then you can't really block them. There are so many ways to get access.'

After seeing Lee I head over to Prego's Italian restaurant at the Stamford Hotel. Prego's is classy without being ruinous and it's a place to be seen. I'm glad it's not exclusively a place for youngsters, there's more of a generational mix at Prego's. I am meeting Professor Chua Beng-Huat of the National University of Singapore, and without any disrespect to the good professor, we are easily the two least fashionable people there. Our table is redeemed slightly by the professor's friend, Ian, a well-connected Brit expat who seems to be able to provide a running biography of almost everyone at the restaurant.

'You see her with the big hair, she's so-and-so's first American wife.'

'You see that man and that woman, they're both senior civil servants but in different government departments. I wonder what they're cooking up. Do you think they're having an affair?'

The lunch is full of gossip and good cheer. Chua is a sociologist of the best kind. He intensively studies the way Singaporeans live. And he tells me they live today differently from the way they've ever lived before. That's why he thinks that while the external or economic explanations for the new groovy Singapore have a basis in truth, they underplay the level of local demand for change.

'A lot of younger Singaporeans just won't put up with the old style anymore,' he says. 'Over the last few years some middle-class parents have been prepared to pay big money for their kids to go to America and do courses in things like film studies. Yes, they say, my son can be a doctor but will he be happy? That's totally new for Singapore.

'Forty-five to sixty-year-old parents have much greater self-confidence and are much more liberal than their forebears. If they went to university they are the richest generation Singapore has known. There is a deep middle-class security about these people. They're secure even to the point of having made financial provision for their kids. Singapore is inhabited by seriously different generations. Lee Kuan Yew's generation knew real hardships. My generation knew poor people though we weren't poor ourselves. My children know no poverty.'

Chua's most fascinating insight is that young people are not so much rebelling against the old ways, much less against the Government, rather these things just don't impinge on their lives to anything like the same degree that they did on their parents' lives: 'There's a kind of post-modern attitude to Government amongst young people now, the idea that government just isn't that interesting one way or the other. They're neither obedient nor disobedient. The Government doesn't enter their space. My generation [fifty-somethings] was completely preoccupied with government.

But in most countries nation-building is not a project anymore. My daughter fully and deeply accepts that Singapore exists already and that frees up a lot of mental energy for other things. My feeling is that the Government has less call on young people now even than it did in the early 1990s.'

Chua is a typically cosmopolitan Singaporean. Informal in an open shirt, with grey hair and a wispy goatee, he grew up in a poor, squatters' area but did well at school and left, age nineteen, in the late 1960s to study in Canada. He married a Canadian woman of Chinese origin and settled in Canada. He did what he calls a 'filial piety' trip back to Singapore in 1980. A couple of years later the Housing Board told him they needed a sociologist because they were building all this housing for people but needed to know what Singaporeans were doing with their lives.

While he was working at the Housing Board an earlier essay he'd written, which proved to be controversial, was published and he later lost his position. He was seriously uncertain of his future for a while but is happy now at the university. His books are regularly published and widely read within academic circles. At the end of the day, he chooses to live and work in Singapore. He points out the day's *Straits Times* to me, in which a local writer suggests Singapore should compare itself to small Scandinavian countries and not just with its traditional Southeast Asian neighbours.

Of course the counter to that is that the Scandinavian countries don't have any of Singapore's security worries.

Most places have changed in a generation but few places on Earth can have changed as much as Singapore in the last fifty years. Paul Theroux, who is a wonderful travel writer but you would have to say doesn't display warm affection for all that many places or all that many people, lived in Singapore in the 1960s and didn't like it, especially its political restrictions.

His novel of Singapore in the 1950s, *Saint Jack*, paints the place as a bawdy, rowdy, seamy American Rest and Recreation stopover, full of triads and cockroaches and phonies, and for most of its

Chinese inhabitants a place of dullness, grind and routine. Theroux wrote: 'The Chinese life in Singapore was mainly noodles and children in a single room, the noise of washing and hoicking. It could not have been duller, but because it was dull the Chinese had a gift for creating special occasions, a night out, a large banquet or festive gathering which sustained them through a year of yellow noodles.'

No doubt even for the 1950s that was a jaundiced view. But there's no doubt too that there's something in what Theroux wrote. A better guide to the past is just to look at the photographs of Singapore in that era, of the tiny shop-houses—indeed often a whole family housed in a single room—the lack of sanitation, the income levels so far below those of the West.

We don't need to rely on a jaundiced observer like Theroux for memories of Singapore's poverty in the old days. Lee Kuan Yew himself has acknowledged the poverty of Singapore before independence, once recalling: 'As Prime Minister of Singapore my first task was to lift my country out of the degradation that poverty, ignorance and disease had wrought. Since it was dire poverty that made for such a low priority given to human life, all other things became secondary.'

Nowadays Singapore is a city of about four million people on what is a pretty small island. They certainly don't live lives anything like that described by Theroux in *Saint Jack*. I decide to get off the tourist trail and take a simple journey around Singapore. The Mass Rapid Transit (MRT) system is underground in the heart of Singapore but goes above ground for a good deal of its length and around much of the island. I get on at the Raffles Square stop and ride around for a couple of hours, repeating the round trip a couple of times. Travelling around the entire network doesn't take very long.

What I see are massive housing developments. The Housing Development Board apartments are the very heart of the Singapore system. The maximum height is forty storeys. There are three-, four- and even five-bedroom apartments available, and apartments have been built all over the island.

Taxes are low but the Government takes a big chunk of its citizens' salaries for the Central Provident Fund, the national superannuation scheme. You can use your CPF money to buy a HDB apartment at a substantial Government discount. But to get the government discount you must form a family unit. I'm told that unmarried mothers with kids don't qualify. Having bought your apartment at a government discount you can sell it later if you wish on the more expensive open market, but then of course you need to buy on the open market to replace it. If you don't qualify as a family unit in the first place you can also buy on the open market, if you've got the money.

The majority of Singaporeans live in HDB units. Only a small minority rent. Many buy 99-year leases. Many aspects of the Singapore system, both legal and social, formal and informal, contrive to create incentives for families to stay together.

Catherine Lim, Singapore's leading novelist, distils the essence of the Singapore view in her lovely book, *Following the Wrong God Home*. There's a *Madame Bovary* in the tropics quality to this book. It's a sympathetic treatment of a Chinese wife who falls in love with another man. But while it is set in the context of adulterous lusts, its broader point is compelling. Lim writes: 'Singapore was dominated by the acknowledged gods of common sense, duty, money, security, power, who could not be put to flight by love. In the end it would always be the good marriage saved, the contrite wife received back, the joint property, so carefully built up over the years, kept intact, the family name untainted by shame, the well being of the children protected. Let passion have its brief hour, but in the long days ahead, it had no place. In the end, said everyone philosophically, it comes down to that heat in the groin, fleeting and passing, which family is not. All else passes away, except family.'

All else passes away, except family.

The importance of family is borne home to me that day as I travel around the MTR system looking at these giant HDB blocks from the outside. The few that I've been inside are comfortable, if compact. Just once or twice in the whole journey do I espy the smallest bit of graffiti. Most of the blocks look good. If you're going to go high-rise, this isn't too bad. They have big green spaces at their base, everything is clean and tidy, and many of them have covered walkways from their front doors to the MTR stops so that you don't even get wet in Singapore's many sudden furious downpours.

The problem for your average Westerner would be noise. No matter how well constructed, apartments can never quite keep out all the noise and your chances of having a crook, noisy neighbour must increase when you have neighbours above and below and on each side.

Still it is a tribute to what seems almost an innate Chinese capacity to put up with lots of each others' company (although of course Malays and Indians live in these HDB units too) that they can live so densely yet so peacefully. High-rise public housing in the US, UK and Australia has been little short of disastrous. One big difference is that HDB units, although government-assisted, are not a welfare provision for the poor in Singapore. Most HDB residents are middle class.

The stress on family is evident in Singapore's popular culture. Many of the HDB units contain three generations—mum and dad and a couple of kids and one or two surviving grandparents. This is the situation in Singapore's funniest sitcom, *Under One Roof.* Like many Western sitcoms of a decade or two ago it is affection-ately built around dad, who is both profoundly wise, a rock of stability, and amazingly gullible and silly. *Under One Roof* is entirely worth watching, with good jokes and a believable central character. What's fun about it is the way it gently mocks, even as it reaffirms, central elements of the Chinese family myth. So wise old dad loves to tell enlightening stories with a moral—except these are invariably cockeyed and meaningless and the family grimaces when it has to hear them. He loves to utter profound aphorisms but these too are somehow always dotty rather than apposite.

Prof Chua tells me of a local assessment. If you don't care about owning two cars and living on the ground, if both partners of a marriage are prepared to work eight hours a day, you can live in the best HDB flat, which is nothing to sneeze at. You can have a couple of kids and a Filipino maid to look after them, you can have the MRT at your doorstep, good schools and great services generally within walking distance of your home and play golf every evening. If you want a house on the ground and two cars you're going to have to do something cleverer and harder than just a normal eight-hours-a-day job. If on the other hand you're really determined that you only want to work eight hours a day and you definitely want a nice house on the ground and plenty of space, the answer's easy, migrate to Australia and live in Perth.

That afternoon I do something I seldom do when travelling, I change my hotel for no good reason. The Furama in Chinatown is fine. The room is very small, but the service is OK and no location in Singapore is really inconvenient. But a friend has told me of a four-star hotel on Orchard Road itself which is remarkably cheap. Orchard Road is the shopping and entertainment centre of Singapore. I like inner cities and I love the sense of life going on twenty-four hours a day right outside my doorstep. Also this hotel might turn out to be good value next time Jessie and I are in Singapore together.

I'm not worried about the noise from Orchard Road. I like the sounds of a city at night. In Sydney we live close to the city and I find the sweet wail of sirens soothing in the night, I like to hear the distant chug of the suburban train, the steady thrum of traffic. In Bangkok I even find the motorcycles' backfiring, like the sound of rain on a tin roof, perfectly relaxing. When I first took Jessie, raised as she was in the noise and bustle of KL, to visit Canberra, Australia's bush capital of only 300 000 souls spread across the land area of London, she couldn't sleep because it was so unnaturally quiet. I felt the same way. Nonetheless when I check in at the four-star, which is indeed right on Orchard Road, the front counter staff kindly suggest they give me a room at the back of the hotel because it is quieter there.

That night I stroll along Orchard Road to look at Singapore and its visitors at play. The funny thing about Orchard Road is that the Government didn't initially plan for it to be the tourist and shopping centre of Singapore. Friends tell me it used to be a slow, predominantly European road. The first big change was the Hilton moving in, and these five-star brand names were incredibly powerful in the early days of Southeast Asia's economic take-off. Then came another five-star hotel, and another.

Now the street is a series of modern shopping temples, many in sumptuous marble, high-class restaurants and hotels. It's tempting to say that shopping is the religion of Singapore. But Singapore also has a high savings rate. It's not just consumption, it's earned consumption. Nonetheless it is true that Chinese civilisation is remarkably materialistic. China is the only great civilisation not to invent a religion, a pantheon of gods, or one God, a true cosmology. Some Chinese have had metaphysical speculations of course but the great Chinese tradition, Confucianism, is almost wholly unconcerned with metaphysics. The *Analects* of Confucius, while profound in their consideration of the best way to live, are almost unconcerned with the soul.

That's not inconsistent with the Chinese being incredibly superstitious. Ghost stories are among the bestselling of fiction in Singapore. But superstition is not religion. The same is true of the many small gods celebrated in statues in many Chinese homes. Their religious significance is minimal. It's not much more than a gambler kissing the dice before he rolls them in the casino, or the man at the racetrack invoking the name of his favourite horse or late jockey. People from all backgrounds can be committed to their superstitions while not really believing in them at any profound level. Professional sportsmen are notoriously committed to their favourite bats, lucky boots or whatever.

There's no reason why Singaporeans should be particularly religious. Just across the causeway, in Malaysia, the concern is about religious fundamentalism. But I do wonder what story Singapore's leaders can now tell their people about the purpose of Singapore. For a long time the purpose was clear—defeat the communists, set up a nation, survive, prosper. They've done that now, done it brilliantly. Is this now to be followed by a certain ennui of the spirit? There's no epic history of Singapore to celebrate, no wilderness either to tame or preserve, no obvious national myth or legend. Nor can there really be the political task of international human rights and United Nations activism that some small, wealthy West European nations go in for. Is it just making a buck in the world's biggest shopping centre and theme park? Perhaps helping its Southeast Asian neighbours to achieve development offers something of a national vocation, although this would be overlaid with all kinds of Chinese/Malay racial and cultural sensitivities.

Walking down Orchard Road I am assailed by these thoughts as I am also assailed by a thousand different sensations. They say the visual style of Ridley Scott's *Blade Runner* movie was inspired by the Shinjuku district in Tokyo, but you can see a hint of it too in Orchard Road. On both sides of the broad street, for example, are giant video screens. On one of the screens music videos are playing. As I am passing a girl group is belting out a pretty raunchy number. The giant video screen on the other side of the street is showing film clips and as I look up it is showing parts of a science fiction film, whose futuristic pyrotechnics fit the mood of the street. At many points along the road fairy lights arc across it.

Well-groomed prostitutes sit on the benches provided for the public. They approach a lone male but do so with much more discretion and restraint than in most parts of Southeast Asia. Presumably if they were too aggressive in their soliciting, if they ever hassled passersby enough to make life unpleasant, the police would clamp down on them. And really, unless you make an enemy of the Government, or engage in drug smuggling or some other criminal activity, nothing is unpleasant in Singapore. It has rightly been called the air-conditioned society.

That night I am giving a talk at Border's Bookstore on Orchard Road. Singapore's bookstores are magnificent. There is one, in the Tanglin Centre at the end of Orchard Road, which specialises in books on Southeast Asia. I am always in danger of massively over-spending when I go there.

Borders has taken bookstores to a new level in Singapore and other big stores have had to respond. It has a prime location, a long, deep, large space right on Orchard Road. There are cafes at either end and above it. At one end of the store itself is a music section, at the other is a magazines and newspaper area with a terrific range of international journals, especially American, which are generally not that easy to obtain. I don't know if Borders makes a profit selling these modestly esoteric magazines, many about culture and politics, but they add to the cosmopolitan feel of the place.

The bookshelves are arranged in spacious bays, with plenty of easy chairs and sofas around. You're welcome to take your time here, to take a book down and browse through it before you decide whether to buy it. I'm told Borders can be a bit of a pick-up joint as people discover they like the same books.

The children's section is brightly coloured, with large distinctive patterns on the floor. The Singapore Government noticed Borders' success in attracting younger readers and incorporated some of its design features into its own children's libraries. Similarly the Community Development Buildings, like the one where I saw 'Circus of Fear', have invited Starbucks to set up coffee shops, to attract young people to the centres.

I am astonished at what a crowd turns up for my talk, which is about a book I'd written on Asian politics. My talk is not very good. Afterwards, in the gentlest way, a Borders staff member tells me I made the mistake of talking about the subject matter of the book. People don't really want to hear that from a writer. They'll get that after all when they read the book. What they are much more interested in is the how of the book—how did you become interested in this subject, how did you go about the writing.

Nonetheless I am gobsmacked at how many people buy the book and come up and get me to sign it. Even the most obscure author, it seems, adds greatly to the allure of a book by signing it.

After Borders, I look in on an Orchard Road disco, way up on the twentieth floor. There's a S$20 cover charge and the kids are so young it's unbelievable. It's hard to imagine they're all above drinking age, although Chinese youngsters can look very young, and in any event a lot of them are not drinking alcohol. The kids are incredibly dressed down. That's obviously the hip look among this group right now.

By the time I head back to my hotel it's late. I look in on the lobby of the Hilton Hotel. It's quiet but a pretty young woman, a strand of black hair curling around a plump cheek, is sitting, legs crossed (a necessity given the micro-mini she's wearing) with her boyfriend. But she is scowling and discontented, smoking a cigarette and looking bored. The boyfriend, with a mop of black hair and shiny black suit, has one hand resting in negligent lasciviousness on her thigh. But his real interest rests with his other hand which, like his eyes, are on his laptop computer, on which he is manipulating some internet transaction or other.

I've been so busy that day that I haven't had a chance to read *The Straits Times* and it's the only thing you can't buy late at night on Orchard Road. The Borders news-stand section has long since sold out of that day's edition. As I wander past Starbucks on the way to the hotel I brazenly and wickedly steal a copy they have for customers to read. It's almost midnight, technically the paper is almost out of date. It's my only criminal act.

Alas my choice of hotel turns out not to have been inspired. My room is indeed at the back, but either the plumbing, or the lift, or perhaps both, sing a rowdy tune all night. It's the sort of irregular noise—whooshhhhh, whirrrrh, clunk!, shhhhhh, whooshhhh, wirrrh, clunk!, shhhhhh (unlike the soothing, steady murmur of traffic)—that repeats again and again throughout the night at irregular intervals and makes sleep difficult.

A few days later I walk up to the Shangri-La Hotel, to its Chinese restaurant, the Shang Palace, to meet Catherine Lim, author of *Following the Wrong God Home* and Singapore's most popular novelist. A strikingly handsome woman in her fifties, she wears a close-fitting cheongsam in a red floral pattern and severe but stylish hair.

We dine at the Shang Palace where the food is expensive and very, very good. Years ago I stayed a night or two at this hotel and it was a pretty good hotel then, but nothing compared to what it is now. Now it has been remodelled into a sumptuousness beyond imagining. It's not cheap either.

The restaurant is not very busy that night. The table nearest us is comprised of four or five Westerners. A huge guffaw of not altogether comfortable laughter breaks out. I miss it but Catherine has overheard the exchange and tells me the waitress has asked one of the men whether this is his daughter he's brought to Singapore. No, he says, it's my wife.

Several years ago Catherine wrote a couple of political commentaries which momentarily got her into hot water and she feared briefly she might be sued for libel. Her novels are sexy and saucy and frequently poke fun at Singapore's pretensions. She is now a redoubtable figure, an icon, one of very few Singaporean writers to have a reputation, and sales, beyond Singapore itself.

She has her own interpretation of the Government's desire to get Singaporeans in touch with their funky, creative sides: 'They [the Government] have achieved so much that they have a huge reservoir of goodwill. There are a few givens in Singapore—the economic imperative, meritocracy, no corruption and the government in control. Once they are established the Government will give way on some other things provided they don't challenge those givens.

'There are a few taboo areas—one is race and religion. A second is the integrity of the Government. A third used to be the Government's style but that is perhaps a grey area now. This Government is much less touchy on sex matters. They are clever, they come down hard on those who violate the core areas but on sex matters it doesn't affect them too much. So then there is a transference strategy, they say the parents won't accept this, or the society isn't ready yet. They move ahead incrementally.

'On gays the Government knows how much they contribute to the arts and the Government mostly leaves them alone but it's quite clear if they provoke the Government it could take unpleasant acts.

'Lee Kuan Yew had a pathological distrust of flamboyance. But that style might have to change for the contemporary economy. Look at Richard Branson or Bill Gates.'

Catherine's own story is a Southeast Asian Chinese classic. She was born in Malaysia, one of fourteen. Her mother lives in Penang. Penang Hokkien is her native tongue. She came to Singapore as a young teacher, when she married. She later divorced.

'I was a young mother, just about to give birth, so I was most concerned about making a living,' she says.

'I got a teaching job and citizenship quickly.'

She later won a Fullbright scholarship and studied at UCLA. Her intellectual development mirrors a lot the development of Singapore itself, though she mightn't see it that way: 'I was born a Daoist. I converted to Catholicism, then I abandoned that and I'm more or less a vague sort of agnostic now. But in the end everyone's a pragmatist in Singapore.'

I press her on her religious beliefs and she reveals unexpected scientific knowledge about the nature of matter and life, the human genome. The closest she'll come to a mantra for life is the comment that 'in the end I think everyone acts from disguised self-interest'.

A lot of rationalists come to that reasonable conclusion but I find it depressing, though this feisty, energetic woman is certainly neither depressing nor depressed. I report my conversation with Deputy Prime Minister Lee about Singapore becoming a funky place and she ripples with laughter: 'Ten years ago the word "funky" wasn't in the [ruling] People's Action Party's vocabulary.'

In Singapore Catherine's books don't sell as well as local ghost stories. But the Chinese, like the Indians, have a great presence in the Western mind, and Chinese writers who interpret Chinese life and traditions and culture to Western audiences are often popular. It's difficult for mainland Chinese writers to do this beause they're not familiar enough with the Western audience they're writing for. Amy Tan has achieved astronomical sales by writing about Chinese women in America, especially multi-generational family sagas. Given that family is so central to Chinese life anyway this is a natural fit.

Chinese writers in Southeast Asia, like Catherine Lim, are much more familiar with the West (living in what were until recently Western colonies) than are mainland Chinese writers so they have a much better shot at connecting with a Western audience. This Catherine has done and as a result has been translated into several European languages, including Icelandic she proudly tells me. *Following the Wrong God Home* takes the Western connection even further by having the married Singapore heroine fall in love with an American academic. (This character was originally going to be a British academic but her American publishers talked her into changing his nationality—there's American cultural imperialism for you.) This role of mediating between Asia and the West is a big part of Singapore's comparative advantage, as it is for Hong Kong too.

Catherine is happy with her perch in Singapore but makes what must be a typical qualification for senior people: 'In order to like Singapore more I need to go sometimes to more raucous cities like London or New York.'

Like so many Singapore Chinese families, Catherine's relatives are spread across continents. A daughter is a doctor in Hong Kong, a son is a journalist in Houston: 'Like a Chinese mother I require that they ring regularly, then I ask typical questions—have you eaten properly, how is your health. Every third family here has someone abroad. We have this wonderful thing called the English language— it's so hospitable, it can service anybody's needs. I admire Lee Kuan Yew's honesty about this. In the 1970s it was fashionable for newly independent countries to kick out the English language. He understood we needed it.'

As it turns out I will have a chance to test with Lee Kuan Yew himself Catherine's assessment of the importance of English.

Shortly after this encounter I make my second hotel change, to the Stamford Hotel. This is a good business hotel, where I've often stayed before. It's more than fifty storeys high, with good-sized rooms and everything works. I am transferring, however, not for reasons of comfort, but to meet my then boss, David

Armstrong. Together we are to interview the redoubtable Lee Kuan Yew.

David is at this time editor-in-chief of *The Australian*. He makes it an occasional practice to apply jointly with correspondents for some interviews with serving or retired heads of government. It makes the interview more likely to occur in the first place and gives us extra range and firepower when the interview itself is taking place.

David is a slim, perennially well-dressed and quiet figure, grey-haired, bespectacled, soft-spoken and a deeply thoughtful man. He is one of my oldest friends in journalism. He was already a star at the magazine where I began in journalism twenty-five years ago. He is something of an old Asia hand himself, having been for several years editor-in-chief of *The South China Morning Post* in Hong Kong.

David comes in on a late flight and we meet at 7 o'clock the next morning for breakfast with Murray McLean, the Australian high commissioner, at one of the smaller restaurants at Raffles. Murray is an old-style foreign affairs professional with an endless love of China. Diplomats posted to Singapore are often China experts rather than Southeast Asianists, because the ability to speak Mandarin is useful in Singapore. It's a plus because it helps Singapore have senior diplomats posted there but it does tend to draw the lion city further away from the rest of Southeast Asia.

David and I lunch with my old friend, Cheong Yip-Seng, the editor-in-chief of *The New Straits Times*, at a spectacular Japanese restaurant in the shopping centre at Raffles City. This is a lunch of succulent sushi and the hottest wasabi I've ever tasted. Yip-Seng is also slight of build, with a bald front pate and large specs. He is a wise old bird deeply familiar with the region's politics. Listening to David and Yip-Seng chat that day is to hear two newspaper professionals, editors to the tips of their fingers, instantly fall into comparing notes about the challenges all newspapers face around the world—a sluggish advertising market, ads seeping out of papers onto the net, how to capture young readers who've grown up with computers and no habit of newspaper reading at all.

Yip-Seng talks of the possibility of hiring journalists but not giving them a desk at the office, setting them up with a laptop and getting them to file from home or wherever the story is. I can see the efficiencies in this, but it sounds monstrous to me. As a journalist, when you're on the road that's one thing, and that has its own joys and rewards. But to be in the headquarters city and to miss out on the cut-and-thrust of constant interaction with your colleagues sounds horrible. You'd miss so much, especially the cascades of information and ideas that flow through newspaper offices—something the health writer passes on to the science writer who tells the local government man who mentions it to a feature writer who sees the germ of a story there. Perhaps this is just another example of my personal attachment to the life-long pattern of travel and return, for a stable base and adventures out among the wider world.

Yip-Seng also tells us disturbing things about surveys which show even established newspaper readers spending less time with their newspapers each day.

I am struck by two aspects of Yip-Seng's conversation over lunch: how much his comments chime with Professor Chua's perception of an emerging post-modern attitude in the young, especially towards Government—after all, reading a serious news-paper, as well as providing you entertainment, is an act of civic participation in your society—and how universal and cross-cultural and familiar are the problems which newspapers confront.

That afternoon David and I prepare the main lines of our discussion with Lee Kuan Yew, which is set for the early evening. When you're going to have an hour or two with an important figure in history, and one of the busiest people in the region, it's best to prepare well so that you make every use of your time. Lee Kuan Yew founded modern Singapore and more than any individual shaped its destiny. He joined a common front with the communists to seek independence but then outmanoeuvred them in the struggle for power. He experienced the shattering break-up with Malaysia. After more than thirty years as PM he voluntarily relinquished power to Goh Chok Tong. He is the only Asian to have a worldwide reputation for strategic sagacity which rivals that of Henry Kissinger.

David and I take a hotel taxi down to the back entrance of the Istana building, set in a small but pretty park in the middle of Singapore, where Lee has his office in the same building as the Prime Minister. The security arrangements are simple and easy, we're expected and whisked into Lee's waiting room in an instant. Like Malaysia's Dr Mahathir, Lee normally starts his interviews on time.

Lee's office is spacious but spartan. He is generous with his time today. David's presence is a big plus for the interview. Most of it concerns the issues of the day but David asks Lee what turns out to be the most productive question of all for understanding what Singapore is today. How important was it to make English Singapore's main language?

Lee surprises us by saying it was perhaps the most important single decision he ever made: 'If in 1965 I'd yielded to the Chinese Chamber of Commerce and the Chinese clan associations to make Chinese our national language because the Chinese were the majority, we would have invited a fight among ourselves. The Malays and the Indians would be dispossessed. And who would we trade with? English was a practical, hard-headed choice. When we were excluded from Malaysia we did not have to make Malay the main language of communication. We left Malay as our national language, the national anthem is still sung in Malay. But we adopted English as our working language. It's such an emotional issue. If we had made English our national language there would have been a row. Not to ruffle feelings, we made English our working language.

'For some years after independence, enrolment in Chinese schools went up. Many didn't believe that they would be better off learning English. When the results were seen in jobs after graduation the tide flowed the other way. The test was: what's your market value? I didn't force them. You could go to Chinese school where Chinese is the main language and English a second language. Had we dictated what they should do, there would have been trouble.

'Without English, in the age of the internet, imagine how disadvantaged we would be. Every time I boot up my computer to access Chinese websites, I have to open up a second program called Chinese WordStar. Then only will the funny squiggles form Chinese characters. We made our decision on practical, pragmatic grounds. We had no room for fancy theories.'

Lee has been a great champion of Confucian cultural values. How difficult is it to transmit your own cultural values to your children in a foreign language?

'It's a serious long-term problem. I'm unable to predict how much of an erosion there will be in one or two generations. If you are unable to use your proverbs, your sayings in the original tongue, it loses that emotional punch. I'm seeing it in my grandchildren. Their parents are Chinese- and English-educated.

'But because of a change in society's language climate, although they go to Chinese schools, their friends all speak English, because they are speaking English at home. Parents want them to be proficient in English so they can score better, so their Chinese has declined.

'The internet is wide open. So is satellite and cable TV. What is the impact on values and attitudes over one, two generations? I'm quite fearful. But we had no choice. We still have none. Take us back to 1965 and my colleagues and I would still have made the same decision.

'I told C.H. Tung [Hong Kong's chief executive] that Hong Kong students grappling with three languages—Mandarin, Cantonese and English—is tough, that the average brain, linguistic IQ 100, can cope with one language. If you put in a second language, something of the first language is lost. The megabytes just aren't there; the vocabulary and the rules, grammar, syntax need megabytes.

'In Singapore, those below fifteen no longer speak dialect [languages of their ancestors, if these are other than English or Mandarin]. Our children speak either Mandarin or English to their parents. They can't cope with three. Grandparents speak to them in dialect, they reply in Mandarin.'

So Lee and Catherine Lim agree—English made Singapore.

David and I are exhilarated from our interview. It's been a fascinating couple of hours with Lee who, apart from talking about Singapore, has given us a grand strategic tour of Asia and the world.

David knows Singapore a little, but hasn't been to dinner in Singapore's Little India before so we take a cab to the start of Serangoon Road and begin a leisurely amble along Little India's main drag.

Singapore's Little India is different from KL's. For one thing it's much smaller. It centres on Serangoon Road which is a long stretch of Indian music and religious artefact stores, clothing shops, restaurants and temples. It's not really a fashionable part of Singapore.

It has undergone many metamorphoses while retaining its Indian identity. Formerly it was overwhelmingly Tamil, with a small presence of the much smaller north Indian Sikh community. But now with many Bangladeshi guest workers on building sites and the like they are a noticeable presence.

David and I take off our shoes and wander into the Veerama Kali temple, dedicated to the militant goddess Kali, consort of Shiva. Among the colourful statuary is one of Kali literally ripping the guts out of some opponent. She's not a woman to be trifled with, clearly, our Kali.

We retrace our steps up Serangoon Road and turn off into Race-track Road which houses half a dozen or more good, cheap Indian restaurants. After the heavy sushi and wasabi lunch this proves to be a big eating and hot spices day, as we consume a feast of lamb, chicken and vegetable curries. The dinner, though flavoursome and satisfying as expected, is not without contention. David asks for a lamb rogan josh, though it is not on the menu. Ours is surely the only Indian waiter in the world who is unfamiliar with rogan josh.

I see that Indian spices tea is on the menu and order a cup. This is a delicacy involving clove, cardamom and other spices blended in a rich, strong tea which carries the medley of flavours perfectly. Jessie frequently makes spices tea at home.

But I like a slight variation. Spices tea is normally made with milk, which is added while the tea is brewing. I like it without milk, which means the tea maker must brew separately for me.

Our small, shy Bengali waiter, disconcerted by rogan josh, is completely flummoxed by spices tea without milk. But miraculously the spices tea *sans* milk arrives at the end of the meal. Singaporean adaptability has won out. It is well-worth the haggling.

I remember visiting Little India more than a decade ago with Warren Osmond who was then my counterpart, foreign editor, at *The Sydney Morning Herald*. Warren was a complete original in Australian journalism. A former student radical, a former academic, he looked a little like Harrison Ford. He combined elements of the bohemian and elements of the dandy and had an exceptional gift for friendship. Though a serious scholar in several fields he also collected all sorts of esoteric information for its own sake, just as he collected friends, for their own sake. He was really too much the intellectual for journalism and he was under-appreciated professionally. Tragically, several years after our walk round Little India Warren died of a totally unexpected heart attack.

That night, more than a decade ago, as Warren and I wandered around Little India we took a turn off Serangoon Road and came upon the foulest red-light district I've ever seen in Southeast Asia, spectacularly unlike the modern, pristine Singapore. It was reminiscent of an infinitely down-market version of Taipei's famous snake alley. There were stalls and tables selling snake's venom and other potency drugs, various charms and amulets and a long row of brothels, dreary, filthy-looking establishments with sad women standing outside. I don't know whether they catered for the poorest strata of locals or for Indonesian and other sailors off ships.

When I try to locate the area again to show it to David I find it's gone altogether, redeveloped into much higher-class accommodation. That's one part of old Singapore whose passing no one would mourn.

David leaves early next morning but I stay for a day or two longer. I go out to the National University of Singapore. Forget

Cambridge, Oxford or Harvard—this is the greenest campus I've seen anywhere. The students seem more relaxed, and friendlier, than they did at the Islamic University in KL. There are also no security guards on the gates. I stop at a convenient student canteen for a cold drink. The heat is almost distressing. A three-minute walk and I'm covered with sweat. Air-con is a luxury in most Western countries but it has been an essential ingredient of modern life in cities like Singapore. Quite apart from human beings, there are all kinds of computers which just couldn't function without it.

Obliging students direct me to Professor Wong Poh Kam, the director of the university's Centre for Management of Innovation and Technopreneurship. He is another ethnic Chinese who has come to Singapore from Malaysia partly because he doesn't like the *bumi* preference system in Malaysia.

He gives me a convincing spiel about the role of hi-tech in Singapore's future and the need to get the juices of business creativity flowing. But it is his own experience with his own kids which is most telling. The school system, which has done so well in the big industrial catch-up phase, may not be well adapted for the demands of the contemporary economy.

'I have kids in the primary system and I can see strong rote learning and discipline in their schooling,' he says.

'Up to a point that's good but I still don't think that's flexible enough. The American system of extreme flexibility is good for bright students but I think it may fail poor students. Part of the difficulty in getting change in Singapore is the teachers. It's very hard to change the style and emphasis of older teachers.

'The other main problem is the parents. A lot of parents in East Asia came from poor backgrounds and have done OK and education helped them. So we have a debate and conclude that the system is too exam-oriented and change to more project work by students. But the parents feel that even the project work is going to be graded eventually so they start doing the project work for the kids. Parents are very conservative.

'I don't want to send my kids to extra tuition. But my wife gets pressure from all of her office mates. Most of my sons' classmates go to tuition.'

Through contacts at the university I am introduced to a young Indian woman, Sheena, who has experienced both the Singapore and Australian education systems. Sheena is a journalist in her mid-twenties. She did a diploma course at the Polytechnic in Singapore and then used that as credit towards a degree at the University of Queensland in Brisbane.

A plump, pert, happy young woman, Sheena enjoyed her time in Brisbane: 'The Australian lifestyle is so relaxed compared with Singapore. Australians work just as hard as Singaporeans but they make time to relax and they know how to relax, they know how to have a good time. In Singapore things are more hectic.

'We are trying to relax more as our standard of living goes up. More people my age, who go abroad, realise the need to have quality of life as well as quantity of life—to stop and smell the roses.

'I live with my parents. It's expensive to live independently. People who live away from home tend to have more freedom to decide how they relax. My family's very understanding but I still call and say I'll be late and why.

'At primary school the teaching was very conservative. The teacher talked and we listened. But at the top end of secondary school I did have teachers who encouraged discussion.

'Right now things are happening in Singapore and I feel good here. I lived in Australia for two years and enjoyed that very much. When I first got back from Australia I felt like, Oh I want to go back, I want to go back. Studying overseas was a good growing-up experience for me, with no mummy and daddy on hand to organise everything and make sure everything's OK. A lot of young Singaporeans who come back from Australia try and recreate their life in Australia back here, they bring some of that Australianness back to Singapore.'

Can that be a good thing for Singapore? I suppose if Singapore is 'trying to relax' it must be.

Commitments back in KL mean I'm flying out instead of taking the train back. Changi Airport remains consistently the best, for my money, in the world. It's not the most beautiful—it lacks the gardens of Miami or Hawaii or a number of other American airports, the grand traditional design of Jakarta, the space-age feel of KL. But it is the airport in the world which gets nearest to the designation that everything works all the time and there is almost never any fuss.

Its strategically placed bookshops have deprived me of many a dollar on my way out or in. They deserve some kind of special award for the contribution they make to Southeast Asian letters.

All the economy seats are taken on the day I need to fly back to KL so I have to buy a first-class ticket. For such a short journey it's not very expensive. It's the only time I've ever flown first class and it provides a glimpse into another world.

At Changi, travelling first class as I am, I don't do anything so vulgar as join a check-in queue. Instead, someone meets me at the first-class entrance, a porter takes my bags and I am directed to a large leather sofa and offered drinks. My personal attendant takes my ticket and passport and does the formalities while I recline in comfort reading the day's international newspapers, which are provided for my convenience.

I pass through immigration and take the elevator upstairs to the first-class lounge where TVs and music, food and drinks in ridiculous abundance, telephones and computers, newspapers and journals of every kind are all provided. There seem to be as many staff as passengers. Despite the abundance of amenities on offer there is a lovely atmosphere of quiet and discretion. There are partitioned areas with full-length beds available if you want a kip. Naturally an attendant approaches you individually when the riff-raff have boarded the plane and you stroll on in languid, regal ease to take your rightful place at the front of the plane.

Hemingway was right. The rich *are* different from the rest of us. They have a lot more money.

It's fashionable in the West to sneer at Singapore, at its controls and its neuroses. Singapore's self-confidence, its growing sense of being relaxed and cool and funky, took something of a blow when it was discovered that a group of Malay terrorists, linked to al-Qaeda, had planned to blow up the US, British and Australian diplomatic missions.

What was particularly shocking for Singaporeans was that those arrested had been to government schools and some had done moderately OK. There was nothing in their background to suggest desperation or even alienation. It seemed instead the pure triumph of an evil ideology. Most terrorists, of course, are not desperate but well-educated and full of purpose. In any event the Singapore authorities responded with their usual speed and effectiveness.

I just don't buy the West sneering at Singapore. I have been at dinner parties in Sydney and New York and, more seldom, London where the talk turns to Southeast Asia and the tone towards Singapore is automatically hostile and sniggering and I am always at a loss to know what my dinner companions are talking about.

Compared to what? I feel like asking.

Southeast Asia is a region of successes and failures. Surely Singapore is an unambiguous success. Would you rather live there or in Rangoon, or Hanoi?

I leave this green and beautiful island and its brilliant and unlikely society with regret. Soon I will have a chance to compare it again with other iconic regional cities, with Hanoi and Saigon, with Hong Kong and Jakarta. It may still be only trying to relax. It may in truth not be quite as funky as it would like. But the bottom line for judging any city is the quality of life it gives to its sons and daughters. You can do a lot worse than Singapore.

Hanoi's Ho, Miss Saigon and three Vietnams

OK, I know I'm obsessed with breakfast, but doesn't every journey really start with breakfast? When Jessie and I travel to Hanoi and Saigon we stay the night before at the Pan Pacific at KL Airport. We oversleep so don't have time for the sumptuous buffet breakfast but grab a couple of muffins and some water for later and race across the covered walkway to the terminal.

For we have a bit of flying ahead of us. All the advice is that the Vietnam Government prefers Western reporters to start their tour in Hanoi rather than Saigon. The problem is that Saigon is so much more lively a commercial centre than Hanoi that there are direct KL–Saigon flights but no direct KL–Hanoi fights.

So our program for the day is fly to Saigon, clear customs there, make the blood-curdlingly tight transfer to a Vietnam Airlines flight to Hanoi. If we miss the connection, which the airline is honest enough to tell us is quite a possibility, we'll be spending the day at Saigon Airport.

Why am I calling it Saigon when its official name is Ho Chi Minh City? The communists, when they took control of the whole country in April 1975, renamed the southern capital after the man they thought of as their national leader and liberator, Ho Chi Minh.

A small central area was still officially designated Saigon but the big sprawling metropolis, of which Saigon was now just a small part, got the new name. Not wishing to cause offence, I trained myself to call it Ho Chi Minh City. But when I got there I found everyone in Saigon, and almost everyone in Hanoi too, still calls it Saigon. The southerners take a positive, perverse joy in continuing to insist on their city's name, the northerners have simply bowed to reality.

So if it's good enough for the Vietnamese themselves, it's good enough for me. I certainly don't plan to be more Catholic than the Pope, so to speak. If they can call it Saigon, so can I.

Jessie and I are hugely excited about our trip to Hanoi and Saigon. I'm a child of the Cold War. The Vietnam War entered my consciousness when I was about eight and ended when I was nineteen. I remember when I was nine or so the head nun in the convent primary school I attended telling us boys that in eleven years' time we would be conscripted into the army and sent to fight in Vietnam. Even at nine this was a sobering prospect, as it was no doubt meant to be, although in retrospect the nun was an extreme pessimist to believe not only that the war would last for another eleven years (which come to think of it, it almost did) but that Australia would still be sending conscripts there to fight.

All my first trips to Asia were following the story of the Vietnamese refugees. Even my first trip to KL, in the mid-1980s, was to visit the refugee camps—one just outside KL itself, and one on the beautiful island of Pulau Bidong, off the east coast from Trengganu. As a consequence I have many Vietnamese friends, but before today I have never been to Vietnam itself. For me, like so many others, Vietnam is a field of dreams.

We fly Malaysian Airlines, which is always a pleasure. Unluckily today we check in a bit late so we are in separate seats, a few rows apart, each of us squeezed into a middle seat in the middle section of the plane, right up the back. But it's only a short flight, a couple of hours. That's one of the great things about Southeast Asia, everywhere is pretty close to everywhere else.

There's an incredible diversity in Southeast Asia. Here we are in the twinkling of an eye travelling from a conservative Muslim, majority Malay society to an officially communist and atheist society of vastly different ethnic extraction.

We touch down at Saigon Airport and I can't help imagining the time when it was the busiest airport in the world, with all the American military supply and transport flights coming through. It's a strange feeling to be here at last. It's certainly not the busiest airport in the world anymore but it offers an instructive introduction to the two cities of the two Vietnams.

Glitch number one is that we can't find one of our bags. This is likely to be a big problem as it could mean we miss our connecting flight. By the time we get to the luggage area the bags have already been taken off the small, inadequate luggage carousel and laid out in neat rows. Here is an axiom of profound cultural insight. Communist societies are obsessively neat at the surface, capitalist societies are inherently disordered at the surface. But in communist societies bureaucratic neatness at the surface merely obscures the larger chaos beneath, while capitalistic chaos at the surface is often an expression of free forces working below which are nearer to rationality and order than obsessive bureaucratic rules. Or to put it another way, communism is anal, capitalism is oral.

The problem this day, however, is not remotely linked to the anality or bureaucratic rigidity of the Vietnam command state. The problem is that we just bought a new bag and forgot that it was black, both Jessie and I thinking, for some reason that escapes me still, that it was blue. After seeing, evaluating and rejecting as someone else's what is in fact our bag we come back to it, try again and discover that yes indeed it is ours. This leads to two bureaucratic reforms in the Sheridan family (which is certainly not a command state). From now on, we attach a label bearing our name, and also a piece of vivid red cloth, to all our pieces of luggage.

Now we are really short of time. Two signs on the airport wall give us some pause. We are to hear a lot about corruption in Vietnam. A society without contending sources of power, independent institutions like courts and a free press, is always going to be prone to massive corruption and Vietnam is no exception, to put it mildly. One sign says simply: Please do not put money in your passport when you give it for inspection.

This is a common way of offering bribes in many parts of the world. Generally in US currency, a $50 bill, or even $20 or $10, folded in behind your passport in the passport pouch itself is discreet and non-provocative. If the traveller strikes an honest official the mere presence of some dollars hasn't constituted the crime of trying to offer a bribe. Maybe that's where you always carry some spare cash. If the official is dishonest he quietly snaffles the money, without an untoward word from anyone, and expedites the traveller's needs. The sign at the airport is at least evidence that the problem of corruption is publicly recognised, and deprives the would-be briber of the excuse that the money was in the passport by accident, though I wonder how often the instruction is breached anyway.

The other sign reminds us that it is illegal to bring food into Vietnam. Now I hate to enter a new country by breaking the law so Jessie and I quickly quaff the muffins we brought from the Pan Pacific buffet and drink the bottled water, all before we approach customs and immigration.

At the official counter we tell the woman that we are trying to make a tight connection to Hanoi. She glowers as though we have breached some important airport protocol and tells us to wait over there, her tone sharp and peremptory. Oh no, I think, here comes some great Marxist–Leninist bureaucratic palaver designed to slow us down. To my immense surprise, another official, also a severe-looking woman, takes charge of us and actually rushes us through the remaining formalities so that we do in fact get the connection.

At this stage we haven't glimpsed Saigon, or really even Vietnam. On the flight to Hanoi we are again separated but it's a short flight. Because we've done all our immigration formalities there is nothing confusing about Hanoi Airport except its scruffy, run-down feel. Hanoi has been the capital of an important country for hundreds of years. I know it's a poor country but still I'm surprised at just how unprepossessing its airport is. (Since our visit, there is a new terminal.) Jessie discovers this first hand. Before we get a taxi she goes off to find a bathroom.

I know you shouldn't obsess about toilet standards in poor countries but the ladies bathroom at Hanoi Airport is something else. Jessie is an experienced traveller familiar with many aspects of life in Southeast Asia. Hanoi's toilet though just grosses her out. First, the cubicles have no doors which lends a performance art aspect to the whole thing which she finds distinctly unappealing. Even worse is that those folks who haven't been able to secure a cubicle simply squat down and do their business on the toilet floor. For a big international airport this is not a good look.

On the other hand it's easy to get a taxi so Jessie decides to wait until we get to the hotel. Driving into the city from the airport I am struck by how undeveloped it all looks. It looks as poor as India and yet the area around Hanoi is unusually rich by Vietnamese standards.

As we drive in I am excited beyond words just to be in this land which has occupied so much of my imagination. Like everyone of my generation I had a passionate position on the Vietnam War. Then the refugees led me into Asia which has become my lifelong obsession. I know how destructive was the tragedy of the war, yet visiting Vietnam is for me like entering the distant worlds of childhood legend, like journeying to Tolkien's Middle Earth.

Then too there is the strangeness of the environment. When you live in a settler society like Australia you are accustomed to thinking of certain groups as minorities. I have met Vietnamese in all parts of Australia, in the US, in Europe, in Central America, in many parts of the world, but I've never before been in an environment which is overwhelmingly and naturally Vietnamese. For reasons that even now I don't fully understand I find it frankly a bit thrilling.

We are staying at the Hotel Sofitel Metropole Hanoi. The world is full of five star hotels but the Metropole is something special. It's a hundred years old and conveys everything that was elegant about French colonialism. Before I get carried away with that thought it's worth remembering that French colonialism in Vietnam—throughout all Indochina for that matter—was mostly not an exercise in elegance but was exceptionally cruel and arbitrary. There were worse colonisers than the French, but the French were pretty bad. All the elegance they created in Vietnam was meant for the enjoyment of the French colonisers and their guests, not the Vietnamese.

Nonetheless they built pretty hotels and the Metropole is one of the great hotels. Its elegance is breathtaking. It runs between two city blocks. Internally its rooms and courtyards gently curl and snake around, while at street front it is perfectly regular. Each facade is a brilliant white, always a good colour in the tropics provided you keep the paintwork up to scratch, with the front entrance covered by a green canopy. Small, white balustrades frame petite balconies upstairs and green wooden shutters open out from the windows.

Our room is vast, with dark, polished floorboards and sumptuous throw rugs, the furniture a mixture of dark and light woods. The size of the room alone bespeaks a more leisured age. There is an expanse of space beyond the door, with the bathroom to the right of the entrace. This gives the room a natural L shape. Around the corner from the door, and out of its sight line, is the huge bed. In the opposite corner, about a cricket pitch length away it seems, is a table setting with rattan chairs, where Jessie and I will eat croissants and sip rich, dark coffee for breakfast. Looking through the french doors from the breakfast table we see a glorious, internal courtyard with a wealth of tropical green—pretty, profuse, yet perfectly still. The french doors, like the other windows in the room, are covered with heavy, gold, brocaded curtains which are drawn back during the day to reveal gossamer-thin, white lace underneath, which lets in the light but maintains your privacy. Graham Greene stayed at the Metropole, lucky sod, and wrote some of *The Quiet American* here.

I gotta be straight with you about all this. I know there's an ethical dilemma about indulging in such luxury when you're in a very poor country. I don't generally seek out top-of-the-range hotels because I can't generally afford them. This one has been booked through local friends at a low season for tourists. Would it be ethically more pure to stay somewhere cheaper? It's hard to see exactly why. If you stay at backpackers' accommodation you make a backpacker's contribution to the local economy. At the Metropole dozens, probably hundreds, of Vietnamese earn a decent living. There's no need to idealise tourism to realise that in a poor country the tourist industry is one of the few to provide the wherewithal for a lot of families to live decently, wherever the ultimate profits go.

If you're going to visit a country like Vietnam it's a bit of an affectation, of no benefit to the Vietnamese themselves, to avoid spending money there.

Jessie and I have developed some habits in our travel, some rigid rituals both practical in their effect and reassuring in their regularity. If we're staying more than one day we always unpack completely. It not only gives you a sense of order, which on a long trip you can lose, but it almost always ends up saving you time as well. You don't spend hours looking for the nail scissors or wondering where some important notebook has disappeared to. This is an innovation which has only come to me with marriage. In our partnership I am the principle of chaos, Jessie is the principle of order. When I travelled as a bachelor I was as disordered as you get. Now, even when I travel alone, I find I continue the routines Jessie and I have evolved together. Our other habit is that as soon as possible after we unpack we go for a long walk. Three or four hours walking around, suitably broken up with a cappuccino stop at a sidewalk cafe, carried out with no more assistance than a city map, is the best possible introduction to a new city.

Today we still have some hours of light and we head off from the Metropole, full of intrepid hopes. Opposite the hotel is a raft of sidewalk cafes which could have come straight out of Paris. Parts of the city do look distinctly Parisian, especially the older, art deco apartment houses, with their curving fronts and 1930s design adventurism. Barely five minutes' walk from the hotel is the city square which houses the French-era Opera House, a squat, boldly yellow but not ungracious building, whose colour scheme has been matched by the adjacent Hanoi Hilton. We wander into the Hanoi Hilton and find it strangely empty. I wonder do Americans feel the slightest hesitation in staying at a hotel whose name was once the slang term for the notoriously cruel prisoner-of-war camp?

We retrace our steps and set out for the city lake, which we have heard is beautiful. Hanoi is an odd sort of city visually. Much of the traffic is bicycles and motorbikes rather than cars. Its centre reminds me of Beijing in the mid-1980s, before the fantastic burst of development in the 1990s totally transformed that city.

As I see more of the city I'm astonished at its variety. Architecturally it's certainly a weird mix. The building boom of the mid-1990s has left a few monstrosities, what seem to be quite a few mostly empty hotels and a cacophony of wildly mixed housing styles, well captured in the phrase 'lego-deco'. Every weird, decorative pink-and-cream addition you can imagine festoon exceptionally narrow concrete houses, frequently built to four or five storeys high. Often in a wealthy family as a son marries an extra floor is added to accomodate the new bride and groom. Sometimes a new storey is set back a couple of metres from the main building (which at its base may go right to the street side) to allow a tiny balcony to be added. The exceptional narrowness is said to date from an ancient period when tax was levied according to the width of a shopfront.

On our way to the lake Jessie and I are assailed by many beggars and hawkers. They're not as insistent as in a similar-sized city in India but they are numerous, poor and in need of a feed. Some sell postcards, others just hold out their hands. Like most Stalinist cities, Hanoi is generally a safe place for a Western visitor. There is not much crime practised against foreigners. The penalties, as with the penalties for political infractions, are just too severe. But there are an awful lot of postcard sellers, many more it seems than there are tourists visiting the city.

We find the lake and it is indeed beautiful. Hanoi, unlike any Indian city I've visited, has clean streets. After all, labour is cheap and the city can afford to hire lots of people to sweep the streets. By the route we've wandered the lake is a fair walk from the hotel and we need to sit down in one of the pretty parks on the lake's shore and rest. This is not wholly a good idea. A succession of postcard hawkers and bottled water sellers and some more straightforward beggars approaches us as we sit. The view of the lake, while lovely, is rendered somewhat bizarre by the city's decision to paint the bottom metre or so of every tree white. The beggars don't bother us much, we face the normal quandary of how much to give and how often, but there is one muscular young man, bare from the waist up, his face set in a grimace of hostility, his upper body rippling with muscles, who has been following us, never more than about ten metres away. As we sit, he sits too. I know what he wants—our money. But I'm not sure how he plans to get it. In any event I don't think we should make ourselves stationary targets for too long. So after a brief rest we start walking again.

Not far from the lake we come upon a real treasure of Hanoi, its old city, or the 'District of Thirty-six Streets'. This district gets its name from the thirty-six guilds which each took a street for its own. Even today each street tends to specialise in one line of merchandise, such as one magical street where every shop seems to sell red lanterns. Here the shop-houses—shop below, residence above—are even narrower than in the rest of Hanoi, again because of the old tax system. They are sometimes called tube houses because they are so long and narrow. The streets too are exceptionally narrow. They are dense and fecund and wholly absorbing. Many of the shops come right up to the street, others have a little footpath on which they frequently display merchandise. Here, perhaps obeying some local unwritten law, the beggars disappear, as does the menacing young man who has been following us. The Vietnamese, like the Chinese, have almost a reverence for commerce and its prerogatives (which makes them among the unlikeliest of communists). Perhaps beggars and muggers and the like, though presumably not pickpockets, are kept out of the thirty-six streets district by some unspoken local agreement or tradition.

The great charm of this district is its antiquity and its historical continuity. It is about a thousand years old. Because it is still today a shopping centre, and because that is a reasonably close relative of its original function, it represents an example of the living ancient which you don't get in KL or Singapore because they are not ancient cities. And although the 'District of the Thirty-six Streets' has certainly become a tourist attraction it is not wholly, nor even primarily, a tourist attraction. Lots of local commerce is transacted there. The streets are filled with every type of Vietnamese—there are motorbikes in great profusion, jostling the streets with women in conical hats carrying chickens or vegetables in baskets suspended from either end of bamboo poles carried over a shoulder. Everyone is delivering, receiving, paying, trading. And certainly most of the people there are Vietnamese. Jessie and I are wholly absorbed by the district of thirty-six streets. We spend a goodly time wandering around this district, buying the odd piece of fabric or tablecloth or some such thing which is always irresistable when you're travelling and useless and untouched when you get home.

We are tired from all our walking and not absolutely sure of the route back to the hotel. So we hop on a rickshaw, or cyclo as they're mostly called in Vietnam, to ride back to the Metropole. Expat friends who have lived in Hanoi a long time, later tell us they use cyclos quite a lot around the city. They're cheap and efficient. But I find this ride deeply disturbing. The cyclo driver has assured us he can take us both and that there is no need for a second cyclo. But really his machine is nothing more than a pushbike mechanism connected to a seat and it's clear after a few minutes that the two of us are too much weight. He strains and groans and pushes to move us. He's muscular but this effort is too much. Surely he can't keep it up day after day. How many people, I wonder, what permutation of extended family, which child's schooling or grandmother's medicine depend on his exertions alone? I've never ridden in a rickshaw before, despite all the time I've spent in different parts of

Asia, and I determine after this never to do it again. There's something demeaning to him and unpleasant for me in the groaning struggle he makes to carry us all back to the Metropole. There's no point quivering in sensitive distress every minute that you're visiting a very poor country, nor is there any point being indifferent to the poverty. No doubt the cyclo driver would rather earn a living this way than not earn a living at all. No doubt too on the scale of Vietnamese deprivation and suffering being a cyclo driver in Hanoi is not near the bottom. I don't begrudge him his right to earn a living this way. But I won't be taking a cyclo again.

The other factor driving this view is the sheer, insane, death-defying nature of the ride. Hanoi's traffic is torrential and its motorists lawless and anarchic. This cyclo driver is the maddest and baddest of them all. He makes the most excruciating, hair-splitting judgments about when he can cut across the line of traffic. And seated in a cyclo you have the well-founded sense that there is absolutely nothing between you and the bone-crunching impact of the oncoming traffic except your driver's skill and strength. The judgements the cyclo driver makes need to be precise because he has no power of acceleration and no other vehicle has the slightest inclination to cut him any slack simply because he has two passengers in his conveyance. Miraculously we make it back to the hotel in one piece and I start to count out the several tens of thousands of dong he asks for the fare. Jessie, her Southeast Asian bargaining instincts ever ready to kick in, inquires about the basis of the fare. But when I calculate the exchange rate I work out we are only going to pay him about US$2 anyway so I double the amount and he is nearly delirious with joy. That is one of the hardest-working guys I've ever met.

Next morning we begin the business of meeting some Vietnamese. As Jessie and I leave the hotel we come upon a sight both infinitely hopeful and decidedly dangerous. A young girl in a maroon-coloured school uniform, maybe eleven or twelve and presumably on her way to school, is crossing the road near the hotel. As she walks across the street she is holding a book up in front of her face and reading while she walks. Given Hanoi's traffic this is truly death-defying, even at a pedestrian crossing, though the motorbikes manage to weave past her without apparent effort. The sight of the girl so absorbed in her book is also the most graphic illustration of the traditional Vietnamese love of learning. Lots of cultures claim this virtue but in the Vietnamese case it is no idle boast. Which makes you wonder how the Government has managed to make such a mess of the economy for so long. It doesn't wash just to blame it on the war. The war finished nearly thirty years ago. Lots of other Asian nations have recovered from even greater devastation to a much higher level of prosperity than Vietnam enjoys now.

Singapore's Lee Kuan Yew once described the Vietnamese as a hard people. He meant it as a compliment, meant that they would be able to undertake the tough decisions involved in economic modernisation and succeed in providing a decent standard of living to their people.

But the pattern has been bouts of reform followed by bouts of stagnation. There has been no authoritative figure like China's Deng Xiaoping to give the imprimatur to reform. The political culture remains resolutely Stalinist. One morning I buy *The Asian Wall Street Journal*. This business-oriented American newspaper, which is always worth reading for its region-wide view, must have a tiny circulation in Vietnam. Amazingly, the Vietnamese state censor has stayed up all night and with a black felt-tipped pen blacked out an offending paragraph. I make a point of later tracking down the original version of this story and find that the offending paragraph reads: 'Ultimately, Vietnam will succumb to the peaceful evolution it fears, as private capital establishes vigorous markets and loosens Hanoi's hold on the country.'

This little episode of censorship demonstrates how petty, almost comic, attempts at controlling information can be in Vietnam, yet the fact that the particular issue of the newspaper was not banned altogether shows that Vietnam is still trying to attract foreign investment and understands it needs to make its environment hospitable. One aspect of this is being able to read *The Asian Wall Street Journal*, even if slightly mutilated.

It is an irony—admittedly, an irony without any power to console—that communism, a purely materialist philosophy which derides religion as the opium of the people, was never able to deliver material prosperity to any of the nations that practised it.

In Vietnam's case a kind of economic nightmare was reached by the 1980s which forced it to change course at the end of that decade. There were in the 1980s food queues and even starvation in Hanoi, a bizarre development in a nation which routinely exports rice. A long-term expat told me that there was a time when prostitutes charged a single cigarette for the night. I would normally dismiss such a story as apocryphal but its source is a senior figure whose knowledge of Vietnam is second to none.

In any event, somewhat following the example of its giant neighbour, China, Vietnam in the late 1980s embarked on its own economic reform program, its own *perestroika*, called *doi moi*, which loosely translates as renovation. This has not been accompanied by political liberalisation but has improved the economy markedly, although it keeps coming in maddening oscillations, fits and starts, stop/go, accelerate/halt. The ruling Communist Party does just enough reform to make everyone a bit richer, then gets scared it might lose some political control and clamps the shutters down again. The party is especially fearful of 'peaceful evolution', which is no doubt why it blacked out the offending words in *The Asian Wall Street Journal*. Peaceful evolution, it fears, means that by subtle degrees the nature of the society will change underneath its nose and it will wake up one day to find that Vietnam is no longer communist, no longer socialist, perhaps even no longer authoritarian.

And you know what? I think the party's right, that is the fate likely to befall it. I think peaceful evolution will get it in the end. Even the paranoid have enemies. You can see it already in the fact that more and more Vietnamese, especially in Saigon but also increasingly in Hanoi, can now live their lives without reference to the ruling party. It's not that they're leading political rebellion.

It's rather that, except when required to pay bribes to state officials they don't need to interact with the state much at all. We would see a lot of evidence of this in both Hanoi and Saigon.

A severe young woman from the foreign ministry meets us this morning. Are all official women in Vietnam severe? Is this an attitude understandably struck just for Western visitors, to counter the bargirl stereotype so many Western movies and novels have inflicted on Vietnamese women?

The official explains to me what is expected of a visiting journalist. Although all my interviews are supposed to be arranged through the Government the truth is there is no attempt to prevent me moving around and talking to whomever I like, if they'll talk to me. This semi-freedom is typical of modern Vietnam and much better than what went before.

The first day is taken up with official calls which are conducted in that strange bureaucratese which communist states specialise in. There is a certain cryptologist's skill required to decipher state officials in such circumstances. I remember it well from my time in Beijing in 1985 where what was left unsaid in an interview was often what was most telling. At Hanoi's Central Institute for Economic Management a bland official tells me that his country is committed to economic reform. Yes, I know, but what shape will that reform take?

'Everything depends on the decisions made by the next congress of the Communist Party,' he says.

'What decisions is it likely to take?'

'It is not my place to speculate on the decisions of the party congress.'

'Well, if you can't tell me what decisions it will take can you at least tell me the specific issues it will be considering?'

'It is not my place to pre-empt the considerations of the party congress.'

We repeat this formulation in different ways many times. Eventually I give up. He's a good communist bureaucrat. Name, rank and serial number is all I'm going to get out of that fella.

Although my official foreign ministry guide is severe, she is not really intimidating. Nonetheless I recognise that the people I interview in the presence of a government official, even if they are government officials themselves, are distinctly less forthcoming than those I meet alone, presumably because one of the jobs of the accompanying official is to report exactly what is said back to head office.

Hanoi's Institute of International Relations is on what seems to be about the twelfth floor of an old academic building although I suspect my memory has distorted the trudge up those stairs and in fact it was only about a half (perhaps a quarter?) the number of floors that I remember. Anyway, there was no lift and it reminded me of the sort of think-tanks you visit in India, where the building is indescribably filthy and run-down but the person on the top floor is nonetheless a genuinely brilliant scholar.

Ha Hong Hai of the Institute of International Relations is a youngish-looking man who speaks excellent English. And what he has to say, at least at the level of nuance, is a little more adventurous than his counterpart at the Economic Management Institute. Ha tells me: 'We have exchanged annual summit meetings with China. Vietnamese are impressed by China's orderly society. In Vietnam in the past we have not had brutal experiences such as China's cultural revolution. But the degree of openness of the economy in China has a lot to teach us.'

It's not exactly Martin Luther King, I'll agree, but in its constipated way it's a call to freedom. Expressing admiration for China is a simple code that means he wants a lot more openness, at least of the economic variety, in Vietnam. Good for Ha.

The mid-1990s were a period of pretty substantial achievement in Vietnamese diplomacy. It withdrew its army of occupation from Cambodia a few years earlier, then got the US to lift its trade embargo and in 1995 achieved the double of joining the Association of Southeast Asian Nations and the Asia Pacific Economic Cooperation forum. It finally achieved diplomatic relations with

160 countries. The world wants to welcome Vietnam but as ever this burst of activism was followed by retreat.

Soon I come across someone a good deal more outspoken than the officials I've met so far.

Next morning Jessie and I have a little time free. We ask the concierge where the nearest good bookshop is and he directs us to a two-storey bookshop not far away. At first this looks promising—two floors of books, yippee!—but like most communist societies Vietnam does not do well in the bookshop department. There are classics in English, French and Vietnamese. But what do you want in a bookshop in Vietnam? Books on Vietnam naturally. Apart from a couple of party-approved, poorly produced publications in atrocious English there is nothing on Vietnam or even on its Southeast Asian nieghbours. None of the good histories and political and cultural analyses of Vietnam in English is available. Not only that, none of the standard travel guides is available. Officially at least. But the market in modern Vietnam has a way of satisfying most demands. While I am browsing disappointedly through the thin shelves of this bookshop a man sidles up to me.

'Hullo, sir, do you want to buy a book?'

That seems an odd question to ask someone in a bookshop. I can see from his furtive manner, however, that he doesn't actually work in the bookshop.

'I'm just looking at the moment.'

'Tell me what book you want, I'll get it for you. I have many books not available here.'

'You have a bookshop?'

'Not a bookshop. You tell me what book you want, I'll get for you.'

Well that seems fair enough. I mention one of the standard travel guides to Vietnam that I'm looking for.

'Yes I have that. I'll bring in ten minutes. Just meet me outside, on the corner.'

He's as good as his word. In less than ten minutes he has brought the book and sold it for the agreed price. When I look more closely I can see it's obviously a pirate copy. Some of the pages are smudged, some prints that should be colour are in black and white. Yet it's a pretty fair copy and well bound. Book piracy is well organised in Vietnam.

After this mild excursion into black market trading, Jessie and I go to see Madame Ngo Ba Thanh, a lawyer, a politician, a member of Vietnam's National Assembly. Again there is a lengthy climb up endless stairs. We are not accompanied by our guide today who must have found us dull yesterday. Madame Ngo's outer office is a tiny broom closet. An elderly, stooped man with extravagantly crooked teeth and the odd tuft of hair sticking out from widely spaced base camps on his cheeks and chin, welcomes us in halting English and takes us through to Madame Ngo's main office, which is bigger than the outer office, perhaps the size of two broom closets, and full to overflowing with knick-knacks and the sort of memorabilia—photos with famous folks, awards from civic bodies—that politicians of all cultures treasure.

The old guy shows us to the two seats opposite Madame Ngo's desk, fetches steaming green tea and then formally introduces himself with a bow: 'Hullo, I am Mrs Ngo Ba Thanh's secretary and I am also her son.'

A few minutes later Madame Ngo bustles in and while she's no spring chicken I would have thought if not told of her relationship with him that she was younger than the man who introduced himself as her son. After effusive introductions Madame Ngo directs our attention to her greatest trophy, almost hidden on the wall amidst so many other photos and bits and pieces. It's a flattering profile of her published in *The Boston Globe* newspaper on 23 October 1973. It tells of her imprisonment at that time in Saigon as an academic critic of the then US-sponsored South Vietnamese Government.

As is abundantly evident from her photograph of those times she was beautiful, feminine, academically well qualified with a string of American and European law degrees and described by *The Globe* as one of the most important female politicians in Vietnam. Now she is still a feisty and energetic woman, much plumper than thirty years ago, white-haired, wily, multi-lingual, as clever as ever and with a reputation for speaking her mind.

She is also one of a tiny minority of members of the National Assembly who is not a member of the Vietnamese Communist Party.

'I come from the south,' she tells us.

'I was part of the third political force, neither a supporter of the Saigon Government nor on the communist side. I was not a communist then and I'm not a communist now. At reunification [of North and South Vietnam in 1975] I represented the third force in politics.'

With the exception of one term when Madame Ngo was not re-elected she has been in the National Assembly ever since 1976. Vietnam doesn't have genuine, democratic elections and Madame Ngo is obviously tolerated as a sort of house liberal. Perhaps in the year she wasn't re-elected it was thought that she was a little too liberal.

She represents a Hanoi district and is bolder than anyone else I meet in the north on the need for Vietnam to embrace the rule of law and become more democratic. Like everyone she has to pay her dues and a good third of our conversation involves Madame Ngo calling for the US to pay reparations for the damage done during the Vietnam War. Now whatever you think about the Vietnam War, it's as likely that the US would offer to pay reparations to Vietnam as it is that the US Congress would strike a national holiday in commemoration of Saddam Hussein's contribution to humanitarianism. Madame Ngo, with all her doctorates and her many international contacts, surely knows this as well as anyone. So why waste her time on such a futile proposal? I think it's fair to assume that this part of the spiel is domestic politics.

She is more interesting on life in Vietnam today. She loves the way her adopted city has changed under the economic reforms: 'Hanoi has just bloomed in the last few years and this is the consequence of the Government's policy of recognising different economic sectors. People buy and sell without any reference to the Government. So the tax people can't work it out, they just ask people to pay a little tax.'

On what her Government should do next she is surprisingly forthright. The Government theoretically adopted a new policy of private enterprise-driven economic reform in 1986, she says, but this wasn't reflected in the constitution, which remained moored in assumptions of absolute socialism.

'So the nation's constitution between 1986 and 1992 did not reflect reality. Only two sectors were recognised—the state and collective sectors.'

This was remedied only in 1992 when a new constitution was proclaimed and the consequences of this landmark decision, Madame Ngo says, are only now working their way through Vietnamese society: 'Vietnam will become more democratic. There are a lot of differences already. But it is the trend as we move towards a more market economy. The state recognises different sectors of the economy now. And a democratic economy draws out more democratic social activity. We start with the economy and move on to politics. So we will avoid East Europe's fate—they started with politics first.'

I hope Madame Ngo is right. By contemporary Vietnamese standards these comments are pretty outspoken. She also has a lot to say about corruption and how the party and the Government need to tackle it energetically. This too might seem adventurous but it is the orthodox party line. Corruption is pandemic in Vietnam. In Saigon I would later meet a former Viet Cong revolutionary who reminisced about how bad it was under the Americans.

'Corruption was terrible then,' he said, 'just terrible. Almost as bad as it is now.'

Official corruption is fantastically unpopular with the people at large, which is one reason the Government these days makes a fuss about it. At the same time it's hard to know how seriously to take the Government's protestations that it's cracking down. When corruption cases do come to light they often disclose bizarre behaviour by officials. The Government also takes frequent decisions which make the eradication of corruption more difficult, such as passing laws that forbid journalists from publishing unauthorised stories or make them legally liable for any commercial damage arising from their stories, even if their stories are perfectly true.

British journalist, Robert Templer, in his masterful book on modern Vietnam, *Shadows and Wind*, describes how corruption has become for the Communist Party the modern equivalent of ideological deviance—that is, it's a perfect weapon to use against adversaries in the endless intra-party struggles. Given that at some level lots and lots and lots of people and their family members are corrupt, or at least engage in irregular practices, corruption is always a plausible charge to make against an opponent and a good excuse to purge someone inconvenient or disagreeable.

In a country whose constitution makes it an offence 'to doubt the fruits of the revolution' and in which the most revered political philosopher remains Lenin, for his grasp of the importance of state power, the authorities can define corruption pretty much how they like.

Nonetheless Vietnam is changing. The changes, though, often involve a return to older traditions rather than a new version of the modern. The economy, so the saying goes, is moving from plan to clan, with big, powerful families now becoming dominant. Especially powerful are the families who combine high state office with control over a corporation. And those who can influence the movement of resources between the state and private sector are often the most influential, and the wealthiest, of all.

One of the weird consequences of the foreign investment Vietnam has attracted over the past decade is that it has improved the state of the economy to the extent that it has propped up the state-owned sector. Many of the foreign joint ventures have been with state-owned enterprises so foreign capital is prolonging the life of the Vietnamese Communist Party. There's a contradiction of history for you.

In an anonymous corporate boardroom in Hanoi I meet one of the icons of Vietnam's private sector. Nguyen Tran Bat, chairman and chief executive of the InvestConsult group of companies, and eighteen or so of his closest advisers, troop into the boardroom after me and welcome me to their firm. Nguyen tells me he realised by the mid-1970s that socialist societies would face enormous economic difficulties, which puts him a decade or so ahead of most Western economists (and two or even three decades ahead of Western sociologists).

'I was an engineer by training and I spent several years in the army,' he tells me.

'From the mid-1970s I decided to study free enterprise theories.'

He established his nation's first partly privately owned company in 1987 and then, when the law was changed, established the first fully private company in 1992.

'Before the open door policy was introduced we had a fully planned economy and our government received most assistance from socialist economies. But then they collapsed and we had to open up our economy. At the time we did not understand how outsiders operated and they did not understand how we operated. The two business communities needed a bridge. I established InvestConsult to be that bridge.'

As he warms to his theme he becomes surprisingly frank: 'Vietnam's politicians hoped they could combine their traditional political system—a political monopoly—with a semi-free internal economy and a free economy outside. There was a conflict between the political theory of the government and the free market practice which foreign investors brought in.'

I am yearning to meet the arts community in Hanoi, to see if any fresh winds are blowing culturally. So I visit the Hanoi College of Industrial Arts and Design. Depressingly, this building is like so many others. There is the obligatory heroic statue of Ho Chi Minh out the front. Ho is ubiquitous in Hanoi. It's a bizarre cult of personality in a society allegedly devoted to egalitarianism. His statue out the front of this college is even more banal and saccharine than most in Hanoi. In this pose he is fondling the heads of two adoring children snuggling at his side. What is it with dictators and children? Lenin still stands in Hanoi too. He went up, also in humourless heroic mode, just as he was about to come down all over Eastern Europe.

While Hanoi's streets are clean there is just no way to describe how filthy many of the buildings are inside. The College of Industrial Arts and Design is a case in point. On the ground floor it contains what is without question the blackest, filthiest, most profoundly grimy latrine I've ever seen anywhere in Asia, Africa, Latin America or the Middle East. The grime is so thick it cannot have been cleaned in decades. It's surely a more interesting cultural exhibit than anything formally on display in the college itself.

Le Huy Van, the deputy director of the college, does his best to live up to the image of the arts administrator as ageing bohemian. He is almost a caricature of the artist/professor, garbed in black French beret, thick black jacket, black shirt and trousers and black brogues. Like almost all colleges in Vietnam now, his college takes a proportion of full fee-paying students. He emphasises that the college trains both industrial and creative artists. Why not come upstairs and see the human form life drawing class?

Why not?

I'm a little surprised that this college would have a life drawing class. Hanoi, like Saigon though not to quite the same extent, has a big, raucous sex industry, but officially it is very demure. I can't imagine any state institution sanctioning the drawing of the human form in anything but the most decorous and covered circumstances, in which case it wouldn't be the human form.

The dilemma is solved as we walk into the classroom. The class is indeed drawing nudes, but without the naughty bits, for their models are plastic, shop mannequins, which fortuntaely don't have the naughty bits anyway. At least they don't have trouble getting the models to keep still.

Le tells me the atmosphere is much better for the arts than it used to be and I have no reason to disbelieve him, but no particular reason to believe him either.

You generally get a better feel for something by talking to a practitioner than to a bureaucrat or state employee. Through a private contact Jessie and I are directed to a tiny coffee shop, run by Nguyen Huu Bao and his wife. Nguyen is an artistic photographer and he too somewhat plays the bohemian. An owlish looking man of middle years with giant, tortoise-shell spectacles and longish hair, his wife is much younger.

But I warm to Nguyen Huu Bao, even though his photography, as displayed on the coffee shop walls, looks pretty cheesy—burnt sunsets and chocolate box pretty girls on beaches, although there's the odd photograph of poor children to balance the moral ledgers. The coffee shop itself is tiny, a single room off a busy street in the District of Thirty-six Streets. There are just a couple of tables with tiny, low stools, so small that your knees seem to be up under your chin when you sit on them.

The couple proudly tell me their coffee shop is a traditional haunt of artists and writers. What is likeable about Nguyen Huu Bao is his obvious passion for life, his delight at having a couple of foreign visitors in his wife's coffee shop and his eagerness to talk.

He started taking photographs in 1974, before the end of the war, and has devoted most of his time to photography ever since. His brothers are all involved in the cinema so artistic endeavour is a family tradition. As we talk hawkers wander in and out. They make their pitch and then leave; Nguyen and his wife don't chase them out, but they don't stay and become bothersome.

Nguyen works part-time for a state photographic agency and for Vietnam Airlines but he prides himself on being an artist and being as independent as it's possible to be.

'We have a more open attitude to the arts now and that is good,' he says.

But Nguyen is not altogether the bohemian radical pushing the boundaries of freedom. He's also a parent, and nothing in life makes you more conservative than being a parent. He has two daughters, one fifteen and one seven.

'I don't know if I'm happier or more concerned at the new generation. They're overloaded with classes and computers and foreign influences, so many things that they don't have time to look at the stars and the moon. My oldest daughter knows all about the Spice Girls and Michael Jackson but nothing about traditional Vietnamese music. So I take my daughters back to my home village to show them the buffalo and rice because the root of all art is nature. I'm afraid she'll be like a machine or a robot when she grows up.

'We have large numbers of students reaching a high technical standard but they don't meet basic cultural standards. Now everyone wants to go to college and university but most graduates can't find jobs. My daughter will leave school in three years' time but for the time being she's not interested in anything. I'm very sorry about this but I don't want to impose anything on her.'

It seems that just a little bit of affluence and a parent starts worrying about his kids losing traditional values. Nguyen almost echoes Lee Kuan Yew in his concern for passing on the culture.

When it comes time to leave Hanoi Jessie and I are reluctant. This city has a lot to offer. The food for one thing. Every night we've eaten at Vietnamese restaurants and it would be a pleasure to go on doing so. Vietnamese food is such a successful blend of influences—Chinese, French, Thai. The heavy use of ginger and bean sprouts and coconut makes it always fresh and clean to the taste, the chillies and garlic and other spices are hot and various, the delicate sauces soften the overall effect—you could get seriously interested in food if you lived in Hanoi. Of course, you'd need to be pretty careful about the hygeine in many places.

Hanoi Airport is more pleasant on departure than it was on arrival. In the airport lounge waiting for our flight I can see what Nguyen was talking about in terms of foreign influences. Over the PA system the Beatles' song, 'Ticket to Ride', is playing, which seems a lame sort of choice for an airport, while on the TV British costume dramas, dubbed into Vietnamese, are showing. At the airport in Saigon the TV discloses the even more remarkable feat of dubbing *The Lion King* into Vietnamese, including the original melody.

Driving in from Saigon Airport it's as if we're in a totally different world from Hanoi. It's as if, in fact, we've returned to Southeast Asia from some other strange place a long way away. The two cities could hardly be more different. For a start there's all the familiar fast-food outlets—KFC, Baskin Robbins, Dunkin Donuts. Then there is the neon, the neon is everywhere. And as we drive into the city I can see another cultural artefact ubiquitous in most Southeast Asian cities and strangely absent in Hanoi—the multi-storey, air-con shopping complexes. These are the undeniable harbingers of a local middle class and their presence cheers me greatly.

I find my spirit lifting overall. Saigon, though its streets are clean by most Southeast Asian standards, is dirtier than Hanoi. I rejoice in this dirt, for it is the dirt of freedom—limited, constrained, fragile, but compared with Hanoi a lot of freedom. Even as we drive in we can see how many bars there are everywhere. If Hanoi is Beijing of the mid-1980s, Saigon is Bangkok 25 years ago.

And the thing about Bangkok twenty-five years ago is that it grew up to become the Bangkok of today—prosperous, middle class, democratic.

My reaction is the opposite of that of most foreigners, who coo and bill over the antiquity of Hanoi and tut-tut at Saigon's racy boisterousness. But antiquity, the living ancient, the survival of very old ways of doing things—these are often a sign of poverty, of a brutal restriction in people's life choices. I recall reading about Mother Teresa picking up a new-born baby left to die in some rubbish dump in Calcutta and exclaiming with wonder: 'Look, there's life in it.'

I feel just the same about Saigon, it's so pulsatingly alive. It's true that it doesn't have some of the comforts for the foreigner of a Stalinist city (even one in which the Stalinism is clearly in decay, like Hanoi). For one thing, you're much more likely to get mugged in Saigon than in Hanoi, as Jessie and I will discover directly.

Saigon and Hanoi differ in countless ways. There is still great discrimination in Vietnam against ethnic Chinese. It was only as recently as the late 1970s that the Vietnamese Government actually ordered all ethnic Chinese to leave Vietnam, an act which hugely boosted the refugee outflow. Ethnic Chinese are disproportionately present in Saigon.

Similarly there is great discrimination against anyone who had anything to do with the old South Vietnamese Government and its military forces. Many of the cyclo drivers in Saigon are ex-South Vietnamese soldiers who cannot get other jobs. This discrimination echoes down the generations. Their children have difficulty getting into state-run universities or getting government jobs. After the war many former residents of Saigon were sent to harsh re-education camps. Many died and many others lost their residence permits but they came back to Saigon anyway.

People in all the persecuted categories are disproportionately located in Saigon.

But with all this discrimination Saigon has thrived. It is wildly successful compared with the rest of Vietnam. The whole metropolis has a per capita income of well over US$1000, about three times the national average, while some rural areas have an income as low as US$100. The city has attracted the vast majority of foreign investment that has flowed into Vietnam.

Both Hanoi and Saigon have plenty of what the authorities call 'social evils'—drugs and prostitution. Robert Templer estimates there are between 300 000 and 600 000 sex workers in Vietnam. It's fashionable among the politically correct to blame this on the money brought in by foreign investment, or even, more tenuously still, to blame the American period. But overwhelmingly the clientele is local. Drug addiction and drug trafficking are a big deal too.

The presence of such 'social evils' does not really lead to any general conclusions except that human beings have the same vices the world over.

———

Jessie and I are staying at the Caravelle Hotel, right next to Saigon's Opera House, which, like Hanoi's, dates from the French era and exudes a certain colonial formality. By staying at the Metropole in Hanoi and the Caravelle in Saigon we have unwittingly stayed at two hotels which once, simultaneously, housed an Australian embassy each. From 1973 to 1975 Australia had diplomatic relations with both North Vietnam and South Vietnam.

The Metropole wasn't quite so comfortable in those days. An old hand tells me the Australian Embassy rented five rooms, one for the ambassador and one each for his four staff. Each bedroom doubled as an office during the day. The ambassador's room was the only one with a working ensuite bathroom. This was not an unmixed blessing for the ambassador as tummy troubles were common and his door often burst open in the middle of the night as a desperate staff member would leap over his bed to get to the bathroom.

Or so the story goes.

You can't avoid war stories in Vietnam. This is a pity in some ways because the Western obsession with the Vietnam War as a Western experience obscures the reality of Vietnam today. We are so used to the stereotypes, especially those promoted in movies, that we don't bother to pay much attention to the Vietnam of here and now.

The Vietnamese themselves don't help the process, especially in Saigon where bars associated with the war are booming. In the Caravelle itself there is an open-air bar on the ninth floor called the Saigon Saigon Bar, where, so local legend has it, reporters used to gather to watch the rockets flair and the bright lights of explosions and combat on the outskirts of the city. The night Jessie and I arrive we go up to have a look and the place is bopping, with a live band, lots of couples and larger groups, the mix about 50/50 between foreigners and locals.

Being with Jessie means I am spared most of the frankest approaches of the Saigon sex industry, which is very in-your-face. But one night Jessie and I are sitting in a window front lounge of the Caravelle having coffee. Jessie goes to the bathroom. Within a second a young woman on the pavement is offering, through unmistakable hand gestures, to come into the lounge and join me.

The Caravelle was very much a reporters' hotel during the war. It's funny how the major hotels in a city develop their special characters and their special clientele. When I was based in Washington in 1986 and 1987, I several times went to El Salvador to cover the civil war. In the capital, San Salvador, I always stayed at the Camino Real, which was full of journalists. The Government and its guests stayed at the El Presidente, whereas the CIA, so it was said, stayed at the Sheraton.

Diagonally opposite the Caravelle is the Rex. During the war it was full of senior US soldiers and somehow, decked out in a shocking red, it still bears that look. It too has a magnificent rooftop bar, much bigger than the Caravelle's, where the military used to hold their briefings. The night we go there the clientele, except for us, is purely Vietnamese.

Just beyond the Rex is the Continental where much of *The Quiet American* is set. Many of these central Saigon hotels openly recall both the Vietnam War and the French colonial period. Saigonese know that a lot of visitors will be interested in this stuff. Their frank money-making desires strike me as almost wholly wholesome. The desire to work hard and earn a living is one of the most constructive instincts known to mankind. Those who deprecate commerce deprecate an innate part of life itself.

Because it's night when we arrive Jessie and I don't get to do our orientation walk until the next morning and then we see what a pretty part of town we're in. The Opera House area has been spruced up and looks a picture. The main drag of Saigon, a wide, tree-lined boulevarde of heavy traffic (like Hanoi lots of motorbikes but many more cars) runs right up to the Opera House with the Caravelle on one side and the Continental on the other.

We walk a few blocks past the Rex and come across air-con coffee houses and pastry shops, designer-label boutiques, little folk art galleries, other art establishments where you can get your portrait painted, others still where famous paintings are expertly reproduced.

Then we come to the Catholic cathedral, Notre Dame. There was a time of communist zealotry when Catholic services weren't allowed in Vietnam, and Catholics generally (like Buddhists) have been much persecuted by the communists. Now the cathedral functions both as a working church and a tourist attraction.

It doesn't have the dead, deserted, locked-up look that the cathedral in Hanoi had when we visited. Instead the old Catholic service of Benediction, in which the Eucharist is venerated but no mass is said, is under way.

The cathedral is open to visitors and tourists several hous a day but when mass or Benediction or some other service is taking place the cathedral's supervisors not unreasonably ask tourists to stay out, to allow the people who actually want to use it as a church to do so without being gawped at by a lot of rubber-necking blow-ins.

I nonetheless proceeded to behave myself just like an enthusiastic if perhaps unusually cunning rubber-necking blow-in. We walk up to the gates and witness a scene that could have come from a textbook on *The Ugly American.*

Don't get me wrong, I like Americans. I'm the opposite of anti-American and most of the Americans I meet on my travels are friendly and almost ludicrously courteous. But the American accent in the wrong hands does lend itself to arrogance and because America is so powerful it's easy for people to feel especially aggrieved at American arrogance.

Jessie and I approach the iron gates of the cathedral which are being held shut by the frail hands of a small, older man.

An affluent young American guy, maybe early twenties, close-cropped hair though not I would think military, a big camera hanging round his neck, is acting as spokesmen for a few of his friends.

'Our guidebook says the cathedral is meant to be open now!' he shouts as though the old guy is deaf.

'Now close, tomorrow open.'

'But I can see the people in there. Why won't you let us in if there are people in there?'

'Now close, tomorrow open.'

'You people do not live up to your promises, you don't meet your obligations.'

There are few things more revolting than watching an affluent young Western man badger and harangue an innocent, emaciated and impoverished old cathedral keeper, but I've got to hand it to the old guy. His will is stronger than the American's and the bumptious young fellow eventually storms off, leading his friends with him.

I wait till the American is well clear and then make my own approach to this admirable old man. I can see that the old guy doesn't have much English but I take a guess that he will speak French.

'Excusez-moi, monsieur, nous sommes Catholiques.'

To tell you the absolute truth my French is pretty limited and I couldn't quite catch every nuance of his reply which was a long stream of French, I suspect mostly about the just departed Americans. But while he is saying all this he opens the gate and lets Jessie and me in. I nod heartily in general agreement with whatever he's saying.

This little encounter is good for my soul. I cannot betray my new friend on the gate by now behaving like a true tourist, wandering up and down, talking all the while and taking some happy snaps of Vietnamese at prayer. Instead Jessie and I slip quietly into a pew and say a few prayers of our own. The congregation is not very big and overwhelmingly it is made up of women, not all of them old but all of them past their first youth.

You have to respect the devotion of these women, their hair covered, heads bent forward in serious prayer. What's the bet that not a single woman in the church was praying for herself but rather asking God's help for a wayward son, a daughter soon to marry, a husband in travail?

That afternoon we explore several of Saigon's indoor markets. Walking down the main drag to get to the first, we see a strange sight. The footpath is covered with informal traders selling everything from fruit and vegetables to knick-knacks and postcards. All of a sudden they pick up their merchandise and disappear. The police are coming by. Vietnam's social structure is so thoroughly corrupt that the police have a lot of trouble when they arrest, on traffic or even drugs offences, a son of a high or even middle ranking partry cadre. This makes the police cautious about who they pull over and limits their ability to collect fines. But the street vendors are frequently people who can't get another job, often because they are from one of the persecuted groups in society. So the police can harrass them for permits and informal considerations to their hearts' content.

The indoor markets Jessie and I see make no claim to antiquity, unlike Hanoi's District of Thirty-six Streets. They are purely functional, just great big barns stacked with all kinds of merchandise, the huge floor areas divided into intricate lattice-works of makeshift alleys and passages. Jessie picks up essential supplies like table napkins and cutlery, stuff they don't have in Australia. Everybody everywhere is bargaining. I don't know what a merchant would do if anyone was ever silly enough to pay the price initially asked. He'd probably keel over with shock. The places are all packed. Saigon is a populous city and everywhere you go is stacked with people.

Except one place. Jessie and I come upon the Revolution Museum. An old ornate French building of imposing proportions, it now bears a series of exhibits testifying to the communist struggle in Vietnam's history. Outside the building, taking advantage of the grand backdrop of the French architecture, a young couple, she in dazzling white Western wedding dress, he in black dinner suit, are having their photographs taken.

Inside the museum there are plenty of official guides but not one single patron other than Jessie and me. Not a sinner anywhere to be found. It is startling, and the more startling the more you reflect on it. In Canberra the National War Museum is always full or nearly full. It's the only place, apart from sportsgrounds, that gives you an authentic sense of the sacred in Australia. In Washington DC there are always people at the Vietnam War monument. In Saigon I can only conclude that the communists' struggle is not something that moves the residents of this city one bit.

When you look at the exhibits it's not hard to see why. One of the unwatched, unloved exhibits concerns the fiendish American plot to sap the will of the former citizens of South Vietnam by promoting pornography and drugs back during the Vietnam War period. Why it is that the Americans would want to sap the will of their allies is left, to say the least, somewhat obscure.

The evidence of this American plot is a photograph of a long-haired young Vietnamese man playing a guitar, and a woman, apparently in some sort of beauty contest, wearing a bikini. By comparison with the raunchiness of contemporary Saigon and parts of Hanoi the American period, on this evidence, seems quite mild.

There's another reason it's difficult to take this anti-American propaganda too seriously. The restaurant which occupies the garden of the Revolution Museum is called—what else?—Miss Saigon.

Every night we are in Saigon Jessie and I go walking, either around the central shopping area or down by the river, just a few blocks from the hotel. That night, walking past the Rex, we see a truly revolting sight. There have been very few occasions in my adult life when I've been tempted to physically hit anybody. But this is one such occasion. I see a fat, oleaginous, middle-aged Western man, his belly bulging over the top of his shorts, sweat glistening on his balding pate, ineffectively covered by a few strands of greasy, brown hair, his thick black glasses sliding down his nose, walking fast with two little Vietnamese kids, two little boys, in tow.

'Look, Jessie, look at that creep with the little kids. What's he doing with those boys? I'd like to smash his head in.'

Jessie looks more thoroughly than I do, and sees things better. She also doesn't rush to judgement so much.

'No,' she says, 'you're mistaken. Look more closely where the man's hands are and where the children's hands are.'

Right!

I have got the scene completely arse about. The guy has his hands stuck firmly in his pockets, presumably holding a wallet in one and keys in another, and is trying to get away from the kids, which is why he is walking so fast. Each kid, on the other hand, is wrapped around one of his arms, trying to pull it out of his pocket, trying to get him to stop, turn around, give them some money, go with them. The poor guy nearly got clobbered and was completely innocent.

The child beggars of Saigon are a formidable crew. There are lots of them and they're tenacious. One young girl, I would guess about ten years old, sells Jessie half a dozen postcards for US$2. She then sells Jessie another batch of postcards for the same amount. Jessie's policy is to make a few contributions per walk and then stop but this kid wants a third sale and is very persistent. Amazingly she keeps up quite a patter in Enlgish as she walks along with us.

'No thanks,' Jessie finally says to her. 'I've bought some from you already. That's enough.'

'Well there's no need to be so rude about it, madame. Why'd you get so angry, anyway?'

These kids are amazing. There is a charity which teaches child beggars to speak English, on the basis that they'll make more money that way. Kids naturally learn so fast that between their lessons and chatting to tourists, a lot of them become quite fluent. Maybe it's a skill that will help them get other jobs later in life.

One night we have dinner with an Australian expat couple, Nick, a lean, tanned, older guy and Maria, a pretty blonde, whom we've been put in touch with through common friends back home. He works for an aid agency, she is in commerce. The posting is basically Maria's and Nick came along as her partner. Nick is a former Australian soldier who fought in Vietnam. He had a strange rush of emotion when he first flew into Saigon but he got over that quickly and found there were endless opportunities to make himself useful. He has now learned the Vietnamese language much more deeply than Maria has because she deals all day either with other expats or Vietnamese who speak English. He spent the first couple of weeks bumming around then learned the language very quickly. Soon enough he got a job with an aid agency and works closely with Vietnamese every day. I get the impression that Nick is really having a ball and Maria is also enjoying herself, but not quite as much.

They take Jessie and me out to a lovely restaurant where you can order Vietnamese or French. Naturally we order Vietnamese and, on their advice, dive into a seafood feast—prawns, whole fish in various sauces, the lot. We have enjoyed the food in Vietnam but we have been a bit cautious about what we eat because we have seen so many rats about. A friend in Hanoi who lives in high class Western accommodation told us she was eating a mince pie one night and had eaten half of it when she decided to get some plastic to cover the rest and put it in the fridge. She was out of the room for a second getting the plastic covering and when she returned a huge rat was up on the sideboard helping himself to the pie. But on this visit we are lucky and there is not a whisper of rebellion from our digestive systems.

After dinner, Nick, Maria, Jessie and I walk past the Caravelle and down to the river. We pass numerous hotels owned by the Vietnam Tourist Authority which are now all tarted up. The service is said to be not great in these places but they are developing a big Vietnamese clientele and a modest line in budget-conscious foreign tourists.

We explore several riverfront hotels. In one, a tall building in wedding cake white and fairy lights, we catch a lift to the top floor then climb a spiral staircase to the uppermost deck. Here we sit down for a drink at their beer garden. The view of the Saigon River is magnificent. We spy a ferry, full of motorbikes, linking a poorer area of the city to the central business district. There are floating restaurants which cruise the river after everyone has eaten. There are rice barges, timeless purveyors of the basic trade good, floating down to the sea. Across the river are a slew of huge neon signs. People love these signs, not only for the colour they bring but because the more signs that are illuminated the better is Saigon's economic health.

To sit above the Saigon River, despite its fantastic pollution, on a warm tropical night, sipping a coffee with your wife and a couple of friends, as the life of the river flows past, is just about heaven.

We have been warned by many friends, and by brochures in the hotel, to be conscious of personal security and on the alert for pickpockets, muggers and snatch-and-grab thieves. Women are advised not to carry handbags, or if they must carry them to carry small ones without any valuables inside, and not to wear jewellery. As we are walking back to the Caravelle, just around the corner from it in fact, Maria lets out a piercing scream.

It takes us all a few minutes to work out what has happened. A snatch-thief riding pillion on a motorbike has ridden close in beside her and, with what must have been an extremely sharp knife, sliced through the strap of her handbag. He has also sliced through her silk blouse but, in what was a matter of millimetres, he hasn't sliced her body. Nick, a man of action, once he determines that Maria is OK, pulls over another motorbike rider and sets off in hot pursuit of the thief, though of course he loses him in the blackness and the traffic of the night.

Maria is uninjured and lost nothing of value, but it's an unpleasant end to an otherwise beautiful evening.

It's difficult in Vietnam to get high-level official interviews. After weeks, perhaps months, of campaigning before I come to Vietnam I get a written interview with the Deputy Prime Minister. It's not very revealing. Written interviews never are because they are composed by bureaucrats whose prime objective is to avoid making a mistake. I have been writing to the Vietnamese diplomatic missions in Australia, and the foreign ministry in Hanoi, over and over for weeks requesting appointments with various officials. Nothing came through in Hanoi until the very last minute. The same goes for Saigon.

I have a number on which to ring a Mr Tran, an official in the local government, my first morning in Saigon. So far my program in Saigon consists of no official interviews. It's never a really joyous experience to go back to a newspaper office and tell your colleagues that you got to see nobody.

So, through the help of a few extraordinarily kind expats, I have semi-independently lined up one or two interviews. These include some private-sector people, some aid agency folk and even one or two government figures, the most important of whom is Le Thanh Hai, the vice-chairman of the Ho Chi Minh City People's Committee. But I'm not quite sure if it will be alright for me to keep any of these 'unofficially' arranged appointments once the ministry is informed and at the moment my official appointments book is as empty as a parliamentary debate.

As it turns out everything comes together at the last minute and I do see a succession of sober bureaucrats. They are praiseworthy people as far as I can tell but they wear me down with an unending barrage of statistics on foreign investment, projected rates of growth, project approvals, corruption trials, reform laws and the rest. All of them, singing in chorus, chant that the Government is in favour of further economic reform. None specifies in any detail what that reform might be. Who knows if their statistics correspond with reality? Until a couple of years ago the state budget in Vietnam was a state secret. Transparency is not the strong point of communist political culture.

I don't start off with a really good exchange with Mr Tran, although he is at least available on the number I ring.

'Mr Sheridan, I have been expecting your call from Hanoi.'

'Oh I'm sorry, Mr Tran, I was dealing with the foreign ministry in Hanoi. They said to ring you when I got to Sai . . . er, Ho Chi Minh City.'

'I was informed that you would ring before this. You should have rung.'

There is a pause. I'm not sure if I should apologise further. I decide that Mr Tran is probably fairly junior and while I'll make substantial efforts to placate him I'll save major sucking-up for someone more senior. After our telephonic silence has stretched on for a goodly time Mr Tran makes an announcement: 'I have arranged your program during your visit.'

'Oh, thank you very much, Mr Tran.'

'On Wednesday afternoon at three o'clock you will see some of the middle-ranking and senior editors of our city newspaper.'

'Mr Tran, that sounds wonderful. Thank you so much, but, er, I believe at that time I am supposed to be seeing Mr Le Thanh Hai, the Vice-Chairman of the Ho Chi Minh City People's Committee. I know that is a privately arranged interview but I hope that is OK with you. Of course I would love to meet the editors at some time but could we possibly reschedule that appointment as it would be very impolite of me not to see the Vice-Chairman?'

A thunderous silence ensues.

'This is most irregular. Mr Le Thanh Hai is my superior. I have not been told of this. This is most irregular. Wait in your room and I will ring you back.'

Sure enough, a couple of hours later, Mr Tran does ring back.

'You will have an appointment with Mr Le Thanh Hai at two o'clock, not three o'clock, on Wednesday afternoon. I must say I find your method of working most disagreeable and unsatisfactory.'

Fair enough.

The editors have been quashed. They are not rescheduled.

Come Wednesday and, as instructed, I arrive half an hour early at Mr Tran's office, in a different building from the People's Committee. He turns out to be friendly enough in the flesh. I guess communist officials just don't like unpredictability. Probably my requests didn't physically reach him until a day or two before I arrived in Saigon. In any event, he has one more instruction for me.

He begins somewhat delicately, with a hint of reticence: 'Mr Sheridan, you are wearing a suit coat.'

This is undeniably true. I am wearing a suit coat. Guilty as charged. I don't see what the problem is, though. Admittedly it's a bit shabby and a bit baggy, but it's a dark blue so you can't really see the soup stains. Anyway, what did he expect, top hat and tails?

'The Vice-Chairman will not be wearing a suit coat.'

Another pause. I still can't see quite where this is going.

'The Vice-Chairman may feel uneasy, perhaps embarrassed, if you are wearing a suit coat and he isn't. So, I must ask you to take off your jacket and leave it here during the interview.'

No easier said than done.

The Ho Chi Minh City People's Committee houses itself in a splendid, nineteenth-century, neo-classical French building, all gold leaf and filigree, chandeliers and thick carpet, soaring ceilings and ornate bulustrades.

When I finally meet him Le turns out to be a gregarious pol, anxious to make me feel welcome and not bad at small talk. An attractive Vietnamese woman in the traditional *ao dai* costume— long flowing blouse cut at the thighs over long pantaloons—serves us tea and coffee. Le is accompanied by a small bevy of officials including an interpreter. The interpreter is also a woman but unlike the tea and coffee lady she doesn't wear the ao dai. Le welcomes me, I thank him for seeing me, he solicitously asks about Australia, I respond modestly and manage to work in a compliment about Vietnam, everything is going swimmingly until the actual interview begins.

Le starts reading a prepared statement and it is only after the first fifteen minutes or so that I realise this is not going to be a perfectly conventional interview. I summon up my courage and tremulously interrupt to ask a question. Le takes this in good spirit, he is not a bit cross with me for interrupting him, nor does he acknowledge the question in any way but merely returns to reading out the statement, which is duly translated, sentence by sentence.

There is something about listening to a lecture as the only member of the audience which makes it harder to concentrate than if you're part of a crowded lecture theatre. You have to work so hard to keep your body at an attitude of attention. It is desperately difficult to take in anything that's being said.

Nonetheless Le's words are not without interest. I'm surprised to hear him boast, for example, that half of Saigon's tertiary students are at full fee-paying universities. I'm also surprised to hear him admit some faults on the Government's part: 'The management of some state authorities had some red tape problems and also some embezzlement and corruption problems.'

I leave Le grateful for his kindness at having seen me but not all that much wiser about Vietnam. However he is a model of clarity and simplicity compared with the Chamber of Commerce and Industry. The chamber has instructed me to hire an interpreter for our meeting and I have engaged the services of one such person who is supposed to meet me at their office at 4 p.m.

As I get out from the taxi I come upon an incredibly cluttered footpath outside the chamber's compound, with all manner of motorbikes and vans and cars squashed onto the pavement. As I thread my way through these higgledy-piggledy vehicles I tread on something soft and squishy.

Uh oh.

I look down to see an enormous dead rat under my foot.

Inside the chamber couldn't be a greater contrast to the rancid footpath. I am ushered into a meeting room which looks like it was designed by Lou Reed in partnership with Mel Brooks. A huge mother-of-pearl table dominates a large, dark room. We sit in enormous red velvet chairs and both sides of the room, in front of and behind me, are covered in heavy black curtains. There is no sign of my interpreter but the two officials who see me speak perfectly good English. It's just that I can't make much sense of what they say. Perhaps the fault is mine. I still haven't recovered from the rat and the black curtains are suggestive of something sinister. It reminds me of the set for *The Rocky Horror Show*. I am inclined to leave.

About 5 p.m. I make my farewells and there in the foyer I meet a lost-looking woman who seems to have something to say to me. But she can't speak English well enough to communicate whatever her message is. One of the office staff comes over to translate for her. Arriving just as the interview finishes and as far as I can make out unable to speak more than a few words of English, the woman is my interpreter.

Commerce also provides my best experience in Saigon.

A young woman meets me at the entrance to the Tan Tao Industrial Park on the western edge of Saigon. She shows me over the premises before introducing me to her boss. This place is spic and span. The offices are all air-con and the computers are humming happily at their business. Tan Tao has, without question, the cleanest toilets in Vietnam.

My young guide can see that I'm impressed with all this, as who wouldn't be, and positively beams with pride.

'The standard for the entire park,' she says, 'is Singapore.'

I am happy to hear it. This is a sensible goal for Saigon to aim at, that business should be as efficient and hassle-free as Singapore. They won't reach Singapore's standards but it's such a good ambition, such a decent idea.

I meet her boss, Mr Pham Thi Ngoc Phuong, of the Business Division. Pham is a nuggety young guy in a crisp, short-sleeve, blue business shirt and bold red tie and, symbol of the up-and-coming businessman of Bangkok circa twenty-five years ago, a clunky Rolex watch. He has a pot plant on his desk, a swivel chair and an air-con unit nearby—these must be some of the best working conditions in Vietnam.

He is all energy and bustle and full of stats about the park—sixty hectares of ninety are leased, eight foreign companies, twenty-five domestic ones, 80 per cent utilisation, all that sort of stuff. I haven't the faintest idea if the park's a roaring success or a white elephant but it looks good and it feels good. If Vietnam has a decent future it's being built here by Pham and his colleagues.

Pham did his first degree in maritime studies and joined a merchant ship. He regularly visited South Korea and Singapore for work and he saw how things were done in these successful Asian tigers. This is one of the most beneficial dynamics in the world. Half of human success comes from watching someone else's performance and thinking: 'Hey, I can do as well as that.' Living in a successful neighbourhood is a much neglected factor in the economic success of nations.

Pham realised he'd like to work in business and did a combined law and economics degree. Now, as well as running the Business Division, he's doing an MBA from a British university. He fairly bursts with pride in his industrial park. God bless you Pham. As the football commentators would say, 'Go, you good thing.'

The young woman who welcomed me initially now shows me out. She takes me downstairs and out through the front office. Pham and I have talked through the whole morning and now it is lunchtime. To my surprise all the workers in the front office have their heads down and are fast asleep.

'They are having a small snap,' my guide says.

The other place I'd expect to meet the same can-do, practical approach to life is at the Red Cross, but it doesn't quite work out that way.

Dr Minh Tam is the president of the city's Red Cross and talks winningly of her work. The effect is spoilt somewhat, however, by having to sit under the baleful gaze of the old tyrant, Ho Chi Minh in yet another of the several million statues of him, this one in Dr Minh's office.

Dr Minh is a good woman who does great work. No one would deride her efforts. No one, similarly, could take her statistics seriously. She tells me there are 15 000 HIV positive people in Vietnam, including 3000 in Saigon alone. This is a ridiculous underestimate.

On the other hand she seems admirably direct in admitting: 'Drugs and prostitution are growing problems. Drug abuse is a big problem among young people and is growing rapidly, especially heroin abuse. Drugs are very cheap here.'

Up to this point I'm listening to a solid health professional. Then she says: 'We don't know where the drugs supply comes from.'

Gimme a break. Lots of people have told me that some drugs are produced locally but most are smuggled in from the Golden Triangle. It's hard to know why saying that, or anything like it, could be so dangerous.

When Dr Minh describes the problems she faces it ends up being a familiar story. Young people without jobs and without education, young people coming in from the provinces chasing jobs and not getting them—these are ready-made victims of the 'social evils'.

Saigon and Hanoi are both fascinating cities. I'd be happy to spend a lot of time in either of them. They are fantastically different. They seem to represent not only different societies but different time zones, different periods of history, as well as radically different outlooks. Yet it is difficult not to leave Hanoi and Saigon without a sense of frustration. Vietnam has so many things going for it—the tradition of valuing education, the proximity both to the giant market of China and the growing economies of Southeast Asia, a large population and a disciplined workforce, the desire of virtually all the international community that Vietnam should succeed. All this surely means that Vietnam should be running at a much higher level than it is.

The Government's performance has got better in recent years and so has the economy's. But it's worth remembering that this is off an extremely low base, as the economists would say.

That there is so little criticism of Vietnam in the West for its human rights record is a testament to the powerful, unresolved and often counter-productive feelings of guilt and error which most Western commentators still harbour about the Vietnam War.

But we should be quite clear about this. Vietnam's modern human rights record is atrocious. I learned this directly because all my first trips into Asia were interviewing Vietnamese refugees. For one project I interviewed dozens of men who had suffered in the harsh, brutal re-education camps. These were monstrously cruel and many, many people died in them. They weren't death camps as such but death was a frequent by-product of the way people were treated in these camps. Most often if Western commentators are forced to confront this human rights disaster they fall back on saying something like, 'Well, at least they weren't as bad as the Khmer Rouge.'

It's true, they weren't anywhere near as bad as the Khmer Rouge.

But they were pretty bloody bad.

The persecution of ethnic Chinese and anyone associated with the former South Vietnamese Government led directly to the huge refugee outflow, what became known as the boat people.

I'll never forget going to Pulau Bidong island in Malaysia in the mid-1980s to interview refugees in a camp which over the years accomodated hundreds of thousands of refugees. Getting there involved a journey of a couple of hours in a tiny boat leaving from Trengannu during the monsoon season. That journey alone made me marvel at the determination of people who would travel by rivercraft hundreds or thousands of kilometres from their home.

The first person I met at Pulau Bidong was Nguyen Dinh Qui, a small, softly spoken man who gave the impression above all of thoughtfulness, that his words were well considered. Nonetheless he had a ready smile or laugh for a friend, even a new friend.

But Nguyen's story was overwhelming. Hearing it was one those times in my life as a reporter when I have felt completely inadequate, that any response I could make was worthless.

That Nguyen could ever laugh or smile again is a testament to the courage within him. He and his wife had left Vietnam on a boat that landed on an oil rig in the South China Sea. They were three days at sea with thirty-six people on the boat and were taken from the oil rig to Pulau Bidong, from where Nguyen, ultimately successfully, applied to resettle in Australia.

Nguyen's story indicates the deep insanity which lay at the heart of twenthieth-century communism. He had come to Australia under the Colombo Plan in the late 1960s. He studied electrical engineering, completing his degree in 1972. He was influenced by the Australian political environment of the time and considered himself to be on the moderate Left. He returned to Vietnam in 1972 and worked as a senior engineer in the state power company.

In April, 1975, with the fall of Saigon imminent, American friends offered him the chance to leave.

'I decided to stay,' he told me, as we sat together outside one of the camp huts in the brilliant sun of Pulau Bidong that day.

'I believed the new Government would remove corruption and I wanted to participate in rebuilding Vietnam.'

The new communist Government didn't see it that way, however. Nguyen had two fatal strikes against him—he had studied in the decadent West and he had worked for the anti-communist government of South Vietnam. That meant he was convicted without offence, and without trial. So even though he had decided to stay in Vietnam to support the new Government, he was sent to a re-education camp for a year. In that time he lost much of what people would consider a normal life—possessions, income, the ability to look after his family. And of course the regime in the camp was extremely harsh.

But still he hoped he could build a new life and help build a new nation. Then in the late 1970s, in a fit of paranoid xenophobia, the Government told its ethnic Chinese that they were no longer welcome. They should leave, though the Government made no orderly arrangements for this, instead expecting people to bribe them to leave. Nguyen's wife is ethnic Chinese so the two, by now despairing of their country, tried to escape. The authorities let many boats leave, others they impounded and put the people in prison.

Nguyen and his wife in 1978 paid all the appropriate bribes and joined 400 others on a boat organised by the Vietnamese secret police. Their boat capsized and their two children—a boy aged five and a girl aged four—were drowned. As he told me this Nguyen's voice was without emotion. In this passage it had that flat, affectless quality I've noticed in others who have gone through similar experiences, as though the way to deal with it is to treat it, in speech at least, as distantly as possible. Nguyen's home was confiscated and he and his wife, half mad with grief, had to sponge accommodation from relatives.

Nguyen and his wife made more attempts to escape. Escape became their obsession, the purpose of their lives. Sometimes they were captured, sometimes sent to prison. Finally, more than a decade after the fall of Saigon, they made it to Malaysia and later to Australia.

Months later I got a letter from Nguyen, happy in Australia, surprised I had written about him, grateful for the attention, simply astounding in his resilience and dignity.

Nguyen's story is why I feel I have experienced three Vietnams. Hanoi is one Vietnam. Saigon is another, totally different. And then there is the third, made up of the one-and-a-half million Vietnamese who fled their homeland in the years after the communist victory and who live now in Australia, the US, France, Canada and many other countries of the world.

The presence of these people in our society is an inestimable benefit for us and a tragic loss for Vietnam.

As an Irish Australian I grew up on songs of exile and flight, laments for the homeland. Of course, as contemporary Australians these songs didn't reflect our lives, but we loved the music and honoured the memories of our ancestors who lived through such experiences.

I found similar songs, similar sentiments, in the countless Vietnamese refugee functions I attended in Sydney. In a sense, my first trips into Asia were to the Saigon of the 1960s, displaced a few thousand kilometres and a decade or two into the western suburbs of Sydney.

As a friend of the South Vietnamese I can't believe how badly they've been slandered by Hollywood. For Hollywood's fake and superficial guilt about the Vietnam War has seen it make an endless ideological reparation payment only to the communists. It is surely possible to criticise US policy in the Vietnam War without endorsing the brutal communist dictatorship which overwhelmed the south in 1975.

In truth Hollywood's guilt is only a symptom of its narcissism. The story in any Hollywood treatment of the Vietnam War is only ever really about the Americans, or very occasionally the other Westerners, in Vietnam. This is true even of a self-consciously arty film such as *The Quiet American*. But if you think about virtually all of Hollywood's treatments of Vietnam after the war the Vietnamese themselves hardly exist as characters. The northern soldiers are without exception rendered as heroically brave, especially if they are women. The only partial exception is if they are guarding US POWs. But the only decency allowed to South Vietnamese is when they reveal themselves as communists, as in Fowler's assistant in *The Quiet American.*

The treatment generally of the South Vietnamese in these films is one of the gross slanders of history. The women are without exception prostitutes or near-prostitutes. The men, if soldiers, are depicted as corrupt cowards or psychopaths, and if not soldiers as corrupt businessmen. It's as if the whole society of South Vietnam had never existed, yet we know in the years 1972 to 1975 especially the South Vietnamese Army engaged in countless acts of heroism. The film, *Good Morning Vietnam*, was remarkable in presenting at least a few non-political South Vietnamese as human beings rather than ideological props and colourful backdrops and even showing a South Vietnamese woman who declined to have an affair with an American soldier.

The Western imagination, in lazy thrall to the left liberal inter- pretation of the Vietnam War, has reduced Vietnam to a kind of *Miss Saigon* of the Soul, full of exotic colours, bright lights and sexual promise, essentially a backdrop to our own twisted morality plays, but utterly divorced from the nation of real men and women struggling to get past the insane ideology of its ruling party and to earn a decent living, provide a decent life.

Hanoi and Saigon induce frustration but they induce hope as well.

They are not twins, but they are siblings in the great Vietnamese family. It's a family worth getting to know.

Getting Canto Kicks at the Hong Kong Flicks

Hong Kong's new airport could be Kuala Lumpur's twin. They both bask in more glass than you could ever imagine, with huge, tall ceilings. Both have high-speed rail connections to the main city. As I fly into Hong Kong from KL I can't help remembering the old airport, Kai Tak. Even after Hong Kong had become well and truly wealthy Kai Tak remained a crowded, dense, foetid little place, with sub-par facilities, jostling corridors, not enough seats at the departure gates. Its great redeeming feature was the spectacular sense you got as you flew in of the old Hong Kong, its crowded housing and cramped, dingy streets. You used to be able to just about see what people were eating for dinner through their kitchen windows, so close did the planes swoop between the high-rise residences in their approach to the old Kai Tak.

The new airport is nothing like that. It had a chaotic opening but today it could hardly be more efficient. It takes me less than half an hour from landing to actually being inside a taxi heading for the city.

In central Hong Kong the traffic is monstrous but the highway from the airport is smooth and fast. Hong Kong has become so affluent now it's hard to remember when it was poor, so much a byword for being rancid and filthy, its future so uncertain: 'on borrowed time in a borrowed place' as Han Su-yin famously described it.

I am travelling without Jessie and the boys. I have come to fulfil a few lecture commitments, promote a book and undertake some gentle enquiries about one of the great cultural artefacts of our time—the Hong Kong film industry.

I am staying at a hotel on the main Hong Kong island, in Central itself, the business and political centre. The tourist ghetto—Nathan Road and Tsimshatsui, with its cluster of five-star hotels, miles of expensive shopping and girlie bars—is across the water in Kowloon, on the Hong Kong tip of the Chinese mainland. Central is much more refined: suits, suits and suits are the order of the day.

The hotel I'm staying at is ghastly expensive. Hong Kong's economy has been having a bit of a rough trot over the last few years but it's still an incredibly affluent and expensive city, as my hotel attests. It's a nice enough hotel, but the room is tiny, as is the Hong Kong custom. However, the location has its compensations. I'm near ferries and subways and all the various public transport systems in which Hong Kong excels.

I'm barely inside the door of my room, wondering how it will accomodate both a suitcase and me, when a reporter and photographer arrive from *The South China Morning Post* to interview me about the book I'm promoting. Somehow they swarm into the room, occupying crevices of space I wouldn't have guessed existed. They're fast, furious and efficient. Although the room is not big enough to swing a cat the photographer contrives a vaguely atmospheric shot involving the bedside lamp, which somehow gives the impression I'm reclining in a spacious study and looks remarkably good in the paper the next day; the reporter extracts whatever information she needs in a trice; then they're gone.

Hong Kong is fast.

Fast, hot, efficient, and maybe a little manic.

Tsimshatsui is not only the tourist ghetto, it's a neon ghetto. If neon were an endangered species, Hong Kong would be its nature park, its wildlife refuge, its heartland. Neon runs wild here. Hong Kong has always prided itself on being the place to shop. It surely sets the benchmark for more neon advertisements per square foot than anywhere.

Central is more dignified. Tsimshatsui has its swanky places too but in Central you just routinely expect to be browsing and sluicing in imitation English clubs with local nabobs.

Hong Kong has been an important trading city for a long time. It's been important politically for a long time too, even though for most of British rule it didn't really have politics, at least in the conventional sense. The events surrounding its reversion to mainland Chinese sovereignty in 1997 were a huge political test for Beijing, which on the whole Beijing has passed pretty well. But Hong Kong's greatest significance, apart from offering a life chance to millions of refugees and their offspring, has not been economic or political. It's been cultural.

Suzie Wong, the Pearl of the Orient, the Fragrant Harbour— Hong Kong has furnished more images in the Western mind of Asia, or at least East Asia, than any other city. The classical images of Hong Kong are out of date now. Today it's an affluent, sophisticated city, with an intricate and infinitely complex relationship with mainland China.

For my sins, my profession is that of a political journalist. I gotta tell you, overall, I love this profession. But it has its drawbacks. It involves not only talking to politicians but also to large numbers of officials. Some of them are interesting, some dull. Covering the economic aspects of politics can be deadly dull, although this is what affects people's lives. Covering the defence and security aspects of politics can be scary, either outright scary like on the border between North and South Korea, or conceptually scary as when officials are telling you all the things that weapons of mass destruction can do and how easy they are to produce and traffic.

But over the years, while still relishing the political assignment, I've become more and more interested in the underlying cultural issues. Some smartie once said human beings of different cultures are 99 per cent the same, but it's the 1 per cent difference that creates all the interest.

I'm inclined to agree with that. Now, apart from just talking to folks generally, I'm increasingly drawn to expressions of popular culture, movies and novels chief among them, for clues to that fascinating 1 per cent. In Hong Kong the 1 per cent is vividly, often luridly, on display in its great film industry.

Hong Kong and Bombay—Bollywood—are the two great non-American centres of film in Asia. No one generally thinks of Hong Kong as a cultural centre yet its films are one of Asia's great cultural achievements.

Hong Kong has had a film industry for a long time and it's remarkably influential and successful, if not today producing at anything like the rate of its glory days. Hong Kong still has the third-largest film industry in the world, after Hollywood and Bollywood, but whereas once it churned out 400 films a year, now it's fewer than 100.

Like all of HK's industries, it has to face up to a raft of new challenges, many of them brought about by those first cousins, globalisation and technology. The industry is under attack from a range of new forces. These include piracy, the mainland, the popularity of Hollywood, the local economy, local demographics, the development—often in imitation of Hong Kong—of competing Asian movie industries and, most important of all, consumer taste. SARS had its doleful effects on audiences too. Who wants to be in a cinema where someone coughing could be dangerous? But SARS was a temporary glitch.

But all this isn't necessarily a death sentence. The film industry is like other industries—it must adapt if it wants to thrive. Wong Jing, a fat, moon-faced man, his neck bulging out of his tight collar and tie, explains all this in a scruffy, disorderly office high up in a grimy old building in Kwun Tung, on the edge of Kowloon.

'Actually I think our peak period was around 1992, after 1994 it was downhill all the way. In '92 it was a bubble industry. Some amateurs got into it and there were some triad cases because it was too easy to make money. All the triads poured money into the business. Most of them made lousy movies.'

He pauses, thoughtful, fair-minded man that he is, and adds: 'Of course, some of them made good movies.'

Wong is a considerable figure in Honkers movies. Mainly a director, he has been involved as director, actor, scriptwriter or in some other capacity in 250 films.

'Piracy and the economic downturn [since 1997] mean there is no hot money for us to make movies anymore.'

Piracy is a huge problem. The HK government tries to crack down but the pirate factories just move over the border into mainland China. Technology makes piracy so easy. Even if a pirate can't bribe someone at a cinema where a movie is showing to let them make a direct copy, they can just sit in the cinema with a souped-up video CD camera and film it while it shows. It won't give you a high-quality print but you can have a DVD on sale for HK$20 (US$2), an hour after the movie is finished. And if the whole family can watch it at home so cheaply why should they bother going to the cinema?

The death or disablement of Hong Kong's Cantonese film industry would be a tragic loss to the world, similar to losing the white tiger or the humpback whale. The Cantonese film industry is one of the great non-American forces of global culture. It has always had a huge following in its own territory and across the Chinese diaspora. It has been especially strong in Taiwan, Singapore and Chinese communities in the US, Canada and Australia. It has been a big force in Malaysia. I have watched a lot of Cantonese movies in KL over the years, not least whiling away a quiet Sunday afternoon at Balwinder's flat watching some high-speed kung fu police comedy with sub-titles. Cantonese film was particularly strong in Vietnam and had a good following throughout Southeast Asia. It was watched by lots of folks in Japan and Korea too.

Most of the Asian faces the West associates with movies are 'cross-overs' from the Hong Kong industry: Jackie Chan, Chow Yun Fat, Jet Li, Michelle Yeoh and before them Bruce Lee.

Despite the recognition these stars are gaining the international market is not what it was, as Wong Jing explains. 'Take Taiwan. It used to be a great support for the Hong Kong film industry. But now the whole of Taiwan has changed—its lifestyle, its social composition. They've got cable TV and lots of other entertainments, they don't need so many movies. And there aren't many poor people, only poor people go to movies all the time.'

Here is a paradox of the glamorous movie industry—it appeals disproportionately to the poor. Witness Bollywood's vast popularity among the poor of India. Thirty years ago going to the cinema in Hong Kong meant a night of affordable glamour and a temporary escape into dreams. It was a night of air-con, an alternative to people's overcrowded, tiny and generally stinking-hot, definitely non-air-con, apartments. These dynamics keep poor Indians going to Hindi movies by the millions every week.

But now Hong Kongers are so hip and affluent and cool and globalised and air-con and sophisticated and well-travelled and English-speaking, you need to do something extra to entice them to the cinema. When they *do* go to the cinema they want quality, quality, quality.

This week in Hong Kong as it happens I see the inside of two apartments. I'm invited to one by Frank, an expat American, an old friend from my Washington correspondent days. He works in a top job for a big international bank and lives at Emerald Hill, a swank expat apartment block. There are security men downstairs, a swimming pool in the complex and all manner of mod-cons. Yet the notable thing about the apartment is that it wouldn't rate as even modest middle-class accommodation for a family of five (Frank and his wife have three kids) in Sydney for San Francisco, simply because it's too small, though Frank has removed one of the inner walls to create a bigger living area.

Then there was Bill's place. He's another American, another old friend. His apartment is halfway up the hill on Hong Kong island towards the Peak. It's in the middle of a busy district and noisy as all get out. To combat this, the landlord has installed the most primitive double glazing. There are simply two sheets of glass, a few centimetres apart, in each window, but they aren't vacuum-sealed as in real double glazing. Bill has a new American wife and an adopted Chinese daughter, cute as can be, since I saw him last. His apartment, unlike Frank's, wasn't designed for expats but for locals so it has three very small bedrooms and two bathrooms. In the old days this allowed several families to occupy one apartment. He has turned one of the bedrooms into a TV room but it's such a small place that you seem to be sitting only centimetres away from the screen.

However, both these apartments represent sybaritic indulgence compared with most apartments occupied by most Chinese. Several years earlier I had visited another apartment on the lower reaches of the hill leading up to the Peak. It was the headquarters of a Catholic charity doing work in mainland China and was occupied by an elderly couple, another single, middle-aged woman and the charity's office. It too was notionally a three-bedroom apartment but its total floor size would have been less than the average Sydney living room. You entered into the main room which was a combined lounge and kitchen and had one wall lined with books. Inside they had turned the main bedroom, which was the size of a large walk-in wardrobe, into the office of the charity and so there were files and, miraculously, two desks with computers. The couple occupied one bedroom and the single woman another. Because there were two minute bathrooms everyone had a semblance of privacy. When I gently enquired as to how they managed to contain themselves in such a small space they were incredulous at my thinking. This was plenty of space for only three people, they said.

OK. Enough with the real estate survey already. You get the idea. Hong Kong flats are not very big. So while Hong Kong has become much more affluent, space is still scarce. But now family sizes are much smaller, and several families to an apartment much less common, apartments are a fraction bigger and everyone has money to be out partying, or enjoying the best electronic entertainments at home. Going to the movies is a bit passé.

I decide to watch a movie being shot. I'm due a bit of glamour here. The idea is I'll be rubbing shoulders with Canto movie stars, hanging out with them in hip bars, watching kung fu stunts, sipping champagne with the crew after a tough take, maybe giving a little advice on how to make the dialogue pithier. OK I'm just kidding on that last one, but you see where I'm heading.

Finding a film being shot while I'm in Hong Kong is not all that difficult because films are being shot all the time. I travel out with a minder from the film company to Sha Tin, a suburb out in the New Territories, still part of Hong Kong but beyond Kowloon, further in towards 'mainland' China. Sha Tin is quite different from either Tsimshatsui or Central. Hong Kong is more diverse than its image would suggest. There are spacious farming areas of Hong Kong near the China border. There are big parks. There are calm suburbs. But the freneticism of Hong Kong island and Kowloon are the city's enduring images.

Anyway there's nothing too frenetic happening in film world tonight. We arrive at a scrabbly-looking golf driving range. All East Asians it seems are obsessed with golf, especially those who live in places like Honkers which are too small to have many golf courses.

For a long time after we arrive nothing happens at all. Finally a camera crew and a production manager turn up. The production manager ambles over to say hello and whines in a good-natured way about his pitiful budget. The whole budget for the film is about US$500 000.

'How does that compare with Hollywood, with American movies, even the independents?' he asks.

Well, what can I say?

Nonetheless, I make an effort: 'You know, they say being poor and clever can sometimes be a powerful combination in the creative fields.'

He looks at me as though I've gone completely crackers, shakes his head and gently drifts off.

The star shows up and starts right in practising his golf driving on the range. The scene involves the star, who is the 'hero' of the movie, although I think he's also the gangsta, practising his golf while watched by two burly bodyguards, and, all unknown to him, two Special Branch agents in a nearby car.

This is certainly all a bit less high-tech than the set of *Titanic*, nor is it even Charlton Heston parting the waves in *The Ten Commandments*. The film company, with commendable frugality, has rented only lanes 100 to 108. The other hundred are occupied, sporadically, by members of the public who evince not the slightest interest in the filming.

When the director yells 'Action!' the extras at lanes 100 to 107 leap up and start swinging their clubs. None of the public is remotely distracted from their pursuit of the little white ball. Some of the extras connect with the golf balls but most would do well not to give up their day, or night, jobs to take up golf as a paying proposition. The movie star, in lane 108, is apparently a keen golfer in real life. He's going to get maximum value out of his time at the driving range. He just keeps swinging all the way through, from the time he arrives until, presumably, long after I've left, whether the cameras are rolling or not. He knows a free session at the driving range is not something to be trifled with.

There couldn't be more than fifteen people from the film company there (including me and the minder and the extras) for the whole production.

'The film company has provided some light refreshments,' the minder announces with relish, with even a little triumph in his voice at the prodigies of movieland hospitality.

I see a small, lumpy woman emerge out of the night. She is short and squat and wearing some kind of apron-cum-overall. She is also carrying a plastic bag and I presume at first she is a Hong Kong bag lady, picking up bits and pieces from people's cast-offs at the driving range. It turns out she is the film company's hospitality dispenser. Wordlessly she reaches into the plastic bag, pulls out a lukewarm can of Coke and thrusts it into my hand.

Ah, the glamour.

This is a lean and hungry industry in a fat and frantic city.

My intrepid pursuit of the industry does not end at Sha Tin. There is Disco Bay to come.

The next night I feel like a minor character in a James Bond movie, much more what I had in mind at Sha Tin. I have been instructed to take the four o'clock boat from the Star Ferry terminal not far from my hotel. A government minder, a dapper little man named Mr Tam, is with me as we sail across to Discovery Bay, on Lantau Island. Disco Bay, as the locals call it, is an enclave of the rich and cosmopolitan in Honkers.

There Mr Tam is rung on his cell phone and passes me a number, of another cell phone (if there are seven million people in Hong Kong there must be twenty million cell phones) which I, and only I, am to ring. This I duly do. The voice at the other end declines to disclose its identity but after a brief exchange and another short pause calls me back, again on Mr Tam's phone, with instructions to walk forward towards the main fountain in the rather Italianate piazza and stand in open view. I will be contacted in due course.

All this secret identity checking and mysterious instruction reminds me of *The Honourable Schoolboy*, John le Carré's best spy novel (which is substantially set in Hong Kong) in which the legendary George Smiley of Her Majesty's Government matches wits not only with the fiendish Chinese but the devilish Americans as well.

One thing I've always liked about that novel is le Carré's description of the HK Foreign Correspondents' Club in which 'a score of journalists, mainly from former British colonies—Australian, Canadian, American—fooled and drank in a mood of violent idleness'.

What a lovely phrase—'a mood of violent idleness'. It describes perfectly the state that often sets in among journalists in a group.

But I must say it's a mood to which I've never succumbed myself. I take my idleness in repose. I like idle, I like it as a verb—I like to idle. I idle well. For me idling is an idyll.

Enough of that. The point is that I'm quite happy to stand here at the piazza at Disco Bay for twenty minutes in the sultry evening with the polite and helpful Mr Tam, unaware what the night may yet hold.

I am seeking to interview Theresa Lee—Lee Yee Hung in Cantonese, twentysomething and one of the hottest stars in Cantonese film. Apparently all the falderol with the cell phones and movement directions and what-not involved Lee's assistant, who comes with her tonight, crouching in the shadows watching our arrival on the ferry, looking me over, finding apparently no insuperable objection to an interview and ringing her boss to say, as the British cop shows have it: 'Go, go, go.'

Lee arrives at last looking, as film starlets always do (I have a pretty limited experience in this area but I'll chance my arm on a generalisation here) even more fetching in the flesh than on screen or in her publicity shots and, as starlets (male or female) also always do, somewhat smaller and even skinnier than one had imagined.

Wearing shorts, dark glasses and a sloppy joe, trailing mineral water and tupperware cartons of fresh fruit, she perfectly embodies film star chic.

I tax her about the parlous times for the Cantonese film industry.

'Making a film these days is like doing charity work,' she jokes.

Lee, in the company of our respective minders, tells me her story as the sun sets over Disco Bay and the twilight brings out the expats and mixed-race couples and their kids for the evening promenade. It's such a cockamamie, unlikely, absurd rollercoaster ride to stardom she's had that, in its way, it perfectly exemplifies Hong Kong's own unlikely successes and resilience.

But Disco Bay deserves a word. There is no access to the Bay by road, so there are no cars, just little golf-style buggies for getting around. It's pedestrian-friendly. In the most frenetic city in the world it's an oasis of high-class cool and laid-back mellow. It's full of beautiful people, the odd Australian reporter and his faithful Hong Kong version Carruthers-from-the-Foreign Office sidekick honourably excepted. It's particularly attractive to mixed-race couples. There are plenty of mixed race couples in Hong Kong and they and their kids don't get hassled or anything but Disco Bay allows a couple like that to meld in with other mixed-race couples and their kids. It also probably offers a sense that neither side of the partnership has had to give up their culture or lifestyle entirely. They're living in Hong Kong but the feel is southern California.

Oh, and it's not real cheap.

Lee was born in Hong Kong but migrated with her parents to Canada at the age of six. She cried herself to sleep every night for a year, missing Hong Kong. Like most immigrant children, however, she determined to be just like everyone else around her.

Lee's is a story of identity lost and found: 'In Canada I wasn't conscious of the Chinese connection much. I went to Catholic schools. I steered away from it. When I was little it was almost like I was ashamed to be Chinese. Little kids don't like to be teased about being different. I hated going to Chinese schools on Saturdays. I'm an only child so I had no one to talk to. My parents worked very hard so they weren't around home much.

'I hated it when my mother gave me Chinese soup to take to school. Couldn't she just make me a peanut butter sandwich? She couldn't even do that right. I spoke half-Chinese, half-English sentences to my parents but basically my Chinese language was stuck at the level of a six-year-old.'

In Canada Lee did an honours degree in psychology and dreamed of being a writer. She and her Canadian boyfriend took a trip through Asia and he got to know Hong Kong for the first time, while she reconnected with the place. She went back home planning to do a masters degree in journalism. The story of how she became a movie star is ludicrously unlikely and as she tells it you get the impression that she can barely believe it herself: 'I thought OK I'll be really serious for the rest of my life but I have a whole summer so I'll just do something goofy that I'll always remember. Let's run for Miss Hong Kong, maybe I'll make some tuition money.

'I called one of my cousins for help. They do have foreign entries but I'd missed the deadline so I sent in the form for a local entry. I was waitressing at the time and I got home at 3 a.m. one night and I had an urgent message. I rang back and found out I'd been selected for an interview but the last interview was the day after. I rang my best friend and she said just pack and go. So I threw my stuff in a suitcase but I was living in Edmonton and I couldn't get a flight to Vancouver so I had to go through Minnesota and San Francisco to Hong Kong. It was twenty-five hours of flights. I got yelled at by US Immigration because my connections were so tight. I got into Hong Kong at 6 a.m. for an interview at 3 p.m., but I couldn't sleep before the interview.'

The interview, apparently, was a scream and offers a small episode of a benign incident of globalisation: 'TVB [a Hong Kong TV station] runs the Miss Hong Kong pageant more as a show than as a pageant really. It's often used as a vehicle by women to get into the business. But I had no idea of this. They were talking about the four Canto gods. These are four Cantonese pop singers. I thought they were talking about religion and started talking about Buddhism. In Canada I didn't keep up with Hong Kong film or TV. None of my friends was Chinese. I only remembered a few like Bruce Lee and Jackie Chan. They just all cracked up and thought that every silly thing I said was just so cute.'

At 6 p.m. the committee rang back and said she was in. It was off to Italy the next week and Lee has really never looked back. She was runner-up in the final judgment which led to a year-long contract with TVB. As her first job she was cast in a long-running soap opera as a CBC, a Canadian-born Chinese. ABCs of course are American Born Chinese, or bananas—yellow on the outside, white on the inside.

'All the people in this show were great actors, they always made it very good. I had to have people translate the script for me.'

The same charm that worked for the Miss Hong Kong committee worked with the viewers who thought the CBC character hilarious. The show's ratings, which had been sagging, shot up and Lee's career as a TV and movie star was launched.

Still, the transition from TV to movie was nerve-racking: 'I was quite picky about my first film. I was a happy hooker from Singapore, which accounted for my strange accent.'

She has the good sense to recognise that all this represents incredible good fortune: 'I'm very grateful for all this experience and everything that has come with it.'

Her success—when I meet her she has made fourteen movies and had lots of TV work—has involved a lot of the traditional manic Hong Kong approach to work: 'Mostly it was just winging it. I never had a break except when I went back to Canada to see my parents. I worked with great actors and directors. I was always the lead or the second lead so a lot of effort went into making my performance good.

'A few years ago I finally did an intensive acting course in Vancouver. It gave me some perspective. I didn't realise how good I had it until I did this. I had experience so there were some things I was real good at. In other things I wasn't as good as them and I was embarrassed. I learned some basic relaxation and breathing techniques. I'd never done auditions, so that was the worst part of the course.'

This is a pattern whole industries have followed in Hong Kong. Just rush in and do it, then when you've been successful for a few years put your head up and see if there's anything the world has to teach you about technique.

Like the production manager at the Sha Tin golf range, Lee laments the lack of resources for films in Hong Kong: 'In Hong Kong we lack time for anything, not just scriptwriting. We can't work on a film for three years and we don't have a budget of US$10 million. We can't take a whole week to make a sitcom episode. But Hong Kong people do get the job done and they get it done well. We are the second-largest exporter of films and the third-largest producer.'

The industry's international following always surprises her: 'My boyfriend [a white Canadian] had done a bit part for a series I did for TVB, because we needed a white guy. Later on he went to Vietnam for a holiday and he was conscious that everyone was looking at him weirdly in a hotel lobby. He thought what's wrong and then the hotel bellperson pointed to the TV, the series was showing right then. Any kind of yellow-coloured skin people all over the world watch Hong Kong movies and TV.

'I still tend to watch more Western films than Hong Kong films but you have to admire the Hong Kong films. But I say to our scriptwriters, how can you write a dating scene when you've been too busy to date for five years?'

Lee recognises that the industry can't take its audience for granted anymore and that the answer must come in quality and marketing: 'Now people want something more, or something different, whether it's faster or better effects or higher quality overall.'

Hong Kong has been very good to Lee and she's grateful for it. She offers an unusual vantage point on the society: 'One of the most attractive things about Hong Kong is it's truly an international society. People are brought here initially by money. In that way it's very materialistic and successful. At first people don't care about your origins because the question is, are you going to make money with me? Then friendships develop, real friendships. I've never found any resistance here as an ousider, I've always been welcomed with open arms. When they see someone can still be a Chinese but have all the foreigner's openness they like that. Now I'm very proud when I see Hong Kong people doing well abroad. China is one of the great civilisations of mankind, it's certainly something to be proud of. Culturally it's a very strong force. I'm also proud when I see Canadians doing well.

'I am always very moved by any example I see of culture shock. Part of my dream is showing cultures how to get along with each other. The entertainment industry is a great way to bring that about. But it brings me a lot of pain and sorrow when I see the culture clashes as well.'

Even in a life as thoroughly fortunate as Lee's there has been a consciousness of occasional racial prejudice: 'Unless you've been a minority you can never really understand what it feels like. Sometimes when I would go out with my boyfriend people would look strangely at us, a racially mixed couple. He would always say something sweet like they're just looking at you because you're so beautiful. But I knew it was different.

'Even now I sit sometimes with caucasian friends who forget I'm Chinese and speak ill of the Chinese in town, as if white people don't push and shove.'

Without wishing to confirm Lee's suspicion that caucasians have prejudices about Chinese pushing and shoving in Hong Kong, I have to report that pushing and shoving is a conspicuous part of the experience if you use the commuter rail system at peak hour.

I undergo this small trial in order to meet Paul Fonoroff, a legendary film critic in Hong Kong, at the Standford Hillview Hotel, which is near a subway stop and just up a little flight of stairs on a steep rise of land. The lobby lounge is tiny but accommodates us for a coffee.

Fonoroff, head shaved, muscular, hyperactive in speech, originally from Cleveland, Ohio, is one of those Western expats who have invested their lives in HK. He is fluent in Cantonese and Mandarin and writes film reviews for newspapers and TV. He has seen the film industry change: 'For a long time the Hong Kong film industry took its audience for granted. Ten years ago all the box office hits here were local movies. It's incredible anywhere in the world to have a community so strongly supporting its local film industry. But now at least half the top hits here are Hollywood movies.

'I don't always enjoy going to the movies here because the audience is so rude, always talking on their mobile phones. They tend to be better behaved for a Hollywood film.

'We've had a big Hong Kong film industry since the 1930s but only now are a couple of actors coming through like Chow Yun Fat and Jackie Chan. It's an irony that the West has finally started to notice Hong Kong films when the Hong Kong audience has started to turn off.'

And of course, *Crouching Tiger, Hidden Dragon*.

Fonoroff thinks the industry's greatest problem has been a focus on the technical wizardry at the neglect of script development.

That may be changing as Hong Kong's films become more quality-conscious in response to their market's preferences. HK's films have gone through distinct phases. The most obvious in the mid-1970s was the martial arts film and the rise of Bruce Lee. Then came kung fu-meets-comedy, especially associated with Jackie Chan. The 1980s were dominated by cops and gangstas—sometimes comedy, sometimes drama, always lots of action. Then came a slew of triad films, then a wave of farces, generally still involving martial arts of a high order. Then there was an ultra-cool, so-hip phase that inspired Qunetin Tarantino. Increasingly, movies explore relationships and reflect the full range of bourgeois concerns which Hong Kong's middle class shares with most other middle classes around the world.

The other new problem the industry faces is the mainland. The international art house circuit is very keen on mainland Chinese movies—*Raise the Red Lantern, Farewell My Concubine,* that sort of thing. Mainland movies offer Western audiences more overt exoticism. Hong Kong movies are, oddly enough, perhaps too familiar, even for Western audiences who have never seen them. The sense of familiarity arises from the mistaken idea that all Hong Kong films are action movies. There is also a Western exhaustion with the idea of Hong Kong as the exotic. It's many years since *Suzie Wong* entranced Western audiences. Despite the incredible staying power of the Hong Kong icons in the Western imagination they are getting by now a little tatty in the living room of the Western mind. Beijing and Shanghai are more alluring.

There's also a Mandarin versus Cantonese angle. Most Hong Kongers speak Cantonese but Mandarin is more widely used in mainland China and internationally. Hong Kong film-makers solve this problem by dubbing their movies into Mandarin, so there is both a Cantonese and Mandarin version of the films, and they might carry English and Chinese sub-titles. Indeed I've watched Hong Kong movies in Kuala Lumpur which are quite disfigured by having Chinese, English and Malay sub-titles all on the screen simultaneously.

As with so many industries, the Hong Kong film industry finds huge opportunities on the mainland. Hong Kong offers technical and financial expertise in abundance, the mainland provides exoticism, variety in locations, cheap labour and ultimately a huge market. Despite the chronic mainland problems of payment, copyright enforcement and regulatory chaos, it should be a match made in heaven.

No doubt in due course it will be. But it would be a tragedy beyond imagining if Hong Kong stopped producing films which reflect its own society.

After talking to all these people about movies naturally I want to go and see some of them. The first I see is *The Kid*. This is a sentimental movie, the opposite of the standard action flick Hong Kong has been so famous for. Based on the original idea for Charlie Chaplin's first feature film of the same name, it concerns a custody dispute. A rich, young securities broker loses everything on the day of the East Asian economic crash in 1997. That night on his yacht he finds a baby boy abandoned by a desperate young woman. Four years later he is raising the boy as his own. The young man has abandoned corporate life and he and the boy are living a life of wholesome, and, for the audience at least, touching and entertaining poverty.

Enter the mother. She has since struck success and comes back for her son. There are many elements of this plot that are unlikely if not implausible but the acting and direction sweep you along in easy suspension of disbelief.

The child is the cutest kid I've ever seen on screen.

I wanna, I wanna, I wanna say that Chinese kids are very cute but that's a pretty dumb statement. It doesn't make any sense to say Chinese kids are cute, as if Australian or American kids aren't. All races' kids are cute in the right circumstances.

Kids R Cute. OK?

Anyway in The Kid the scenes between the young man in his penury, happily working odd jobs, and his adopted boy, are infinitely affecting. The audience bawls their eyes out at the screening I attend. *The Kid* is also full of character and sub-plot. Shaun Tam, a legend in kung-fu films, shows he can really act by playing a middle-aged neighbourhood policeman who falls in love with a local spinster but is so shy that he is utterly ineffectual in his wooing.

I find *The Kid* a much more affecting and absorbing film than, say, the Dustin Hoffman–Meryl Streep hit *Kramer vs. Kramer*. It's also a million times better than the later Bruce Willis/Hollywood version of *The Kid*. Western audiences would love it if they ever saw it but it's neither exotically Chinese nor does it contain any super stars recognisable to Western audiences. So only a tiny number of Westerners will ever get to see it. That's a loss for Western audiences.

I go see another, *Beast Cops*, which is more the typical gangsta–bad guys–triad–rebel cops–dark hero sort of stuff. It's full of gangstas and gangstas' molls and tough guy cops right on the edge, and way beyond the edge. It has an element of character study to it and a few little film noir touches but the action is furious and incredibly grisly.

Another affecting Hong Kong movie I see is *In the Mood for Love*. This concerns a man and woman who are neighbours. They discover their spouses are having an affair with each other. The philandering spouses are never seen on screen and slowly the neighbours themselves fall in love. But their love is unconsummated, though their respective marriages break down. This movie is pure art house stuff, and indeed did well enough in Western art houses. It is infused with aching regret and loss and the sense of paths untaken. It is striking for its devastating deployment of understatement and restraint. But powerful as it is emotionally, that's really all secondary to the visual delight of the film. It is set between 1962 and 1966 and is a masterful celebration of the aesthetics of that period in Hong Kong's life. Each scene is precisely framed, as perfectly constructed as the finest painting, and the director and cinematographer wring a lyric beauty out of the cramped living quarters, the narrow hallways, the small, smoky offices and laneways where it all takes place.

Christopher Koch, in his beautiful novel of the Vietnam and Cambodian conflicts, *Highways to a War*, recounts the experience of an innocent young Australian making his very first acquaintance with Cantonese sensuality: 'The radio is quite close, and a female Chinese voice is singing . . . hovering on the edges of both discord and sweentess: the melody a blend of Chinese and Western. He's never before heard a Cantonese love song, and it flowers for him as that most telling of all hybrids, beauty crossed with strangeness.'

Beauty crossed with strangeness.

Although in Koch's novel, his young hero, Mike Langford, has the experience in Singapore in the mid-1960s, the sense of it could just as well apply to Hong Kong. Beauty crossed with strangeness is just the way Hong Kong has often struck the Western imagination over the years.

Hong Kong has done surprisingly well under mainland Chinese sovereignty. That reflects well on Beijing and it reflects well on Hong Kong too. It offers everything as a city, every type and form of vulgarity and crass commercialism, but also sublime cultural achievement and many, many folks making a good life and a good living.

As Theresa Lee points out it's increasingly cosmopolitan. On my last night in Honkers I go to the Happy Valley races as the guest of a local panjandrum of business and politics. My host has assembled a little party of half a dozen or so foreign guests. We are accommodated in a steward's box where we dine sumptuously on about eight tonne of Chinese food spread out over endless courses throughout the evening. From time to time we stroll out to the balcony to watch the horses run by, having placed bets at a little window down the corridor.

We are an eclectic group. Opposite me sits a pasty-faced English member of parliament, on some far-fetched junket, who keeps thanking us all for taking an interest in him as nobody is interested in backbench English members of parliament, still less if they're conservatives like him. His daughter, a loud blonde with prominent upper teeth, has been working in Honkers for some months in a bewildering number of positions and keeps explaining why her last employer but three was no good because he didn't give her proper opportunities, her last but two messed up her visa, her last but one couldn't cope with her creativity, while the current one seemed at first to like input from outsiders but then became jealous and defensive.

Next to me is a white-haired woman of spectacular antiquity, a white Russian from Harbin in northern China who migrated to Australia, married an Indian, now long deceased, and now divides her time between Melbourne and New Delhi. She has relatives in Melbourne but prefers Delhi.

'I find Melbourne so lonely,' she says.

'In India I have twelve servants in my house and I'm never lonely.'

Indians keep loneliness at bay by the cultivation of constant conversation. Hong Kong Chinese have traditionally kept it at bay by working so hard and so long and living so much cheek by jowl that there is neither time nor space for such an affliction.

As I fly out next day, back to the familiar pleasures of family and friends in KL, I feel well satisfied with my week in Honkers. Coming to Hong Kong to seek out self-conscious culture is an eccentric choice. People come to Hong Kong to make money, to escape—famously because they failed-in-London-try-Hong Kong (the 'filth').

But Hong Kong's conversation is expanding as never before. It's a point of intersection, a point of contradiction, a point of creation. It's also a point of hope. Once a barren rock, it's now a society. It's worth listening to.

Jakarta is Not a Bit Insane

Indonesians sometimes call Malaysians their little brothers. This I think is a wholly unreciprocated sentiment. I've never heard Malaysians call Indonesians their big brothers. Jakarta's Hatta-Soerkano International Airport couldn't be a greater contrast to KLIA. It does however seem to bear out the older brother–younger brother relationship. Jakarta's airport lacks all the gadgetry and whizz-bang modernity of KLIA but it is one of the most beautiful in the region. It doesn't have anything like KLIA's retail outlets. It's not nearly so modern. But it uses traditional Indonesian architectural styles in a deep red to create one of the most distinctive national airports in the region. Its spaciously laid out and widely dispersed departure gates are linked by corridors in which the walls are glass but are shaded by the eaves of the roofs so that you enjoy the light without being overwhelmed by the furious, tropical sun. And through the windows you see lush, green gardens.

I am perennially puzzled that more tropical airports don't make their lush vegetation a visual feature. Maybe the locals are so accustomed to the dense greens that they don't think it's worth bothering about. But for the visitor it's magical, especially for an Australian, accustomed as we are to our washed, stark, pale landscapes. As far as I'm concerned, when it comes to tropical vegetation: if you've got it, baby, flaunt it.

Of course Jakarta flaunts quite a lot else. You couldn't acuse it of not flaunting. On the whole you'd have to say its citizens aren't at all bad at flaunting, but that's another story.

I arrive in Jakarta after the shortest of flights from KL. Once again I've left Jessie and the boys behind in KL. I find now that I love to travel with them. Far from cramping my style they open up all manner of new possibilities. People, especially perhaps Southeast Asians, treat you differently when you have a family with you. You're more human, less institutional, less threatening; people want to be kind to your family even if they don't automatically like you that much. A colleague and friend of mine, an Australian living in Jakarta, discovered this when he had his octogenarian mother visit from Australia. Indonesians in every social situation you could imagine were so naturally solicitous for the welfare of an elderly woman that they treated my friend like a prince while ever his mother was there. He thought it might be useful to have her along whenever he confronted one of the city's demonstrations, her presence would part the waves of demonstrators, or so he imagined. I'm not sure his mother had signed up for this and luckily he didn't put the theory to the test.

Anyway this time I'm on my own. I'm in Jakarta for just a few days, to give a lecture and try to take the temperature of the Islamic debate. In fact I'm going to interview the president as well but I don't know that yet. That's a little roller coaster I haven't yet boarded. Jakarta is often a roller coaster. Get on for the ride and you don't know where you're likely to end up or what you'll see along the way.

I've had a few modest adventures even at Jakarta's airport. I was detained at the airport once—arrest would be too strong a term— way back on my first visit in the time when Australian journalists weren't generally allowed into Jakarta. I had a three-day visa and, although I had only been there for three nights, I had come in on the morning of the first day and left in the evening of the last. The airport official said I had been there four days and three nights and this was a breach of my three day visa so I was taken under armed guard to a detention room. To this day I don't know whether the official was being especially bureaucratic or expected some modest consideration to accompany my passport. You never quite know in Jakarta.

But that was the old days. Nowdays the airport is reliable and sensible and no hassle.

The taxi into the hotel brings me back to the smells of Jakarta, a very distinctive set of aromas. We pass some padi fields but are soon into the urban sprawl of Jakarta, a city of well over ten million souls. It's a surprisingly short and easy drive considering how bad the traffic can be when the mood takes it, or when it rains and the drains overflow and the streets flood. Soon enough we are approaching the broad swathe of skyscrapers that dates from the economic development that took place under the now reviled Suharto. I am staying at the Mandarin Oriental, which is located at the square opposite the Hotel Indonesia on one corner and the Grand Hyatt on the other.

Indonesia's fabulously eccentric first president, Sukarno, once described Jakarta as the Paris of the East.

But then, Sukarno was nearly mad, by the end.

Don't get me wrong. I love Jakarta. Its human variety is fantastic. But I'm not quite sure I'd describe it as the Paris of the east.

I wanna say that Indonesians are incredibly friendly, but that's like saying Chinese kids are cute. It's true but almost meaningless. I suppose you can find people in the world who are not spontaneously friendly. Probably the richer people are, the more they are naturally suspicious of strangers, the more they have to protect, the more cut off they are from traditional customs of hospitality. So you get less immediate friendliness on the streets of New York, or even Singapore, than you do in Jakarta. But when I cast my mind across Southeast Asia there's no national group who I'd say are actively unfriendly to strangers.

Quite the reverse. Almost all Southeast Asians are naturally friendly. Certainly Malysians and Filipinos and Thais and . . . oh, damn all these qualifications. Indonesians *are* incredibly friendly. There's an automatic sense of humour, a willingness to come to the rescue of the helpless foreigner, a desire to make a joke of most things most of the time. Of course Jakarta can be murderous too, in every sense of the word, literally and metaphorically, but such contradictions are the stuff of big cities.

The Mandarin Oriental Hotel, a favourite for journalists, is my home whenever I go to Jakarta. It's not quite as much my second home as the MiCasa in KL but it's comfortable and familiar. It specialises in being unobtrusive. The lobby is modestly large but somehow, with only a relatively small front door, which is itself in shadow, never bathed in light but discreet and subdued in its lighting. Most of the hotel has a theme of the sort of dark teak colours that are so common in Indonesia. This is not depressing but soothing. And everything always works. I've stayed at this hotel when the city has been paralysed by riots but still everything proceeds without interruption. Running a big hotel well, like writing a good novel, is full of that art which conceals an art.

After checking in and changing some money I go for my compulsory, arriving-in-the-city, orientation walk. Outside the hotel is the huge Welcome Statue, at the centre of a gigantic roundabout. Sukarno's edifice complex led to the construction of many such monumental and heroic statues in the city centre. They have been given properly irreverent nicknames by Jakarta's residents. The Spirit of Youth statue is of an heroic figure holding a flame on a plate—it's called Pizza Man. The Welcome Statue is at the centre of one of the busiest roundabouts in Jakarta. The statue itself is of a young man and woman with hands cheerfully raised and is sometimes called 'Donnie and Marie'.

Crossing this roundabout takes a bit of care. The traffic flows around it like two giant rivers, moving in great sweeping currents which eddy around the roundabout itself. I walk half a block away to cross at a side street and crabwise work myself halfway around the roundabout. Then I head along the main drag, Jalan Thamrin, up past the President Hotel, along past the Hard Rock Cafe. The streets are dense with traffic and at first the pungent fog of car smog is overwhelming. Every now and again, to avoid this for a moment, I take an excursion down a side street. These are pretty noxious with vehicle fumes too but the other smells of Jakarta make more of a contribution here. There is the infinitely attractive smell of the streetside food stalls. Like Malaysians, Indonesians love eating at roadside food stalls. They're more numerous at night but there are plenty to be found operating at any time of the day. In the city centre they're especially frequent at traffic lights, where pedestrians have to stop to cross the road. The secret Indonesian recipe for roadside food stalls is simple: whatever it is you're going to eat, it must be deep fried in vast quantities of oil. Only the American south can love deep fried as a cuisine statement as much as Jakartans do.

Two other smells make up the contrapuntal melody of Jakarta's air. One is what can only be described as human ordure mixed with all the swelling, pulsating, crapulous junk that open drains carry.

The other is the most characteristic and distinctive Jakarta smell of all, the *kretek* cigarette. It seems that almost every male in Jakarta smokes these clove-based cigarettes. They are to Jakartans what Gitanes once were to Parisians. I find their sweet, sticky aroma tugs at my heart for nothing is so redolent of Jakarta. I can still rememeber the distinctive smell from the first time I ever visited the city, all those years ago.

Today all the smells mix together—the trafic fumes, the roadside fried-food stalls, the drains and the ordure, the *kretek* cigarettes— all are elements of the strange symphony of the senses that impress themselves on you when you visit Jakarta.

I wander back to the main road and keep walking up to the Arjuna Statue, centre of another huge roundabout, and branch off into the giant park at the centre of which stands Jakarta's National Monument, dubbed by some locals with characteristic indecorous-ness Sukarno's Last Erection, in part no doubt because it is just across from the presidential palace.

This is central Jakarta's biggest park. I find it today strangely deserted. In Jakarta life teems everywhere except sometimes the places designed for its gentle relaxation. Like many cities where unemployment and poverty are rife, there is not all that much gentle relaxation at street level in Jakarta. The rich relax, but they do so in private, in secluded, guarded and exclusive environs. The poor, even the unemployed—especially the unemployed—are too busy assembling the elements of survival for gentle relaxation. Relaxation is a function of plenty. It is the opposite of the apathy of despair, or even the idle unhappiness of near despair.

I'm slightly uneasy in this park. Since the economic meltdown in 1997 and the fall of Suharto in 1998, Jakarta's streets have become less safe for foreigners, and for Jakartans too. Robberies, sometimes with violence, are far more common than they were. I don't think as far as foreigners are concerned there is any racial motivation for any of this. It's purely economic. There were always a lot of poor people in Jakarta, now there are a lot more newly poor people as well. And crowded and swollen as the city is, it remains a magnet for some of the 240 million people spread across the sprawling Indonesian archipelago.

There are fortunes in Jakarta, they know this in the countryside, fortunes and despair.

People have been coming from the countryside to seek their fortunes, and sometimes find them, and sometimes find despair, for a long time. In *Tales from Djakarta*, Pramoedya Ananta Toer, Indonesia's most celebrated writer, tells us many such stories. Although as a volume it was published first in 1963, the stories were mostly written in the 1940s and early 1950s, more than half a century ago. Yet in many ways they could have been written yesterday. The saddest is 'News from Kebajoran' about a married woman, Aminah, whose husband turns dissolute and sells their small village farm and then gambles away the money. Without any money or any prospects the woman accepts the offer of another man to drive to Jakarta with him and try her luck there. But her new man, Diman, works as a garbage collector for such a pitiful wage that they cannot afford even a hut and the two of them sleep each night in a park. Aminah ends up a prositute, thoughts or news of her home village increasingly a torture to her. She plies her trade not far from where I am wandering today, 'no more than two hundred and fifty metres from the [presidential] palace fence'.

These stories are Dickensian in their conception, Dickensian in their effect and Dickensian in their sadness and the rendering of the central place in a human's life of even the smallest ambition, even an electric light: 'Now she has finally fallen asleep. Her face is turned straight upward to the place where the heavens spread out. The stars are in competition with the street lights, with the lights that decorate the verandah of City Hall, and the lights of the Yen Pin restaurant, not to mention the lights that decorate the palace fence. When she was a child, she always wanted electric lights in her room. But that wish has never been fulfilled until now. Until now—when she no longer needs even a handful of rays from any man-made light.'

Aminah's fate is finally sealed when Diman is promoted to foreman. Now they can rent a hut and live like normal people, he tells her. No, she says, now that you're a foreman you'll want a better woman and respectability. And so it proves. In the end she dies, alone and in full Dickensian horror.

Jakarta is still Dickensian. The basic pattern in Pramoedya's story has been repeated time without number and goes on being repeated today. Jakarta can still today stir all the Dickensian anger and pity that informs 'News from Kebajoran'.

I am roused from these reveries by the approach of an adolescent boy. He looks to me about fifteen or sixteen. He could well be a year or two older, for when you grow up hungry you often grow up small. He has no English but makes a gesture that is unmistakable. He wants some money. He puts his hand, shaped to hold food, up to his mouth. He is hungry. It's very simple.

Surely he has a right to eat.

I am neither particularly generous nor particularly hard-hearted. I'm just an average guy. But here alone in this park I feel uneasy about getting out my wallet and giving him money. Is he alone? It must be hard for him to beg, I know. Apart from pride and self-respect, it's hard to beg because young men don't arouse pity.

Children do supremely, and old folks, and sometimes young women. Young men in contrast arouse caution, wariness.

Hoping that he is on his own, I tell the young man to walk with me and although he doesn't speak English he gets my drift. At the edge of the park, back on the main drag, I give him a handful of rupiah notes, in their denominations of tens of thousands, no more than a few dollars. He doesn't, as I irrationally fear, follow me back to the hotel asking for more, but accepts the transaction is finished and leaves.

Ah Jakarta.

Next morning I start telephoning. Naturally I have arranged as many appointments in advance as possible. But Jakarta is pre-eminently a city where it's always worth turning up and seeing what happens. I ring around friends and acquaintances, making arrangements to meet some. I try to ring Ratih Hardjono. Ratih is an old friend. She has an Irish-Australian mother and an Indonesian father. She spent her first seventeen years in Indonesia and the next seventeen in Australia and is superbly fluent in both cultures. For a long time she was the Australian correspondent for the Indonesian daily, *Kompas*. She went back to Indonesia to act as the spokeswoman during the election for Abdurrahman Wahid, the nearly blind, Muslim leader who went on, to everyone's astonishment, to become president.

Now, at the time of my visit, Wahid is president and Ratih is in charge of his office, an immensely powerful figure in her own right. I have been sporadically trying to ring her for a week or so before my visit but we haven't connected. Once or twice she has returned my call, but each time we've missed each other. I'm not going to ask her, as every other Australian journalist has done, for an interview with the president but just see if we can catch up for a coffee or some such. Once again she is out when I ring but I leave a message asking her to get back to me.

Later in the morning I take a taxi round to the Australian embassy for briefings on the political and economic situation. The diplomats are very professional. I've never met an Australian diplomat in Jakarta who doesn't like the place, though naturally it has more than its share of frustrations.

About two in the afternoon I go out for a late lunch and walk across the Welcome Statue roundabout once more but this time to the shopping mall, the Plaza Indonesia, underneath the Grand Hyatt Hotel. First stop is the Times bookshop. This is a good general bookshop but apart from a few places in Singapore and Bangkok, Southeast Asian English-language bookshops generally disappoint me. Some, like the Kinokuniya in KL, are magnificent general bookstores but very few make a serious effort to stock, promote and sell books on Southeast Asia itself. They are especially negligent in promoting novels and creative writing by their own authors, whether it is written originally in English or appears in translation.

Plaza Indonesia is one of the most exclusive shopping locations in all the nation. There are security guards on the doors. I don't know that they formally exclude anyone but I've never seen anyone poorly dressed in the Plaza Indonesia. Without alleging any grand conspiracy or apartheid, clearly the poor are not welcome in these environs. In many Southeast Asian cities the relatively poor can still enjoy at least the air-con, and some of the free entertainments, on offer in the big shopping malls. But Plaza Indonesia, apart from a smattering of Western expats, seems overwhelmingly a locale for Jakarta's yuppies. The poor it seems are not to enter this realm of public comfort and luxury.

Not that there is anything wrong with yuppies. It was a good feature of Suharto's economic modernisation, despite the corruption and its many other faults, that Indonesia, especially Jakarta, started to develop a real middle class.

In Plaza Indonesia you will not be approached by beggars. Other approaches, however, are common. A local band is performing in the open area on the ground floor under the escalators, adjacent to a cafe. As I get up to leave after a sandwich I stand for a few minutes on the edge of the cafe, watching the band. A young woman, sleekly dressed but, it appears on closer inspection, somewhat fragilely perched on high heels, approaches and says: 'Hullo, sir, I be your friend?'

No thanks.

This is not, however, the oddest proposition I've had in Jakarta. Years ago, wandering back late one night to my hotel, a young creature in a garish wig stepped out of the shadows and declaimed, in a deep, throaty voice, 'Sir, I am a girl', perhaps the least effective come-on line known to man.

I wander upstairs to the Grand Hyatt Hotel. This is truly a palace of luxury. Marble, chandeliers, giant escalators connecting its several levels, a huge atrium, giant glass frontage. On a middle level, between entry and reception, is a coffee and drinks lounge, where two young Indonesian women are singing soprano duets of surpassing beauty. I come here for the first cappuccino of my visit. In the West, cappuccinos are now passé. It's latté and macchiato for the in-crowd. But I tend to get stuck in my tastes. I never move with the times. Here's a confession: I'm hide bound. The foaming milk and the sprinkle of chocolate sitting atop my caffeine injection, that's what I like. Well, we all have our prejudices.

Next morning it's an early start. A friend has arranged for me to meet Al Habib Mohammed Ridzieq Husein Shihab of the Islamic Defenders' Front (or, to give it its Indonesian acronym, the FPI). It's often best to get an appointment in Jakarta about seven in the morning, before the traffic gets too bad and before your quarry starts to fall behind in his appointments. My friend knows the location of the FPI headquarters and he comes along to show me where it is. It turns out to be in a lower-middle-class suburb, neither poor, certainly not an urban *kampung*, of which there are many in Jakarta, nor yet either truly affluent.

We leave the car and walk down a series of back alleys and lanes, through a long, narrow garden and up a few stairs to french doors opening on to a small room. In the background a classroom of kids are chanting something, presumably the Koran. We are in a small room, crammed with Koranic texts, posters in Arabic and photos of Ridzieq.

Ridzieq himself is a small, friendly man in flowing white robes, orthodox Muslim moustache and goatee, and he receives us sitting cross-legged on the floor. This I have to admit poses a real problem for me. In order to be polite I too need to sit cross-legged on the floor while I take notes. But frankly my body is just not designed to sit this way for long periods. My sons can do it but my body lacks the flexibility. Not only is there no back support but you need to fold your legs under you like they're a work of origami and can be arranged and re-arranged in any decorous pattern. After a little while the excruciating pain of this arragement stops but then when you decide to stand up and leave you find your legs have gone on strike because they haven't had any blood delivered while you've been sitting down.

Such, such are the sorrows of journalism! But I am prepared to endure this minor torture in order to hear Ridzieq's point of view.

The FPI, I should stress, are in no sense representative of mainstream Islamic opinion in Jakarta. They were allied to the Laksar Jihad, an extremist group responsible for dreadful killing in Ambon. The FPI's claimed speciality was 'sweeping', or harassing foreigners to chase them out of Indonesia, while its main real activity seemed to be going round smashing up nightclubs and brothels.

Despite his in-principle opposition to even having foreigners in Indonesia, Ridzieq is the model of geniality and friendliness during our interview. His genial manner, however, belies the militancy of his words: 'There should be a country to stop American arrogance. That's why we want to make a strategy to pressure the US by encouraging all Muslim countries to sweep Americans.

'We don't only support sweeping. We are the ones who led it first. We want to ask Americans to leave the country, so they will tell their government it's difficult to travel. Americans love to travel, especially in Islamic countries. So let them put pressure on their governments and tell them it's not safe to travel. We want to expel Americans from the country and take control of their assets here.'

Ridzieq also supports *jihad* against the US, although he won't say that his organisation has been involved in sending Indonesians abroad to join any foreign conflicts.

I ask him how he feels about Jakarta: 'The situation here—prostitution, gambling, drugs, ecstacy and so on—is very bad. We also don't like to see unfair treatment of Islam by the Government and others. So we want to have a group of young people who dare to fight frontally against these social problems. The mission is to have a religious society struggling against those social evils. The movement of the FPI has become the movement of many people.

'We are already the moral leaders of the people. Whenever a group attacks a place where drugs are sold, or a place of prostitution or pornography, people say it's the FPI. This helps us to recruit more people.'

He wants Islam to be the basis of the Indonesian state, but not, he says, to force non-Muslims to abide by *shariah*, or religious, law: 'We cannot deny that part of the mission of the FPI is to make Islamic people more Islamic. Islamic people have a duty to follow *shariah* law. That does not mean we want to force non-Islamic people to become Islamic, that is a calumny on us.

'We will succeed in our aims eventually through socialisation. Socialisation has greater impact. It's rooted in the realisation that the US is our enemy. They are terrorists, criminals, arrogant.'

But here's the real kicker, the real significance of everything he has said before: 'We have many kindergarten teachers in the FPI. We indoctrinate kids of five and six against America.'

Friends in Jakarta note that the FPI's operations never touch a disco or hotel or any other place of disrepute that has a close connection, as some do, with the Indonesian military. Ridzieq also somewhat surprises me by calling for the Indonesian Government to re-conquer East Timor, not really a popular idea and one that would bring back nearly a million non-Muslims into Indonesia.

It would be wrong to overstate the importance of a group like the FPI. Sweeping never became a significant movement in Jakarta. The FPI's activities ultimately petered out. But I'll never forget the sound of the children chanting in the FPI compound, or Ridzieq's claim—and who am I to deny it?—that he had many kindergarten teachers indoctrinating kids as young as five and six.

The truth is though that Indonesians are incredibly friendly (there, I can say it now without a shudder of qualification). It's almost against their nature, as well as against their economic interests, given the role of tourism and foreign investment in the economy, to carry out an anti-foreigner campaign. Even as he was saying such hostile things to me about foreigners Ridzieq was personally friendly, solicitous even.

Back at the hotel I try again to ring Ratih in the president's office, again without luck. In the afternoon I go see a much more mainstream Muslim leader, Din Syamsuddin, the secretary-general of Indonesia's Ulama, or highest Islamic council, known by its Indonesian acronym (hey, I told you about Southeast Asians and acronyms) as MUI. He is also vice-president of Muhammadiyah, a huge movement of modernist Muslims with millions of followers, one of the largest Muslim organisations in the world.

Din Syamsuddin is pretty close to head *sharang* of the whole outfit. He's a busy guy and hard to get to see. I meet him at the MUI office underneath MUI's huge Jakarta mosque. The office, with its green carpet and fluorescent lights, is not my ideal of a work environment but then I'm not the secretary-general of the MUI.

In any event he is wholly reassuring. Like everyone in Indonesia, he has his criticisms of US foreign policy but this doesn't drive him into seeing the whole world and all politics as Islam versus the West. He absolutely rejects the FPI's violent programs, telling me that, root and branch, he and his organisations utterly reject sweeping, harassment of foreigners or any attempt to further a political agenda through violence.

Syamsuddin, who was partly educated in California (at UCLA), is also explicit about the direction he thinks Islamic politics should not go in his country: 'I don't believe fundamentalism has a future in Indonesia. It emerges because of sociological deprivation and then religion is used as a justification for politics, but it's contrary to our traditions.'

Yet although he identifies Muhammadiyah as being involved in the project of liberal Islam, he also observes: 'Muhammadiyah is a cultural, religious and social organisation. We believe there is no separation of politics from religion so it's open to us to play a role in politics.' Muhammadiyah doesn't directly run candidates in elections but it certainly is a big political force.

Although Syamsuddin is a moderate, his complaints about America are passionate (which is not to say they are necessarily justified), and representative of much Indonesian Islamic opinion: 'America continues to support Zionist Israel and the killing of thousands of citizens who are Muslims, we are also concerned by American actions against Iraq, Sudan and Libya. America is perceived as applying double standards in the fields of justice and human rights. The other factor is the stereotyping of the American Government, who always attribute any terror attacks to Islam and Muslims. Then there was real anti-Muslim violence in the US, Britain and Australia where mosques were burned.

'Americans are welcome here, they're our guests, they're human beings, they have liberties and rights. Muslim people don't hate Americans but object to the foreign policy of the American Government, especially towards Muslim countries.' Needless to say, Syamsuddin opposed America's war in Iraq.

Like so many Muslim leaders in Southeast Asia, Syamsuddin spent substantial time in the US, time which left him with both good and bad impressions of the West: 'From 1986 to 1991 I lived in California. It was a very great experience. We learned democracy and freedom. We also learned—we also saw—decadence and immorality and we don't agree with that.

'This moral breakdown, through secularisation and globalisation, influences Muslim countries. It's another factor of possible conflict between Islam and the West. The West is destroying the Islamic world through its secularisation agenda. This is the background behind the call to *jihad* by the MUI and other Muslim organisations. *Jihad* of course has a bigger meaning than conflict. It's not just war but striving to create an ideal society in many ways.

'We don't reject modernity. We believe Islam is compatible with modernity. But secular modernisation that creates hedonistic, individualistic society is really a threat to human society. This is the ambivalent aspect of globalisation. We accept the positive part of globalisation. The call to *jihad* is a reaction to the negative part of globalisation.

'The industrial powers dominate the international order for their own interests. We have witnessed asymmetrical acculturation between superior industrial countries and developing countries. The industrial countries dominate science, technology and commerce and then they dominate third world countries in culture and politics.'

Alright, I fairly respectfully counter, suppose all this is true, what is the alternative Islamic model, and which country comes nearest to it?

I admire the honesty of Syamsuddin's answer: 'In terms of comprehensive, balanced development there is no model yet. Many Islamic countries show great dependence on superpowers and launch modernisation without a good balance between spiritual and material development.

'Indonesian and Southeast Asian Islam occupy a peripheral place in the Muslim world geographically yet these countries have the opportunities to develop their own models and open themselves to modernity. Indonesia is fertile soil for modern and moderate Islam though in the last decade this has been disturbed by political factors. But the mainstream of Indonesian Islam is moderate and tolerant.'

I hope he's right. Like Islamic leaders in Malaysia, he identifies cities, specifically Jakarta, as a source of corruption. He lives in Jakarta and travels to the countryside on his many activities most weekends: 'The mosques are full, but the bars are also full. The majority are good, I think, but the attack of external values has the potential to destroy this society.'

I have enjoyed meeting Syamsuddin. I don't agree with everything he says, but there is an attempt being made here to fashion a coherent and moderate Islamic response to the world and all its complications.

I check back at the hotel, ring Ratih again, still with no luck, and head across town to the Indonesian Institute of Sciences, known as LIPI, there to see one of Indonesia's most formidable women, Dewi Fortuna Anwar.

LIPI's office is an odd-looking round tower, standing incongruously on the side of the road. LIPI loves the modern idiom and Dewi, a strikingly pretty woman, is one of its most effective exemplars. Originally from West Sumatra, she has all manner of high academic achievements but was perhaps best known when she was the senior foreign policy adviser to the former president, the wildly eccentric B.J. Habibie.

She is also the main figure in the Indonesian chapter of V.S. Naipaul's influential book, *Beyond Belief: Islamic Excursions Among the Converted Peoples*. It is in this book that Naipaul famously advances his essentially insulting thesis that Islam crushes the converted peoples by making their non-Islamic history illegitimate, by glorifying only Arab history. He even argues that in converted lands such as Indonesia the Muslim fundamentalist 'rage' is directed against the local past, in an attempt to erase its non-Muslim aspects. That may be true in some converted lands but it seems wildly overdrawn in Indonesia, where most people are proud of their country's complex and diverse history, with its long Hindu period and its Buddhist and animist and mystical traditions.

Dewi, whom I meet in a large, private office at LIPI, rejects Naipaul's arguments altogether.

'Naipaul came to this thesis through his dislike of Islam,' she says.

Dewi herself is a strong Muslim, a member of Muhammadiyah, but also a strong opponent of fundamentalism, rejecting the idea that Indonesia should be an Islamic state or implement *shariah* law. As Naipaul describes in his book, she unites at least three strands, as a modernist, a serious Muslim, and a traditional West Sumatran who values those indigenous traditions and their influences on her life. I've seen her wearing traditional Muslim headdress and with her head uncovered. A lot of modern Indonesian and Malaysian women will take the headdress as a matter of occasion, depending who they are mixing with.

Like so many Indonesian intellectuals, Dewi stresses the mixture of Indonesian tradition with Islamic teaching which is the great tradition of Indonesian Islam: 'We accept Islam as our belief and at the same time we continue with a lot of traditional and cultural practices. I am a West Sumatran. I'll continue to be very feminist. Islam is part of my identity. Islam is the single unifying factor of our 500 ethnic groups but our strong culture moderates this desert religion. If it insists on living like seventh-century Arabia it won't last for very long. Indonesia can show to the Western world, but also to other Muslim nations, a different model of Islam.

'Islam doesn't have a Pope. In Indonesia we can all go to each others' mosques . . . '

She also won't accept the idea that Islam is inherently intolerant: 'When the Muslims ruled Spain the arts flourished, including among Christians and Jews.

'Indonesia sometimes has a love/hate relationship with the West. We can be suspicious of major power interests because of our colonial heritage. But this co-exists with the recognition of Western power and the thought that you must join the West.'

Indonesia's critics sometimes accuse it of being inward-looking and preoccupied with itself. This can be particularly so in Jakarta. But here we come up against the Chinese kids are acute, Indonesians are friendly, syndrome. Self-obsession is a feature of all big nations. Chinese, Indians and Americans (except when they are pursuing a vital national interest through a war) are all incredibly self-obsessed. The same is true of most really big cities—think of New York, London, Beijing or Shanghai, Delhi or Bombay. Of course it's true of Jakarta too. We're only surprised because we're not accustomed to thinking of Jakarta as the vital metropolis, and one of the world's biggest cities, at the heart of a nation of 240 million.

Dewi, like many Indonesians, sees a lot of virtue in this nationalism, even if she does express it in a high-falutin' way. She tells me: 'International factors have not impacted on domestic Indonesian discourses on Islam. With democracy, naturally the voice of Islam will be greater.'

I used to think that anyone who used the word discourse was automatically talking baloney. But Dewi is a smart, smart woman. If she says the Islamic discourses are domestic, I'm willing to believe her.

Later that night at the hotel I am sitting at the first-floor lounge, waiting to meet a friend. The lounge looks down into the lobby and gives a view of a grand, spiral staircase which makes an elegant arc up to the first-floor landing. I'm contemplating Indonesia's unequal power relationship with the West and how resentful so much of the Islamic world feels about similar power disparities, when I espy a scene which shows me that it is not only between Islamic societies and the West that power disparities are played out.

The scene I witness is of a family group ascending the stairs. In front, labouring somewhat up the stairs, is fleshy, flashy papa. He is an ample man of early middle age, in flashy, and one must say rather bravely tight, black polo neck shirt. He looks as though he has never gone without a meal, or indeed a mid-meal snack, in his life. Following a pace or two behind is mama, a little younger than papa, and she carries their infant son. Another pace behind is grandma. She, like papa, is unencumbered. All these people are fleshy and full of figure. A pace or two behind mama comes a small, young woman, much slighter of frame than any of the others, slimmer and much darker of skin, probably from one of the outer islands. She is the maid or the baby's *amah*. She is carrying, completely alone, a vastly elaborate stroller replete with a swag of parcels from what must have been a family shopping expedition. A lot of Jakartans, whether new money or old, are to the manor born, and there are a lot of servants in this city.

As I sit in the lounge I feel increasingly unwell. Some tropical fever has struck. I'm scheduled to go to a dinner party with some old Jakartan friends, a journalist I know as Wir and a group of his political and writerly friends, at the home of a benevolent tycoon. We head off in Wir's car with me feeling distinctly under the weather. Wir is an old and good friend but even his best friend would say a prayer before entrusting his life to Wir's driving. His car is disturbingly already missing a side mirror, a small victim of Jakarta's frenetic traffic wars. He has parked in the hotel driveway— how he squared this with the concierge I'll never know—and he talks as he takes the wheel. We hurtle up side roads, squeeze in between other cars, run it desperately close with motorbikes. Often when we are stopped at a red light or just in the general crush of traffic countless adolescent boys and young men approach the car windows. They are all selling something, either bottled water, the day's newspapers or increasingly lottery tickets.

'These young boys selling lottery tickets,' Wir turns his head to remark to me, thus radically increasing our already high chances of a collision, 'it's really disguised begging.'

We seem to drive for hours before reaching a big, ranch-like compound, the home of Wir's friend, scion of an industrial family. Down a long drive there is a central house, another building houses a pergola-like structure and faces on to a huge swimming pool, next to which are changerooms and showers. But we are dining in still a third compound, an open cabana-type structure, in which chicken satay sticks are fried over one cooker, while an array of dishes are served buffet-style on other tables. The dinner is sumptuous and riotous, but I am heavily subdued with my fever. The conversation swirls around. Much of it I can't catch as it flows between English and Bahasa Indonesian, in which I am seriously less than fluent. The night is stifling hot but this is depressing no one's spirits but mine.

We repair for coffee to an outer room in the main house, which surprisingly is also not air-con. The walls of this room are covered by face masks, implements of war and other artefacts from the tribes of Borneo. I sit quietly opposite a huge face mask which says to me, in the weird mechanical tones of a Dalek from *Dr Who*, 'Hello.' There seems to be a glottal stop at the end of this word so it sounds almost like 'Hellop'. I look round, waiting for a reaction from the rest of the room.

Nothing. Am I the only one who can hear this talking face mask? I study my friends. Is this some practical joke of Wir's, a mechanical device inside the mask which says this single word to disconcert new visitors?

My brow is perspiring. I have not brought any batik shirts to Jakarta with me. This is a stupid oversight because batik shirts are acceptable for almost any occasion. So, knowing we are going to an upper class home, I'm wearing a jacket and tie, which was a dumb move. But so often the air-con is so arctic, so often Southeast Asia is a conspiracy of coldness and noise, that it can be a good idea to have a jacket. In any event, between fever and jacket and talking face masks, I am quietly and not very peacefully melting.

I take an orange juice rather than a coffee from a passing waiter. The scene settles a little. I almost convince myself that fever has made me imagine the talking face mask. I lean towards a group who are talking and laughing and shouting, pretending I'm on the edge of their conversation. I can't quite follow its drift but I'm happy to pretend to be part of the group and sit there quietly.

'Hellop!'

The face mask has increased its volume. This is getting out of hand. I must be deranged.

'Hellop! Hellop!'

I lean back in the chair. I am unequal to this. I have no interpretation of it.

'Hellop! Hellop!'

Wir sees that I'm under the weather and wanders over to sit beside me. He seeks a neutral conversation opener.

'So, what's happening in Australian politics these days?'

'Hellop!'

'Wir,' I say in desperation, 'did you hear that face mask talk?'

'That's just a cicak.'

A cicak!

All this grief over a noisy lizard, of the type that infests every non-air-conditioned space in Indonesia, just a noisy lizard sitting behind the face mask driving me crazy. Wir drives me back to my hotel and I sleep the troubled sleep of fever.

Next morning the fever is gone but I feel like I have the worst hangover of my life. Normally I like to go down to the coffee shop for breakfast but today I order toast and orange juice and decaf coffee in the room. Feeling so hungover is not good as today I have to give my big lecture to a luncheon audience of several hundred business types somehow or other associated with the American Chamber of Commerce. I'm going to talk about regional political and economic trends and intend to give a severe tongue-lashing to the International Monetary Fund for what I consider its ham-fisted interventions in Indonesia.

The phone rings.

'Greg! Ratih Hardjono here. Welcome to Jakarta. I've got all your messages. I'm sorry I couldn't get you before this but I'm glad in a way I didn't. I wanted to make sure I could get your interview with the president lined up before I rang back. Come over to the Bina Graha building at one and I'll give you some lunch and then you can see the president straight afterwards.'

How typically Jakartan!

Here I hadn't even asked to see the president but Ratih had assumed that was what all my calls were about. Her generosity and kindness and loyalty to a friend have as usual gone beyond the call of duty. Her call is welcome, of course, it's great to hear from her at last. She is a fine person and has made a big contribution to both Indonesia and Australia. Both nations should be proud of her. Nonetheless, this is slightly tricky. It's not really very polite to turn down lunch at the president's office but a couple of hundred people are expecting me to lecture at them over lunch.

I express my thanks and explain my dilemma to Ratih. The lunch will finish by 2 p.m. and I can be at Bina Graha by 2.15. OK, she says, thinking and calculating quickly, do that.

I ring Fred, the convenor of the business lunch, and tell him the whole story, concluding that I must be out of the room by two because I'm going to see the president.

The lunch, at one of the city's many five-star hotels, doesn't get off to a good start as I find, sitting at my table, the IMF's Jakarta representative. It would be seriously unJavanese to give the IMF a roasting with him sitting there. Oh well, I'll just tone down a bit.

Fred is a big guy, a big, ebullient yank. When the eating is done and it's time for the talking, Fred gives me a generous, you might even say fulsome, introduction, with words to the effect that I stood up the president for lunch in order to be with the group today but I've rescheduled the president for the afternoon so I'll have to leave early.

Yikes!

What an incredibly boastful prat I must sound. Fred's version of my appointment making and swapping is pretty radically different from what I had told him, and of course I didn't expect him to make any mention of it at all.

Straight after lunch I scoot across to the presidential compound, hopeful that no one from the lunch has rung the palace to tell them of my bandying of the president's name. Interviewing the president of the fourth-largest nation in the world (China is number one, India number two and the US number three) is an incredible privilege. I don't want to appear cavalier or boastful about it.

Abdurrahman Wahid is the fourth president of Indonesia, after Sukarno, Suharto and B.J. Habibie and he would in due course be replaced by Megawati Sukarnoputri, Sukarno's daughter. I interviewed Habibie once at the Istana Merdeka, the presidential palace, a grand, white, colonial building which stands next to Bina Graha. It is as sensuous on the inside as it is majestic on the outside, full of paintings from Sukarno's collection, with bronzed, voluptuous maidens in idyllic village scenes.

Indonesia sets a high standard in eccentricity among its presidents. Sukarno was the nation's independence hero but he led it down mad, bad and unproductive paths of regional confrontation, rhetorical excess and economic devastation.

Quite the most astounding book ever produced out of Indonesia's frequently unbelievable politics is Sukarno's autobiography, as told to the American writer, Cindy Adams. It begins, with Sukarno talking of himself in the third person, with the following declaration: 'The simplest way to describe Sukarno is to say that he is a great lover. He loves his country, he loves his people, he loves women, he loves art, and, best of all, he loves himself.'

Later, Sukarno, who is endearingly free of any false modesty, recalls: 'Now, I must admit that in my youth I was so terribly handsome that I was almost girlish-looking. Because there were few female intellectuals in those days, there weren't many girl members and when Young Java put on a play I was always given the ingenue role. I actually put powder on my face and red on my lips. And I will tell you something, but I don't know what foreigners will think of a President who tells such things . . . Anyway, I will tell it. I bought two sweet breads. Round breads. Like rolls. And I stuffed them inside my blouse. With this addition to my shapely figure, everybody said I looked absolutely beautiful. Fortunately my part didn't call for kissing any boys on stage. I couldn't waste any money so after the show I pulled the breads out of my blouse and ate them.'

It would be wrong to deny Sukarno's achievements, which, in unifying the country, gaining it independence, electrifying his countrymen with nationalist fervour, were very great. But so were his failings. His successor, Suharto, was almost exactly the opposite—aloof, reserved, no orator. As his critics say, the longer he was in office the more he practised a kind of Suharto Sultanism, a highly personalised rule. For a long time he delivered great economic growth and gave Jakarta, among other things, a middle class. Famously he also tolerated corruption and the human rights record was poor, at times brutally so. The part German-educated, hyper-talkative, diminutive dynamo Habibie, with his nervous hands and high-pitched giggle, whose pet name for his former boss was SGS—Super Genius Suharto—was another original.

Abdurrahman Wahid, or Gus Dur as he is almost universally known, is pretty clearly the most decent and democratic man to be president of Indonesia.

After a coffee and a quick chat with Ratih, I sit waiting for Gus Dur in the large, anonymous waiting room as he finishes a press conference mainly concerning the proper timing of the Muslim holy day of sacrifice. Then, in his private office, he receives a delegation of Indonesian military brass, resplendent in their green uniforms; men who not so long ago were accustomed to running Indonesia and don't necessarily look all that comfortable taking orders from Gus Dur.

When I finally see him I feel guilty for trespassing on a brutal schedule. He looks a frail figure. He has survived two strokes and he looks it, his eyes closed in blindness, crumpled into a big chair at what seems a small desk, hiding in the corner of the vast presidential office.

It is partly his blindness that makes interviewing Wahid this day a perplexing business. He is mentally alert, sharp, wise. Yet his face has that peculiar vulnerability of the blind—sometimes his mouth is open, sometimes he seems to be chewing.

I met him first in Ratih's living room in Sydney many years ago. He and his wife used to stay with her sometimes when they visited Sydney. Now, with the weight of our conversation so serious—the economy, democracy, sending the army permanently into its barracks and out of politics, reconciliation with East Timor, separatist movements in Aceh and West Papua—he is bowed down with the momentous affairs of state and the old laughing, joking Gus Dur is temporarily absent.

His presidency would end a few months later sunk between the machinations of his enemies and the administrative chaos he himself created. But his achievements, and not just in the presidency, were substantial. For many years he was leader of the Nadhlatal Ulama (known naturally as NU), the movement of Islamic scholars. With more than thirty million followers this is the largest Muslim organisation in the world. That the NU has for so long been committed to pluralism, democracy and moderation is real good fortune for Indonesia and due, in part at least, to Wahid's leadership.

He tells me in effect to chill out about the threat of Islamic fundamentalists in Indonesia: 'The majority of Indonesia refuses to be fundamentalist, including myself.'

The generally calm Islam practised in Indonesia has come about as a result of hundreds of years of cultural development and won't be easily disturbed.

'Islam is a religion of peace. It rejects any violence, except of course self-defence.'

While not uncritical of the US, he even has kind words for Israel, a most extraordinary thing for such a powerful Muslim leader: 'Tolerance has to be shown towards everyone. If we can recognise the Soviet Union and China, which are officially atheist, how can we not recognise Israel? It's a democracy in a sea of misunderstanding.'

Wahid is a good man and I'm grateful for his time today. He has a habit of self-contradictory and undisciplined talking which is one of his great charms, but also gets him into a lot of unnecessary trouble.

Indonesians have wicked jokes about their presidents. One goes that Sukarno was mad about women, Suharto was mad about money, Habibie was just plain mad, while Wahid drove everybody mad. A later joke, drawing on Megawati's famed reluctance to speak, said that in shifting from Wahid to Mega, Indonesians had changed a blind president for a mute one.

Jakartans love to joke about their politics, except when it hits them over the head in deadly violence. Jakarta is always a city of intrigue and mystery. For one thing there are so many different ethnic groups there from all over Indonesia that this produces dozens of different power lines, lines of influence, kinship and obligation. There is fabulous wealth here and desperate poverty, but despite the events of 1997 and beyond there is also a substantial middle. How I love those words—the sweetest in any developing city's life—a substantial middle. There is classical learning, Islamic fanaticism, neighbourliness, a welcome for strangers, paranoid nationalism, Christian churches, a big and sometimes persecuted Chinese minority, nightclubs and temples, reflex Malay hilarity and ubiquitous mysticism, and—everywhere—*kretek* cigarettes and the smell of clove.

The best novel I have read about Jakarta is *The Year of Living Dangerously*, by Chris Koch, who has figured, I know, several times already in these journeys. No lover of Jakarta can ignore this book. It is not purely an interpretation of Jakarta itself but rather an interpretation of a Western experience of Jakarta. It is no less authentic for that. It concerns the experience of an Australian-English journalist, Guy Hamilton, and his group of journalist and diplomat colleagues in 1965 as they cover the disintegration of Sukarno's rule and his eventual eclipse. It has become a classic of the city and the foreign services of several countries recommend their diplomats read it when they take up a post in Jakarta.

Koch writes of the city as it slides into a kind of despair: 'There is a definite point where a city, like a man, can be seen to have become insane. This had finally happened to Jakarta when we reached the seventeenth of August: Merdeka Day, and the end of Sukarno's year. Amok is an old Malay word; and Jakarta had now run amok with classical completeness.

'For a long time, a man may be unbalanced, given to irrational hopes and irrational rages; and though these signs are disconcerting we continue to think of him as eccentric but sane. It's always difficult to believe that someone we know well has crossed into that other territory where no one from our side can reach him, and from which messages crackle back that no longer make any sense. But finally something happens to jar us into seeing this. That's how it was with Sukarno's Jakarta, in the middle of that weird August, the end of the dry monsoon.'

Koch was right. Jakarta did go temporarily insane at the end of Sukarno's reign. Although there have been terrible events on odd occasions since then, the city has never gone quite insane again. Sometimes it has been neurotic, sometimes delusional; there is always talk of ghosts, murmurings of saints and ninjas and angels; there have been strange fevers and spasms. It is often running a temperature. But it is robust.

I find it a lucid city now. If at times it is brutal and ruthless, Jakarta has a tender heart still.

The Heart Divided

KL and Sydney

We're on the plane. When you are a family of five leaving, like arriving, is a big deal. Last night we helped the boys pack at Balwinder's, then went back to the MiCasa to pack ourselves. Leaving is a rolling operation. We get a car from the MiCasa, load it up with our stuff, then call round to Balwinder's. The driver kindly waits downstairs for us for ten minutes so we can say our goodbyes and start loading the boys' luggage. When you are staying somewhere for a couple of months you can't really travel light, no matter what resolutions you make in advance.

The family is all very matter-of-fact about farewells. The deep currents of emotion run below the surface. Just perhaps as she is shooing us into the car Balwinder might have a tear, and Jessie too. The rest of us, Ajay, Lakhvinder, Jagdave and me, are gawky Aussie blokes after all. It's our national heritage at moments like these to shuffle our feet, say 'aw shucks, or try to make a joke.

At the airport one year one of the boys had a plastic rifle. After the toy pistol in Sydney you'd think we'd have learned our lesson, but parents can be as silly as kids sometimes. But they let us take that on the plane, in the old pre-terrorist days. Another time we had a passport crisis. One of our bags is regularly diverted into the excessive size category and we always have to be careful that it doesn't weigh more than thirty kilos (with a few books on board you'd be surprised how easy it is to get to that weight). One year two of the five seats we were supposed to occupy on the plane were broken and had signs saying 'Not to be Occupied'. Their backs wouldn't stay in the upright position. But the plane was packed in all classes and there were no other seats for two days so we happily put up with that minor inconvenience.

Here's the thing. Even when you've been spending time in a place you love, like we all love KL, when it comes time to go home, you really want to go home. I mean *really* want to go home.

And for us there's no doubt about home.

I love these Southeast Asian cities. For as long as I breathe I guess I'll be preparing, undertaking, returning from or planning a trip to Southeast Asia. But I love home, too.

The better part of a hundred years ago one of my favourite Australian authors, Martin Boyd, wrote a whole swag of novels about the heart divided between Australia and England. Many of his characters spend much of their lives unsure at which of the two furthest points on the globe they call home. That was how many people of his generation and background felt.

Now we Australians are much clearer that we're Australians.

Wherever we are, we're Australians.

But still we can yearn for the Other Place. I'm much luckier than Martin Boyd because my Other Places are only seven or eight hours, and a flimsy excuse, away.

In the half-dozen or so years we've been coming to KL as a family I can't believe how the boys have changed. When we first came Jagdave couldn't swim, was even a little scared of the water. Now he's like an electric eel flashing through the MiCasa pool. Lakhvinder just keeps getting taller and smarter. Ajay is an adult. I admire the young men they've become and yet I miss the little boys they were, when dad was such a big part of their universe. All the time they're little you want them to grow bigger so they'll be less vulnerable to the world, then when they do you miss the little guys who used to rely on you so much.

These are commonplace thoughts for a dad, I'm sure. I'm glad that KL has been part of the boys' growing up.

Now on this plane we have seats with backs that work. Jessie and I are sitting side by side and the three boys are one row behind us, having negotiated in statesmanlike fashion the disposition of window, middle and aisle for equitable periods.

The boys tell me they don't sleep on these overnight flights, but play the computer games, watch the movies, occasionally even read their books. But sometimes, when I check on them, I find their eyes shut, dreams of football and cricket playing as substitute movies for them.

I always find these flights so terribly short. Not enough time to read, not enough time to sleep. The boys can barely believe it when I say that. The flight is an endless expanse of time to them. But like others I've noticed that the older you get the faster the time goes.

We approach Sydney not long after sunrise. The boys are awake now, well and truly. They're all smiling at the prospect of going home. For just as we like the cities of the hot zone, we love our home as well. This Sydney is a special, special place. Who wouldn't love it?

The plane banks and turns and suddenly there it is again, the breathtaking splendour of the harbour, the coruscating beauty of the Opera House, the dazzling brightness of the morning.

The city is washed in light, that special quality of light that our artists can never quite believe, that light that on a hot summer's day like this seems as if it must go forever, leaving not a single place of darkness anywhere on the face of the Earth.

Home.

Thanks

I want to record my deepest gratitude to the late John Iremonger, who was present at the creation of this book, who was involved in every stage of the many different forms it took before even I had written a word, who was not only a great publisher but a wonderful friend, and who encouraged me to strike out in a completely new direction. I also want to thank his colleague, Rebecca Kaiser, who took the project over and ministered to it with tea and sympathy. I want to express sincere gratitude to Chris Mitchell, editor-in-chief of *The Australian*, and to Mike Stutchbury, the editor, and to their predecessors Paul Kelly, David Armstrong and Campbell Reid. They encouraged and indulged and sometimes endured my Southeast Asian obsessions. None of these journeys would have been possible without the hospitality of Balwinder Kaur, hospitality far beyond the call of duty. Thanks, too, to Amy, Dipi and Harry for helping to make Kuala Lumpur so enjoyable, and to Harmick and Raj, who helped to make the times good. Thanks, too, to Jessie, for everything, and to Ajay, Lakhvinder and Jagdave, mainly for being themselves.

Some episodes in this book have been amalgamated from more than one episode in real life, some divided, and a very few names have been changed for the usual reasons.